INSIDERS'GUIDE®

FUN WITH THE FAMILY™ SERIES

fun WITH the Family™

MAINE

HUNDREDS OF IDEAS FOR DAY TRIPS WITH THE KIDS

BONNIE MERRILL

FOURTH EDITION

INSIDERS'GUIDE®

GUILFORD, CONNECTICUT

AN IMPRINT OF THE GLOBE PEQUOT PRESS

INSIDERS'GUIDE®

Text design by Nancy Freeborn and Linda Loiewski
Maps by Rusty Nelson © The Globe Pequot Press
Spot photography throughout © Photodisc

ISSN 1536-6162
ISBN 0-7627-2979-1

Manufactured in the United States of America
Fourth Edition/First Printing

For my sister, Patty Rector, whose motto is:

A lobster a day is the only way to visit Maine.

MAINE

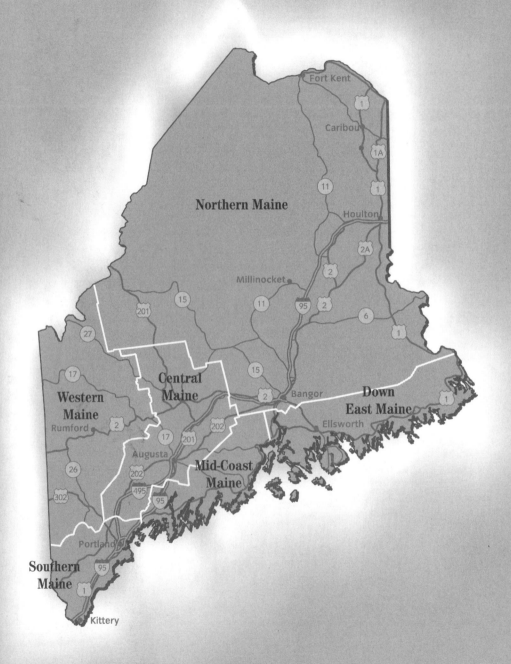

Contents

Acknowledgments vi

Introduction vii

Southern Maine 1

Mid-Coast Maine 51

Down East Maine 95

Northern Maine 119

Central Maine 143

Western Maine 159

General Index 184

Activities Index 193

About the Author 198

Acknowledgments

I have always dreamed of writing books. Like most worthy pursuits, however, writing is not easy; therefore, help is often necessary. I was blessed to be surrounded by a group of gracious and talented people who were willing to give me the help I needed.

Elizabeth Taylor, my editor, and The Globe Pequot Press gave me a chance to write. The Maine Office of Tourism, the Maine Tourism Association, and local chambers of commerce answered all my questions and furnished me with a library of information. Proprietors of establishments listed in this guide enthusiastically provided me with updates.

Friends and family were always there for me, offering love and support. Reneé Fellows, thanks for your enthusiasm about the book and for tips on new attractions. Your friendship is a real blessing. Kristie Bourkas, offering to take the girls so I could get some work done was a lifesaver. All the teachers at CCS—your friendship, support, prayers, and laughter have meant more than I can say. Mary Spidaliere, my forever friend and kindred spirit, it is an encouragement to know you are one of my biggest fans. I just wouldn't be me without a friend like you. Laura Vidal, you are the perfect mom. Thanks for your prayers and for believing in me. Kaitlyn and Jaclyn, my precious angels, thanks for all the strength your hugs and kisses bring.

Finally, I must express my deepest gratitude to my husband, Ken. You are my partner in so many ways, for you are not only my husband, you are my best friend. Thanks for being the hero of my heart and of our home. I thank God for the opportunity to write this book. It's a dream come true.

Introduction

Vacations are meant to be extraordinary and memorable. A Maine vacation is guaranteed to be both. Called Vacationland, Maine offers you and your family so many opportunities for fun that you'll have to come back again and again. I know, because since my family and I moved back to the Pine Tree State we've had swarms of "vacationing" friends visit us. They all leave with the same remark: "It's so beautiful here. We'll be back." Whether it's the state's natural beauty or its variety of activities and culture, Maine is magnetic.

Come for a weekend. Come for a couple of weeks. Enjoy the quiet of a lakeside cabin, or spend time hiking up mountains or around islands. Comb the coast touring lighthouses, or surf the waves. Take a cruise, ride a train, or soar in a hot air balloon.

Whatever the season, Maine is full of fun. Take a quiet vacation in the North Woods, where your days are filled with fishing, canoeing, and cooking over an open fire. Or ride the rapids out of The Forks for a really wild outdoor adventure. Savor a weekend of skiing at Sunday River. Thrill to a downhill run, explore tranquil cross-country trails, or cruise on a snowmobile.

If you're looking for culture and entertainment, visit a museum, drop in on a festival, or take in a play. Over the years, Maine has been the backdrop for numerous films. Come at the right time to the right town, and you might spy movie stars as they film their latest flick. Better yet, make your family the stars as you capture Maine's beautiful landscapes for yourself with home movies and still photos.

If shopping is your bag, explore L. L. Bean in Freeport. Spend a day at the outlets in Kittery. Meander through quaint specialty shops in Boothbay Harbor, or scope out antiques in Hallowell.

These are just some of the vacation possibilities available in Maine. Through this book, I hope you'll allow me to give you a tour of this beautiful state and the variety of fun it has to offer you and your family. And like my friends, I hope you'll visit Maine again and again.

Rates for Attractions

$	$5.00 and under
$$	$5.01 to $15.00
$$$	$15.01 to $25.00
$$$$	Over $25.00

Rates are based on a single adult ticket. Prices are usually lower for children, and at some attractions little ones even go free. Free admission is noted in the listing. It is also noted if attractions offer special family deals.

Rates for Lodging

$	up to $80
$$	from $81 to $120
$$$	from $121 to $160
$$$$	$161 and up

Rates are based on double occupancy. Extra charge for additional occupants are noted in the listings. Also, rates can vary greatly in and out of season. This is also noted (e.g., $–$$$$).

Rates for Restaurants

$	most entrees under $10
$$	most $10 to $15
$$$	most $15 to $20
$$$$	most over $20

Rates are based on the dinner menu. Most restaurants offer similar menus for lunch at reduced rates.

For Quick Reference. Besides local chambers of commerce, there are several state tourism offices ready to send you brochures and magazines sure to help in planning your Maine vacation.

Maine Office of Tourism
DECD
SHS-59 33 Stone Street
Augusta, ME 04333
(800) 533–9595
www.visitmaine.com

Bureau of Parks and Lands
Maine Department of Conservation
22 State House Station
Augusta, ME 04333-0022
(207) 287–3821
www.state.me.us/doc/parks.htm

Maine Tourism Association
325B Water Street
Hallowell, ME 04347-2300
(207) 623–0363
www.mainetourism.com

Department of Inland Fisheries and Wildlife
284 State Street
Augusta, ME 04333-0041
(207) 287–8000
janus.state.me.us/ifw/index.htm

The prices, rates, and hours listed in this guidebook were confirmed at press time. We recommend, however, that you call establishments to obtain current information before traveling.

Attractions Key

The following is a key to the icons found throughout the text.

SWIMMING			FOOD	
BOATING / BOAT TOUR			LODGING	
HISTORIC SITE			CAMPING	
HIKING / WALKING			MUSEUMS	
FISHING			PERFORMING ARTS	
BIKING			SPORTS/ATHLETICS	
AMUSEMENT PARK			PICNICKING	
HORSEBACK RIDING			PLAYGROUND	
SKIING/WINTER SPORTS			SHOPPING	
PARK			PLANTS/GARDENS/NATURE TRAILS	
ANIMAL VIEWING			FARMS	

Help Us Keep This Guide Up to Date

Every effort has been made by the author and editors to make this guide as accurate and useful as possible. However, many changes can occur after a guide is published—establishments close, phone numbers change, hiking trails are rerouted, facilities come under new management, etc.

We would love to hear from you concerning your experiences with this guide and how you feel it could be improved and be kept up to date. While we may not be able to respond to all comments and suggestions, we'll take them to heart, and we'll make certain to share them with the author. Please send your comments and suggestions to the following address:

The Globe Pequot Press
Reader Response/Editorial Department
P.O. Box 480
Guilford, CT 06437

Or you may e-mail us at: editorial@GlobePequot.com

Thanks for your input, and happy travels!

Southern Maine

outhern Maine is filled with enchanting places for you and your family to explore: quaint fishing villages wrapped around snug coves; long white beaches washed smooth by the cool Atlantic surf; harbor ports alive with pleasure crafts and fishing boats; lighthouses poised majestically on rocky cliffs.

The distinctive beauty and charm of southern Maine are captivating. But that's not all. A variety of activities and attractions ensure a vacation packed with one adventure after another. Journey back in time, touring homes and forts centuries old. Thrill to the rides of various amusement parks. Search antiques shops for a rare treasure, or shop the outlets if what you're really looking for is a bargain. Admire masterpieces in art museums. Watch in awe as humpback whales frolic in the deep.

This is just a sampling of what awaits you in southern Maine, and it's only the beginning of a diverse and delightful vacation when you choose to explore the Pine Tree State.

Kittery

The gateway to Maine, Kittery is also Maine's oldest town. Settled in 1623 and incorporated in 1652, it was the state's early center of shipbuilding. The town's maritime heritage is celebrated at the Kittery Historical and Naval Museum.

Kittery Point boasts some of Maine's, and possibly the country's, oldest buildings. Beautiful mansions also dot this area, which was once the summer haven of literary and artistic giants such as Samuel Clemens (Mark Twain).

Today, beyond an intriguing history, Kittery offers travelers a modern-day shopping extravaganza. There are more than one hundred factory outlets along Route 1, and they're ranked among the best in the nation for quality and variety of name-brand stores.

SOUTHERN MAINE

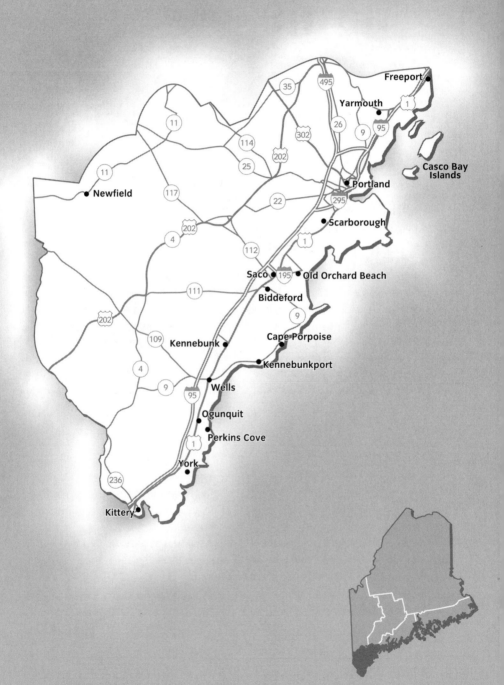

Kittery Trading Post (all ages)

301 Route 1; (888) KTP–MAINE (587–6246); www.kitterytradingpost.com. Open daily 9:00 A.M. to 9:00 P.M., Sunday 10:00 A.M. to 6:00 P.M.

What began as a one-room trading post/gas station in the 1930s has become a Maine attraction, with 42,000 square feet of retail space. Racks of clothes, unbelievable amounts of sporting goods, and much more are all at this one store. You can buy fishing gear, a canoe, picnic items, or souvenirs. Departments for camping, rock climbing, archery, and fishing, as well as winter, water, and shooting sports, will provide you with equipment for every outdoor adventure imaginable.

Your children will marvel at the larger-than-life chain-saw carvings of pioneers. They'll love playing in the tents set up in the camping area. Several natural history exhibits throughout the store are guaranteed to capture their attention. This is one store the kids won't be begging to leave.

If that weren't enough, the trading post also offers special events like Ski Fest, Fishing Fest, Kayak Demo Day, and On Snow Demo Day to help you learn more about enjoying the great outdoors.

Bonnie's
Top Ten Picks for Southern Maine

1. More than 10,000 pounds of goodies at Yummies Candy & Nuts in Kittery; (207) 439–5649.
2. A Ghostly Tour by candlelight of historic York Village; (207) 363–0000.
3. A seaside walk along the Marginal Way in Ogunguit; (207) 646–2939.
4. The Discovery Program at Laudholm Farm in Wells; (207) 646–1555.
5. Homemade doughnuts from Congdon's in Wells; (207) 646–4219.
6. Revisiting the 1800s at Willowbrook at Newfield Restoration Village; (207) 793–2784.
7. Whale watching aboard *Nick's Chance* in Kennebunkport; (800) 767–2628.
8. Watching movies the old-fashioned way at the Saco Drive-In; (207) 284–1016.
9. Riding the roller coaster at Funtown/Splashtown USA in Saco; (800) 878–2900.
10. Enjoying the view from atop the Ferris wheel at Palace Playland in Old Orchard Beach; (207) 934–2001.

Amazing
Maine Facts

Frisbee's General Store in Kittery is said to be America's oldest family store. It has been owned and operated by the same family since its establishment in 1828.

Yummies Candy & Nuts (ages 2 and up)

Route 1 and Haley Road; (207) 439–5649 or (877) 498–6643; www.yummies.com. Open daily 9:00 A.M. to 6:00 P.M.

If you've spent the day shopping and the kids have been good, reward them with a treat from Yummies. Their eyes will light up at the sight of more than 10,000 pounds of candy and nuts. There's everything from homemade fudge to gourmet jelly beans. Sugar-free candies are also available. Chances are the kids won't be the only ones nibbling on a treat on the way out the door.

Kittery Historical and Naval Museum (ages 4 and up)

Intersection of U.S. Route 1 and Route 236, Rogers Road; (207) 439–3080. Open from June 1 to October 31, Tuesday through Saturday, from 10:00 A.M. to 4:00 P.M. $. Children 6 and under are admitted free.

This museum, founded in 1975, traces the region's shipbuilding heritage from the American Revolution to the present. John Paul Jones' ship, the USS *Ranger*, which was launched in the Piscataqua River in 1777, is on display here.

Other artifacts include seventeenth- and eighteenth-century English wine bottles, a belt and shoe buckle from the same era, and a redware clay milk pan, all discovered during a 1978 dig at the site of the Mitchell Garrison farm in Kittery Point.

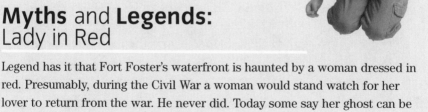

Myths and Legends:
Lady in Red

Legend has it that Fort Foster's waterfront is haunted by a woman dressed in red. Presumably, during the Civil War a woman would stand watch for her lover to return from the war. He never did. Today some say her ghost can be seen drifting near the pilings of an old pier.

Fort McClary State Historic Site (all ages)

Route 103; (207) 439–2845. Open daily, Memorial Day through October 1, 9:00 A.M. to 8:00 P.M. $ For children under 5 admission is free.

Originally named Fort Williams, the fort now bears the name of the Revolutionary War hero Andrew McClary. Built in 1690, it has proved crucial to the area's defense. Expanded during the American Revolution, the War of 1812, and the Civil War, the fort also underwent further changes during the 1898 Spanish-American War. The most memorable aspect of this landmark is the hexagonal wooden blockhouse, built in 1812 and reputed to be the last blockhouse built in Maine.

This is a great place for the kids to explore. Picnic tables are also available if you want to bring a lunch, eat outdoors, and enjoy the beautiful views.

Fort Foster (all ages)

Off Route 103, Pocahontas Road, Kittery Point; (207) 439–2182. Open 10:00 A.M. to 8:00 P.M. weekends only in May and September, daily in June, July, and August. There is a set admission fee of $10 per vehicle.

Now a municipal park on Gerrish Island, Fort Foster offers swimming at pebble beaches, fishing, a ball field, a pier, picnic spots, and nature trails.

During World War II, Fort Foster anchored one end of a submerged net that was intended to keep prowling German submarines from spying on the Portsmouth Naval Shipyard.

The fort provides nice views of Whaleback Lighthouse, at the mouth of the Piscataqua River.

Kittery Outlets (all ages)

Route 1, Kittery; (888) KITTERY; www.thekitteryoutlets.com.

More than a mile. More than a hundred stores. Sounds like a challenge most vacationers would be willing to take. Start off with a cup of java from Starbucks and you're ready to go.

Ladies can find new duds at Old Navy, J. Crew, or Banana Republic. Men can suit up at Polo Ralph Lauren, Eddie Bauer, or Gap. The kids will be styling with outfits from Carter's, OshKosh B'Gosh, or The Children's Outlet. Afterward, take a leisurely lunch break at Weathervane Seafood Restaurant, or Noel's Cafe and Coffee Shop, or grab a quick bite at McDonald's or Burger King. Then it's back to shopping.

Amazing Maine Facts

Kittery boasts Maine's oldest home, the Bray House, built in 1661, and Maine's oldest church, built in 1730.

Spruce up the house with something from Linens 'N Things, Pfaltzgraff, or Yankee Candle. Take home a special souvenir to a friend from Mostly Maine, Perfumania, or The Sweatshirt Shop. By the end of the day you might have worn a hole in your shoes from all the walking you've done. No problem. Timberland, Dexter, or Nine West will fix you right up.

When all is said and done, you'll rest well—not just from all the exercise but from all you've saved at these outlet stores. The Kittery Outlets give a whole new meaning to shopping on Maine Street.

Where to Eat

Bob's Clam Hut. 315 Route 1; (207) 439–4233; www.bobsclamhut.com. Open year-round, Bob's is frequented by locals who enjoy outstanding fried clams. Kids will enjoy such fare as hot dogs, hamburgers, and grilled cheese. $

Cap'n Simeon's Galley. 90 Pepperrell Road, Kittery Point; (207) 439–3655. Located behind Frisbee's General Store, Simeon's offers dining with a view. Look out over beautiful Pepperell Cove as you enjoy house favorites like broiled haddock. Sandwiches, burgers, quiche, salads, and steak are also part of the menu. Prices are reasonable and fit for large families. $–$$

Warren's Lobster House. 11 Water Street/U.S. Route 1; (207) 439–1630; www.lobster house.com. Lobster, lobster, and more lobster is what you'll find here. Have lobster puffs or lobster cakes for starters and lobster thermidor, alfredo, or scampi for your main course. If lobster claws are your favorite you can order a pile of claws, and not have to mess with the rest. Check out their Web site for coupons and specials. $$–$$$$

Weathervane Seafood Restaurant. 306 Route 1; (207) 439–0335; www.weathervane seafoods.com. This is a favorite of tourists and locals alike. There are special deals on the kids' menu, and you can check out the Web site for other savings (i.e., a World Wide Web VIP card good for a **free** appetizer). If you want to enjoy fresh Maine lobsters back home, the Weathervane will be happy to ship them for you. Burgers and fries and other entrees also available. $–$$

Where to Stay

Blue Roof Motel. 59 Old Post Road; (207) 439–9324. This motel offers comfortable rooms and an outdoor pool. Pets are welcome, and kids 12 and under stay for **free**. $–$$

The Coachman Inn. 380 U.S. Route 1; (207) 439–4434 or (800) 824–6183; www.coach maninn.net. If you love to shop, you'll love this hotel because it's the only one within walking distance of the Kittery Outlets. A full complimentary breakfast, outdoor pool, and Jacuzzi rooms add to its charm. Best of all, children under 14 stay **free**—giving you more money for shopping. $–$$$

Enchanted Nights Bed & Breakfast. 29 Wentworth Street; (207) 439–1489; www. enchanted-nights-bandb.com. Most bed-and-breakfasts have an age restriction for children or don't allow them at all. Not this one. Here, even infants are welcome. You have your choice of seven rooms, some with large whirlpool tubs. The Cottage Room, which features a private entrance and two rooms, is great for families. Breakfast served on antique floral china is also part of the package. $–$$$$

Northeaster Motel. 79 Old Post Road; (207) 439–0116. Choose from eleven rooms or five cottages. There's an outdoor pool open in-season. Rates are reasonable, but with a $5.00 charge for each additional person, this is not a great choice for larger families. $–$$

Super 8 Motel. 85 Route 1 Bypass; (800) 800–8000 or (207) 439–2000. Travelers will appreciate the twenty-four-hour complimentary coffee. Kids will like the outdoor pool. Pets can stay the night for an extra $10. $–$$

For More Information

Kittery-Eliot-South Berwick Chamber of Commerce. (800) 639–9645; www.southern mainecoast.org.

Other Things to **See** and **Do**

Don't miss these other sites in Kittery: John Paul Jones Memorial, Lady Pepperell House, Portsmouth Naval Shipyard, Brave Boat Harbor Trail, and Seapoint Beach.

York

Just up the road from Kittery you'll find York, which comprises four distinct areas: York Village, York Harbor, York Beach, and Cape Neddick. So varied are these communities that locals don't even refer to them as one town but rather as "the Yorks." During the summer, these communities are linked via a trolley service. This is something you'll want to look into if visiting between Memorial Day and Labor Day, when the population of York nearly quadruples and getting around can be difficult.

So hop the trolley and see all that York has to offer families looking for fun. Get a taste of yesteryear in the Old York Historic District. Make rubbings of early tombstones at the Old Burying Ground. Enjoy a walk along Long Sands Beach. Watch spellbound as taffy is stirred and pulled at Goldenrod's. Stare into the eyes of Maine's only white tiger at York's Wild Kingdom.

Amazing
Maine Facts

Chartered in 1641, York (named Gorgeana at the time) was America's first chartered city. Years later, when Maine became the northern province of Massachusetts, York was demoted to a town and remained such even after Maine became an independent state in 1820.

Old York Historical Society Museum (all ages)

207 York Street; (207) 363–4974; www.oldyork.org. Open daily, except Monday, mid-June through September. Hours are 10:00 A.M. to 5:00 P.M. Tuesday through Saturday, 1:00 to 5:00 P.M. Sunday. $$. Free for children under 6.

This museum is made up of seven historic buildings: Jefferds Tavern, the Emerson-Wilcox House, the Elizabeth Perkins House, Old Gaol Museum, the George Marshall Store, John Hancock Warehouse, and the Old Schoolhouse. The tavern, a watering hole for travelers as far back as 1759, is now the visitors center for the museum. Tickets and parking are available here, and you'll often find food cooking on the hearth.

The **Emerson-Wilcox House**, dating in part from the 1740s, has served as everything from a tailor shop to a post office. Today the house contains period rooms complete with furnishings, ceramics, and glass. The Declaration of Independence bears the signature of the man who once owned the John Hancock Warehouse. Today it houses exhibits depicting life and industry along the York River during the 1700s. The **Elizabeth Perkins House** is a farmhouse decorated with colonial-era antiques, and the George Marshall Store brings the maritime history of the area to life.

The building bound to have the greatest appeal to youngsters is the **Old Gaol Museum**, built in 1719 and used until 1860 as a jail for debtors and criminals. Kids will stare wide-eyed at the dungeons, cells, and jailer's quarters furnished as they might have been around 1790. The chilling exhibit of instruments of torture is sure to get a reaction.

Cape Neddick Lighthouse (all ages)

Sohier Park, Nubble Road, off Route 1; (800) 639–2442; www.gatewaytomaine.org/visit/lighthousesframe.html.

When Captain Bartholomew Gosnold landed on the tip of Cape Neddick in 1602, he met with local tribes. Two years later Captain John Smith charted the area. He is credited with

Scary Stories

A chilling way to learn about historic York village, and one the kids won't soon forget, is to take a Ghostly Tour (207–363–0000). Escorted by a hooded guide, you'll tour the village by candlelight, listening to authentic ghost stories, witch tales, and folklore of the eighteenth and nineteenth centuries. Tours run nightly June through October.

Amazing
Maine Facts

Old Gaol, a jail dating from 1719, originally served as the king's prison for the entire Province of Maine. It is the oldest remaining municipal building of the English colonies.

the term *knubble,* for which the little island at the tip of the cape became known. The term apparently stuck. Today the lighthouse perched on that island is best known to locals as Nubble Light, or simply the Nubble. Built in 1879, Nubble Light's tower stretches 41 feet from ground to beacon. The tower and a group of red-roofed, white buildings are picture-perfect. Indeed, Nubble Light is one of the most photographed lighthouses on the East Coast.

The light was automated in 1987, at which time the last keeper left the island. Today the light is maintained by the U.S. Coast Guard, and public access to the island is prohibited. However, you can get a great view from Sohier Park, located at the tip of the peninsula. The park includes a parking area, rest rooms, and a seasonal Welcome Center complete with lighthouse information and mementos. You can also take a cruise and view Nubble Light from sea.

York Wild Kingdom Zoo and Amusement Park (all ages)

Route 1, 102 Railroad Avenue, York Beach; (800) 456–4911; www.yorkzoo.com. Open daily May through September from 10:00 A.M. to 5:00 P.M. (times may vary). Combo tickets for both the zoo and amusement park or tickets for the zoo only are available. $$

Come investigate the exotic birds and animals in this "wild kingdom," which houses Maine's only white tiger. Children enjoy petting deer and handling friendly snakes. They

Galas Galore

The people of York like to celebrate, so no matter when you choose to visit, chances are you can join the party. The summer festivities of **York Days** (207–363–1040) include concerts, contests, and carnival fun. **Harvestfest** (207–363–4422) brings in autumn with hayrides, apple pressing, and colonial crafts. Numerous activities, top-notch entertainment, and samplings from local restaurants will make you thankful you came. Winter is never dull, as the **Festival of Lights** (207–363–4974) illuminates historic York Village with parades, fairs, caroling, and jolly old St. Nick himself. Finally, you can swing into spring at **York's Annual Golf Tournament** (207–363–4422).

Check It Out: Wiggly Bridge

If you're traveling from York Village toward York Harbor along Route 103, be sure to stop and walk across the smallest suspension bridge in the world. Don't forget the camera.

can also feed and pet goats, marvel at prairie dogs, be mesmerized by monkeys, and laugh at lions. If you and the kids are lucky, a camel will spit on you. It's said to bring good luck. Elephant rides are big business here, as are the pony rides.

In addition to the animals, the Wild Kingdom Zoo facility also has paddleboats, a gift shop, shows and demonstrations, and a small playground. A centrally located snack bar can help put hunger behind you, and the well-kept grounds provide places to rest and relax.

If animals don't quite meet your energy or interest levels, you can spend most of your time in the complex's amusement park. Rides, games, and other entertainment typical of carnivals are here.

The Goldenrod (all ages)

2 Railroad Avenue, York Beach; (207) 363–2621; www.thegoldenrod.com. Open daily Memorial Day to Labor Day from 8:00 A.M. to 10:30 P.M. $–$$

Rain or shine, you'll find people standing outside The Goldenrod, staring spellbound through the large plate-glass window. The reason—Goldenrod Kisses, said to be the original saltwater taffy. Folks love to watch this chewy delight being made.

At the heart of York Beach, this cozy restaurant has been around for more than one hundred years. Always packed, the full menu is served all day, making it easy for you to enjoy any meal at an off hour, when the line won't be so long. Even if you have a short wait, you can spend it watching the saltwater kisses being stirred, pulled, and wrapped.

Eat in the dining room amid the glow of the stone fireplace, or indulge in some homemade ice cream served up at an old-fashioned soda fountain. After a great meal at affordable prices you'll have a little left over to spend at the gift shop. And if you're inclined to enjoy an after-dinner stroll, the beach is within walking distance.

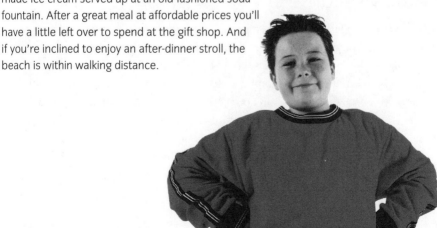

Surf's **Up** in York

The beach is a wonderful diversion for kids who are tired of riding in the car. So succumb to the pull of crashing waves and warm sand, because no matter where you are in York, there's a beach nearby.

- The little ones need wide open spaces, and **Long Sands Beach** provides plenty of that. Aptly named, Long Sands stretches for nearly 2 miles from York Harbor to Cape Neddick. Your children can explore the coarse, gray sand and the nooks and crannies of this shore while enjoying the playful action of soaring gulls. If your family prefers surfing to playing in the sand, there's a designated spot to ride the waves. Metered parking, a bathhouse, and food vendors within walking distance from any spot on the sand all work together to make this a family-friendly beach.

- **Short Sands Beach** is also popular with families. What this beach lacks in length it makes up for in playground equipment. Adjacent to Ellis Park, Short Sands Beach enables kids to go from swimming to swinging, from building sand castles to climbing monkey bars. York Beach village provides a beautiful Victorian-era backdrop, and a large metered parking lot and bathhouse provide modern-day conveniences.

- **York Harbor Beach** is a small, pebbly beach with hard, dark sand. It's a beautiful place to watch boats as they sail in and out of the harbor. The beach is an easy walk from village shops, and metered parking is available, though limited. A hike along Cliff Walk is a sure bet for draining some of the kids' excess energy. However, the trail can be difficult and is not recommended for younger children.

Where to Eat

Frazios. 38 Woodbridge Road; (207) 363–7019; www.frazios.com. This Italian eatery serves up everything from manicotti to seafood tecchia. All meals are prepared from scratch and can be complemented by desserts such as triple chocolate truffle cake or pumpkin swirl cheesecake. Kids' meals include drinks and desserts. Home of award-winning LaStalla pizza, the prices are praiseworthy as well. $–$$

The Goldenrod. See previous page.

Rick's All Seasons Restaurant. 240 York Street; (207) 363–5584. Located in the middle of York village, this is a real find for families. Good prices. Good food. Good service. Enjoy a hearty breakfast for next to nothing. Warm up with homemade clam chowder for lunch. Stop by for a dinner of beer-battered fish. $

Sweet Josie's Candy Shoppe. 7 Railroad Avenue, York Beach; (207) 351–1169. What saltwater taffy is to Goldenrod's, fudge is to Josie's. You'll find fifty different flavors of fudge here. Tough decision? Then don't even look at the varieties of candy, ice cream, doughnuts, and, yes, even taffy that round out this quaint candy shoppe.

When Pigs Fly. 40 Brickyard Court; (207) 363–0612; www.sendbread.com. If you're on the Atkins' diet, this is not the place for you. If not, you're in heaven. Hog Heaven, one of their most popular breads, is made with sun-dried cranberries, homemade granola, and cinnamon. Tuscan Wheat, New York Rye, Sun-dried Tomato, Multi-Grain Anadama, and more are all baked with organic, natural ingredients. So skip the salad and have a slice of Veggie Bread instead. $

Wildcat Pizza. 449 Route 1; (207) 351–3378. Create a pizza with personality. Choose from a variety of crusts, including Bavarian six-grain and San Francisco sourdough. Add any combination of more than forty unique toppings, including fresh shrimp and artichokes. Of course, you can always stick with something more traditional. Dine in, carry out, or get a Take 'n' Bake pizza—just pop it in the oven at dinnertime. This is a fantastic idea for families. Another family plus: Kids get a free drink and slice of pizza (cheese or pepperoni) with any adult dine-in order. $–$$

Where to Stay

The Anchorage Inn. 265 Long Beach Avenue, York Beach; (207) 363–5112; www.anchorageinn.com. The inn has more than one hundred oceanfront rooms with a picturesque view of Nubble Light. An indoor and outdoor pool, fitness room, poolside cafe, and oceanfront restaurant are some of the extras. $–$$

Long Beach Motor Inn. 271 Long Beach Avenue, York Beach; (207) 363–5481; www.chickadee.com/longbeach. This motel sits on three acres of beachfront property. Beautifully landscaped, it stands out in the crowd of motels lining Route 1A. Families will appreciate the thirty-two large efficiency units complete with eat-in kitchen. A family-style backyard with heated pool, shuffleboard, badminton, and barbecue areas makes this a real home away from home. $–$$$

Stage Neck Inn. 22 Stage Neck Road, York Harbor; (800) 340–1130; www.stageneck.com. If you prefer being pampered to being frugal, this is the place for you. Enjoy a massage after a workout in the fitness room. Relax in the Jacuzzi after a swim in the indoor or outdoor pool. Indulge in fine dining after working on your golf swing or tennis serve. All this and you haven't even left the hotel! Rates are high, but gourmet get-

Other Things to **See** and **Do**

If you're staying awhile, York has a few more surprises for you. Hike, bike, or ride horseback on Mount Agamenticus. See the mix-up at the Civil War Monument, where a statue of a Confederate, not a Union, soldier stands. History buffs will want to check out the First Parish Church and the Sayward-Wheeler House, or for something a little different try taking a ghostly tour of the Historic District. Lighthouse enthusiasts will admire the view of Boon Island Light, 6 miles offshore.

away packages are available year-round. $$$$

Sunrise Motel. P.O. Box 1044, Long Beach Avenue, York Harbor; (207) 363–4542 or (800) 242–0750; www.sunrisemotel.net. Open year-round, this motel offers twenty-five units with ocean views. $–$$$$

For More Information

Greater York Region Chamber of Commerce. (207) 363–4422; www.gatewayto maine.org.

Ogunquit and Perkins Cove

While vacationing in Maine, plan to spend some time in the Ogunquit area. Drive up the Shore Road (off Route 1 in Ogunquit). It provides scenery that has to be seen to be believed. The village of Perkins Cove will be encountered as you pass through Ogunquit's southern end. This picturesque spot was once home to fishermen and artists. Restaurants, shops, cafes, galleries, and similar attractions now consume most of the real estate, and parking can be a problem. But it's hard to imagine a spot that feels more like Maine than Perkins Cove. Artists still perch upon the waterworn rocks and bring their canvases alive with images of a salty seaport.

As you walk the streets of this tourist town, you will come across dozens of shops offering everything from jewelry to crafts. Golden Sails, Cove's End, The Country Shop, and the Strawberry Bazaar are fun shops to explore. If you or your kids have a sweet tooth, visit Ayla's Sweet Shop. The Artist's Gallery and Ocean Winds Art Gallery are good places to look for something to take home with you.

You and your children can venture out on the pedestrian drawbridge that spans the harbor entrance. If you're lucky, a large sailboat will blow its horn to request the raising of the bridge when you are nearby. This is done with a series of buttons, and it's common for the nearest person to the drawbridge keeper to become honorary operator of the bridge. Kids get a real kick out of this.

If you don't feel like walking, you can take advantage of the local trolley. The service runs from late May through Columbus Day from 8:00 A.M. to 9:00 P.M. in the fringe season and 8:00 A.M. to 11:00 P.M. between July 1 and Labor Day. Trolley rides are $1.50 per person. Children under 10 ride **free.**

Myths and Legends: Painted Rocks

At the turn of the twentieth century, inspired by the town's exquisite scenery, painter Charles Woodbury formed the Ogunquit art colony. Legend has it that the area was soon so flooded with artists that the cliffs were actually colored by the painted spray of those who washed their brushes in the ocean mist.

Marginal Way (all ages)
Perkins Cove. Free.

This favorite footpath stretches for more than a mile along the shore between the villages of Ogunquit and Perkins Cove. Artists of all types flock here for inspiration. The walk is beautiful as you weave your way along granite cliffs and look down on crashing surf. Plenty of beaches along the path allow you to rest and linger over the view. The trail begins next to the Sparhawk Resort on Shore Road in downtown Ogunquit.

Children enjoy the tidal pools that can be explored as you walk this path that once served as a cattle highway. A farmer, Josiah Chase, gave the Marginal Way to the town of Ogunquit in 1923. In doing this, he preserved a right-of-way to drive cattle down the path and around rocky Israel's Head each summer to graze on the marsh grass in Wells. Parking for this path is difficult to find, but check around the mini lighthouse on Israel's Head and at the town police station on Cottage Street.

Perkins Cove **Cruises**

Water-related activities are abundant in Perkins Cove. For sight-seeing trips or fishing trips, bring your deck shoes and hop a boat to take in all the salty air you can stand. Try Finestkind Scenic Cruises (207–646–5227; www.finest kindcruises.com), if you would like to go out on a lobster fishing excursion or take a cruise by Nubble Light for some breathtaking photo opportunities. Cruises run from mid-May to mid-October, and prices range from $10.00 to $15.00 for adults and $7.00 to $10.00 for children. Some cruises may be more. If deep-sea fishing is more your style, the *Bunny Clark* (207–626–2214; www.bunnyclark.com) or the *Ugly Anne* (207–646–7202; www.uglyanne.com) can fix you right up. Be prepared to see whales and seals as you drift over the wild Atlantic. From April to mid-November half-day cruises are $40 per person. Reservations are recommended for all cruises.

Ogunquit Beach (all ages)
Beach Street. There are five municipal parking lots with varying rates. $–$$

A wonderful destination, Ogunquit Beach sprawls out over 3 miles of sand and surf. As you see the dunes, you might think the waving sea grass is beckoning you to visit. Another welcoming feature this beach has to offer is its location on a large sandbar between the Ogunquit River and the Atlantic. You have your choice of swimming in the river or the ocean.

The most popular access to this beach is from the foot of Beach Street. Your kids can get a snack along the boardwalk, change into swimming gear, or use the rest rooms along the way.

Amazing
Maine Facts

Maine boasts 3,478 beautiful miles of coastline.

Another means of reaching Ogunquit Beach is the Footbridge Beach access. You arrive here by taking Ocean Street off Route 1, about 1 mile north of the center of Ogunquit. This access is less crowded and offers rest rooms for visitors. Moody Beach also has an entrance to Ogunquit Beach; Eldridge Street off Route 1 in Wells is the road to take for this access. Moody Beach is private property above the high-water mark, so don't stray onto sections where you may get into trouble with landowners and police.

Ogunquit Playhouse (ages 7 and up)
Route 1, P.O. Box 915, Ogunquit 03907; (207) 646–5511; www. ogunquitplayhouse.org. Open late June through August with productions Monday through Friday at 8:00 P.M. and Saturday at 8:30 P.M., matinees on Wednesday at 2:30 P.M. and Saturday at 3:00 P.M. $$$$ (Saturday Kid's Korner at noon; $$)

Broadway talent has gained the Ogunquit Playhouse a reputation as "America's Foremost Summer Theater." Stars having graced this grand old stage include Sally Struthers, Bette Davis, Jeff Bridges, and Olympia Dukakis.

The curtain first rose in 1933, and the audience has been yelling "bravo" ever since. The four to five productions (depending on when Labor Day falls) presented each summer include dramas, comedies, and musicals.

Saturday at noon is devoted to plays the kids will really enjoy. *Charlie and the Chocolate Factory, Pinocchio,* and *The Princess and the Pea* are just a sample of the wonderful productions for children. General admission is only $8.00 per person, sweetening the appeal of Saturday Kid's Korner.

Where to Eat

Barnacle Billy's. Oarweed Road, Ogunquit; (207) 646–5575 or (800) 866–5575; www.barn billy.com. This seasonal harborside restaurant is packed during the summer. Lobster stew, made by Billy himself, is a house favorite. Dine on deck watching boats drift in and out of the harbor. Good food and a great view are reasons for its popularity. $$$

Hurricane. Perkins Cove, Ogunquit; (800) 649–6348; www.hurricanerestaurant.com. Extraordinary in its menu and the fact it's open year-round, this trendy restaurant offers deviled Maine lobster cakes and rack of lamb served over a French white bean cassoulet. Here you can indulge in a true surf and turf—filet mignon and lobster tail—or enjoy Sunday brunch while listening to live jazz. Definitely a place for families

Amazing
Maine Facts

Named by Abenaki Indians, Ogunquit means "beautiful place by the sea."

with older children and deep pockets. $$$$

Lobster Shack. Perkins Cove, Ogunquit; (207) 646–2941. If you're a lobster lover, this is one of the best bets in town. Reasonably priced, this old-style restaurant has been serving up new and hard-shell lobster for more than fifty years. Don't forget your bib. $$

Oarweed Restaurant and Lobster Pound. P.O. Box 1889, Perkins Cove, Ogunquit 03907; (207) 646–4022; www.oarweed.com. This is one of our family's favorites. If you prefer the view of the open ocean to the crowded harbor, and baked and broiled seafood to fried, this is the place for you too. The large, rustic dining room is cozy, and the stuffed baked potatoes are delicious. The kids will enjoy coloring their special placemat menus. $$–$$$

Vinny's East Coast Grille. Route 1, Ogunquit; (207) 646–5115; www.vinnys.com. Vinny's is worth mentioning because of their family room especially designed for kids. The room is full of sights, sounds, lights, and action. The kids menu is reasonable, and the full menu includes everything from pizza and pasta to seafood and sirloin. Definitely merits a visit. $$$

Where to Stay

The Beachmere Inn. 62 Beachmere Lane, Ogunquit; (207) 646–2021 or (800) 336–3983; www.beachmereinn.com. Open March to mid-December. You'll have a choice of

accommodation at this secluded yet spacious facility. Stay in the hundred-year-old Victorian Inn, the sixteen-unit motel, or the cozy seaside cottage. $–$$$$

The Dunes. 518 Main Street, Ogunquit; (888) 285–3863; www.dunesmotel.com. Located on twelve acres fronting the Ogunquit River, The Dunes is just a short walk from Ogunquit Beach during low tide or a short ride in complimentary rowboats at high tide. More than half of the thirty-six units are New England cottages, most with fireplaces. $$

The Grand Hotel. 276 Shore Road, Ogunquit; (800) 806–1231 or (207) 646–1231; www.thegrandhotel.com. Large suites featuring refrigerators, a wet bar, cable TV, and VCR. **Free** continental breakfast and underground parking. $$–$$$$

Ogunquit Resort Motel. 719 Main Street, Ogunquit; (877) 646–8336; www.ogunquitresort.com. The model is totally renovated and open year-round. Your family will enjoy the heated pool and hot tub. There's a fitness room for adults and a game room for the kids—if they're 12 and under, they get to stay for **free**. Refrigerators in the room and a complimentary continental breakfast make this a good deal for families. $–$$$$

For More Information

Ogunquit Chamber of Commerce. (207) 646–2939; www.ogunquit.org.

Other Things to **See** and **Do**

The cove and the beach are big hits. Still, there are other places to investigate: Leavitt Fine Arts Theater, Footbridge Beach, the Ogunquit Museum of American Art, and Ogunquit Wooden Toy store.

Wells

Wells became Maine's third incorporated town in 1653. A mill town, it suffered frequent attacks from local tribes and other enemies. The Battle of 1692 changed all that, when just twenty-four valiant settlers took cover in the Joseph Storer House and successfully fought off 400 French and Indian raiders. The house still stands on Route 1. Today Wells provides 62 square miles of land for its 9,000 year-round residents, who live in named sections that combine to form the town. Moody Beach accounts for the southern coastal area, Wells Beach is part of the makeup, and Drakes Island is the most northerly beach. The western end is flanked by sections called High Pine, Wells Branch, and Merriland Ridge. Until 1980, Ogunquit was also part of Wells.

Wells Recreation Area (all ages)

Route 9A; (207) 646–5826. The park is open daily from dawn to dusk. Admission is free. Tennis courts are available for daytime play, May through November.

This seventy-acre playground for young and old alike includes four asphalt tennis courts, two basketball courts, and a baseball diamond, among other attractions. Picnic tables welcome visitors, while those interested in staying fit can work out along a 2-mile fitness course. The sound of horseshoes clanking together can be heard as good sports try to ring the peg. A dirt track surrounding an all-purpose sports field provides a place for walking and running.

Putting Around

Enjoy outdoor fun with the kids at one of these miniature golf courses conveniently located on Route 1 in Wells. **Wonder Mountain** (207–646–9655) offers two eighteen-hole courses and a mountain complete with waterfalls and caves. **Wells Beach Mini-Golf** (800–640–2267), part of a resort campground, is open to the public. Wells Beach features various terrains including bridges, fountains, and a roaring cave under a 25-foot waterfall, all surrounding an eighteen-hole, par 42 course.

Visitors here can also enjoy Hobb's Pond, adjacent to the recreation area. A dock is provided for visitors to use in launching their own canoes and kayaks. Children will want to spend hours on the massive playground, and adults will welcome the fresh Maine air as they take a breather during their busy vacations.

Wells Harbor (all ages)

Walk along a granite jetty or rent some fishing tackle and bait. You and your kids can fish from a municipal dock or from harbor jetties. Surf casting is available near the mouth of the Mousam River. A variety of fish inhabits these waters, so every tug on the line can bring in a surprise. A recreation area offers a playground for the kids and concerts under a gazebo for all.

A Merrill Family Adventure:
Playing Bridge

When we lived in Wells, strolling the Marginal Way was a favorite pastime. The explosive drama of sea meeting rocks never failed to amaze me. Our walks were unhurried. Often we'd stop and sit on one of the benches along the path, watching the white sails of boats turn amber from the setting sun.

We'd make our way to the Oarweed Restaurant (see Ogunquit), in the clearing at the end of the Marginal Way. We'd enjoy a succulent dinner of lobster, salad, and baked stuffed potato, with piping hot steamers for starters and the sweetest homemade apple pie as the grand finale. (Most locals won't spend the money to eat lobster out because fish markets provide them so cheaply. However, being a transplant from Virginia, I just can't help myself.)

Our bellies full, we'd walk out onto the pedestrian drawbridge for an unencumbered view of the harbor. Kids are always aching for a chance to raise and lower the bridge, allowing sailboats to pass through. But let's face it—adults are always aching to act like children. Once I just happened to be at the bridge controls when the toot of a large sailboat pierced the air—my chance had come. I pushed the buttons, the alarm bell rang out, and the bridge went up.

We watched as the sailboat entered the harbor, the captain and crew waving their thanks. I handed the controls over to one of the kids nearby. There were squeals of delight as the alarm rang and the bridge came back down. Later, as we headed back along the Marginal Way, we all agreed it had been a particularly good evening.

Museum at Historic First Meeting House

(ages 7 and up)

Route 1 and Buzzel Road; (207) 646–4775. Open
during summer Monday and Wednesday
10:00 A.M. to 4:00 P.M., Thursday 1:00 to 4:00
P.M., and every second and fourth Saturday
10:00 A.M. to noon. Off-season hours: Wednesday 10:00 A.M. to 4:00 P.M. and Thursday 1:00 to
4:00 P.M. $

Operated by the Historical Society of Wells and Ogunquit,
the First Meeting House is a National Registered Landmark. This museum, once a church,
traces the birth of religious freedom. Artifacts, memorabilia, and genealogies of early
Wells residents also shed light on this historic seaport town.

Wells Auto Museum (all ages)

Route 1; (207) 646–9064. Open daily 10:00 A.M. to 5:00 P.M. mid-June through mid-
September, weekends only in May and October. $. Free for children under 6.

Like antique cars? Then this museum, housing more than seventy classic automobiles, is
paradise. Among them you can see a 1955 Chrysler 300A, a 1918 Stutz Bearcat, and a
1941 Packard convertible. Antique car rides are part of the fun here, and most children
enjoy the sensation of a jaunt in a Model T Ford. If your kids don't like cars, chances are
good that they will stay entertained with the museum's arcade games and nickelodeons
while the adults enjoy the exhibits. A gift shop holds treasures for souvenir collectors.

Rachel Carson National Wildlife Refuge (all ages)

321 Port Road; (207) 646–9226. Trail open from dawn to dusk. Information Center open
from 8:00 A.M. to 4:30 P.M. Monday through Friday, limited weekend hours during summer.
Admission is free, although donations are accepted.

Protecting critical coastal wetlands from Cape Elizabeth to Kittery, the nearly 5,000-acre
refuge provides migration and wintering habitat for waterfowl and other migratory birds.
More than 280 species of birds, mammals, reptiles, and amphibians have been observed
here. A 1-mile self-guided trail begins at the refuge headquarters. The trail offers spectacular views of coastal marshes in season, beautiful wildflowers can be seen. Bikes are not
permitted on the trail, and pets must be leashed at all times.

Wells National Estuarine Research Preserve (all ages)

342 Laudholm Farm Road; (207) 646–1555. Trails open daily May 15 to September 15 from
8:00 A.M. to 8:00 P.M. The gift shop and Visitor Center is open Monday through Saturday
10:00 A.M. to 4:00 P.M. and Sunday noon to 4:00 P.M. Admission is free. A parking fee is
charged in July and August, except on Tuesday, and varies up to $10 per car.

A wonderful way to experience nature, this is one place you can't pass up. Dedicated to
preservation and research, the reserve's 1,600 acres encompass fields, forest, wetlands,
and beach area. Three rivers—the Merriland, Webhannet, and Little—meet the ocean on

Check It Out: Magical History Tour

Give your kids a chance to explore history and mystery as you take a walking or driving tour of Wells monuments. Various markers found throughout the town stand in memory of Wells's rich past. Contact the town hall (207–646–5113) or the Wells Historical Society (207–646–4775) for a complete list of markers.

this property, creating a rich estuarine habitat for wildlife. Many endangered species call this reserve home. Black ducks, least terns, peregrine falcons, and piping plovers are the most noted residents. Native wildflowers like arethus and slender blue flag can be seen on the premises.

The heart of this reserve is **Laudholm Farm,** a historic saltwater farm that allows visitors to view nature at its best. Whether your interest is cultural history, natural history, or just a day of fun, this is one place you must visit. Many exhibits, programs, and trail sessions are open to the public, and children thrill at exploring the reserve with Annie Otter, Mitchell Mummichog, and other special family tour guides. One section of the reserve includes five trails used in the children's Discovery Program. Junior researchers (kids between the ages of 9 and 11) can attend day camps that last a full four days. Older children (between 11 and 13) can participate in their own special research program.

Family tours give children a chance to exercise their senses of sight and smell along the trails laced throughout this reserve. Guides and instructors instigate hands-on learning. When the tides are agreeable, your children can explore the intertidal rock pools on Laudholm Beach. Scud, crabs, and snails are common finds in these tidal-pool explorations.

If you're up for an easy walk along a 7-mile trail, you can take a ninety-minute guided tour to see the watersheds of the Little River and the Webhannet estuaries. Birds, flowers, and butterflies command a great deal of attention on this walk. Orchids are the star players of the wildflowers. Butterflies hover over milkweed, and bees visit snapdragons. Ferns are abundant. Any trip into the flowering section of the reserve is sure to evoke long-lasting memories.

A special program called Skywatch offers night visitors a chance to use telescopes in their hunt for meteor showers and lunar eclipses. The Full-Moon Walk puts you in touch with wildlife that is seldom seen. Deer may be caught grazing in the glow of a full moon, or you might see and hear the nearly silent swoop of an owl.

History buffs will be interested to learn how this Native American encampment area came to be a wildlife reserve. Colonial highways, Indian shutters, antique weathervanes, and century-old buildings are only part of what you will discover in this slice of American history.

Pinching **Pennies**

Many restaurants offer early-bird or two-for-one specials. Call ahead to find out. Also, local papers and yellow pages often contain dining coupons.

Where to Eat

Billy's Chowder House. 216 Mile Road; (207) 646–7558; www.billyschowderhouse. com. With a knotty pine interior and salt marsh outside, Billy's sets the tone for Maine favorites like grilled swordfish and lobster. Open from mid-January until the first week of December. $

Bull and Claw. 2270 Post Road; (207) 646–8467. True to its word, this restaurant promises fun family dining with big helpings at little prices. The kids' menu is great, and the breakfast and brunch buffet is not to be missed. $–$$$

Congdon's Donuts Family Restaurant. 1090 Route 1; (207) 646–4219. Wake up to a doughnut at Congdon's, a family favorite. This restaurant has been famous for homemade doughnuts for more than fifty years. If you're craving a heartier breakfast, the Congdon Special is a good bet (and you still get a doughnut). In addition to scrumptious muffins, breads, and pastries, you can get ice cream made right on the premises. A scoop goes well with a burger, sandwich, or fish and chips from the lunch menu. Take-out orders are quickly available using their new drive-thru service. You'll want to get some doughnuts to go. $

Grey Gull Inn. 475 Webhannet Drive; (207) 646–7501; www.thegreygullinn.com. In dining rooms with water views you'll be served up a fancy feed. Prime rib, broiled haddock, pasta, and other entrees fill the menu here. However, the prices tend to be a little high for large families. $$–$$$

Litchfield's. Route 1; (207) 646–5711. Litchfield's is frequented by many locals who rave about the lunch sandwiches. Seafood and prime rib are also readily available at affordable prices. $$–$$$

Maine Diner. 2265 Post Road, Route 1; (207) 646–4441. www.mainediner.com. Take a trip back to the good old days at this classic diner. Enjoy a breakfast of blueberry pancakes or eggs Benedict and corned beef hash anytime. Award-winning seafood chowder is served up here, and the famous lobster pie

Other Things to **See** and **Do**

When visiting Wells, explore these additional sites: Moody Beach, Drakes Island Beach, Webhannet Falls Park Bridge of Flowers, and the Lighthouse Depot.

has been featured on the *Today* show. Family friendly, the diner offers a kids' menu as well as lunch and dinner specials. Crowded in season, you can spend your wait browsing the gift shop. Check out the Web site for a chance to win a **free** T-shirt. $–$$

Where to Stay

Beach Acres Campground. 563 Post Road, Route 1; (207) 646–5612; www.beach acres.com. If camping is your idea of a good time, this is a great choice, situated less than a mile from the beach. You can swim, enjoy the on-site playground, play shuffleboard, or picnic. A twenty-four-hour security guard is on duty, and fireplaces and laundry facilities are available. Pets are not allowed. $

East Winds Vacation Resort. 371 Mile Road; (800) 638–3366. Located within easy walking distance of the beach, this facility offers furnished rooms, fully functional kitchens (including dishwashers, garbage dis-

posals, and microwaves), cable TV, and carport parking. $–$$

Seagull Motor Inn. 1413 Post Road/U.S. Route 1; (800) 573–2485; www.seagullvacations.com. Motel units and cottages are available on twenty-three acres. A playground, pool, and lawn games add to family fun. $–$$

Water Crest Cottages and Motel. 1277 Post Road, Route 1; (207) 646–2202; www. watercrestcottages.com. You can rent a one- or two-bedroom cottage, complete with modern kitchen, screened porch, and air-conditioning. A playground, a picnic area with gas grills, and an on-site laundry facility make this a great choice for families. A heated pool and spa are added incentives for staying here. $

For More Information

Wells Chamber of Commerce. (207) 646–2451; www.wellschamber.org.

Kennebunk

Originally founded at Cape Porpoise in the 1600s, Kennebunk once supported a thriving fishing and shipbuilding industry. Today, period homes grace the town's historic district, a lasting tribute to the wealth and craft of that time. Take a tour of the Storer House, birthplace of author Kenneth Roberts. Snap a picture of the "Wedding Cake House," a private residence off Route 35.

Shopping along Main Street, you're bound to find something to take home. The **Lafayette Center**, a converted shoe factory, houses upscale shops. The **Brick Store Exchange** showcases locally crafted items. You'll also discover antiques shops and art galleries in abundance.

The Brick Store Museum (ages 4 and up) ⓜ ⓛ ⓧ

117 Main Street; (207) 985–4802; www.brickstoremuseum.org. Open May to December, Tuesday through Friday 10:00 A.M. to 4:30 P.M., Saturday 10:00 A.M. to 1:00 P.M. Museum admission is **free,** although donations are accepted. Walking tours are offered on Wednesday and Friday. A booklet for self-guided tours can be purchased for $5.00. $

Edith Cleaves Barry founded the museum in 1936, using the second floor of the 1825 brick store built by her great-grandfather, William Lord. Today, the museum encompasses three adjacent buildings, the Barry Workshop, complete with barn and carriage stalls, and the Taylor-Barry House, her family home dating back to 1803.

Surf's **Up** in Kennebunk

Kennebunk Beach has a reputation as a family beach. In fact, the beach is commonly referred to in three parts: Mother's Beach, Middle Beach, and Gooch's Beach.

Sheltered in a cove at the south end of the main beach, Mother's Beach is perfect for young children. They can play in the gentle waves or on the brightly colored playground. Middle Beach has a rougher attitude. Still, the rocky shore makes for good walking, and kids will want to explore the tidal pools they discover here. Gooch's Beach offers fine sand and good surfing.

A sidewalk stretches the entire length of Kennebunk Beach, if you want to walk without getting sand in your shoes. Parking is limited, and permits are required. Permits can be obtained from the town office on weekdays or from local lodging facilities. Picnicking is prohibited.

Parson's Beach is another option for sun lovers. A small, private beach with public access and free limited parking, there are no facilities or lifeguards here. However, being adjacent to the Rachel Carson Wildlife Center, it is popular with bird-watchers. A variety of seabirds can often be seen along the shore.

Myths and Legends: A Piece of Cake

The tale is that duty called local sea captain George Bourne back to sea before a proper wedding cake could be baked. Wanting to make it up to his bride, he laced their house with white wooden latticework. Today the ornate 1828 house is known as the Wedding Cake House.

The Lord Gallery features pieces from the museum's permanent collection, which totals more than 40,000 artifacts. View paintings by such artists as Abbott Graves and Thomas Badger or heirlooms from the estates of celebrated authors Kenneth Roberts and Booth Tarkington.

Changing exhibits are displayed in the museum gallery, program center, and carriage stall. Some past exhibits have focused on the Shakers, Maine in the Civil War, vintage wedding gowns, and the Maine forest fires of 1947.

Guided architectural walking tours will give you a better understanding of Kennebunk's National Register Historic District. The museum offers these tours on Wednesday and Friday from mid-June through August.

The Kennebunk Plains (all ages)
Route 99; (207) 490–4012. Free.

Known by locals as the "blueberry plains," this is a great spot for walking and mountain biking. Boasting 1,100 acres of grasslands, you might spy a rare grasshopper sparrow nesting or the unusual blazing star in bloom. In July the wild blueberries are ripe for the picking. A pleasant, relaxing place to spend the afternoon.

Tom's of Maine Inc. (all ages)
302 Lafayette Center; (207) 985–2944 or (800) 775–2388 for tour reservations; www.tomsofmaine.com. Free factory tours offered twice daily Monday through Thursday. The Natural Living Store is open Monday through Saturday 10:00 A.M. to 5:00 P.M.

It was nearly 40 years ago when Tom and Kate Chappell decided to make and sell their own natural personal care products. Beginning with nonphosphate liquid laundry detergent, they now offer natural toothpaste (the first on the market), baby shampoo, deodorant, mouthwash, shaving cream, and soap.

By 1983 Tom's products were on the shelves of supermarket and drug store chains across the country, but their commitment to using only natural ingredients in their product line remains. You'll find pure flavor oil, not saccharin, in their toothpaste, and a preservative mixture of rosemary and vitamin C, not EDTA, in their soap.

Drop in on this multimillion dollar mom-and-pop operation and take a free tour of their manufacturing plant (reservations required). Then shop at the Natural Living Store, where you'll find great deals on factory seconds. Buy a T-shirt, hat, or tote made with organic cotton. No matter how you look at it, a trip to Tom's is naturally fun.

Atlantic Exposure Cruise & Charter Ltd. (all ages)

12 Fairway Drive; (207) 967–4784; www.atlanticexposure.com. Cruises offered May through October. $$$

Forget dinner and a movie. Enjoy a cruise and a video—a live underwater video at that. Using Remotely Operated Vehicle (ROV) technology, you will go on a virtual scuba dive to the bottom of the ocean. Will you see octopus, a sea horse, or seals? Will you be attacked by a lobster or crab? One never knows as each "dive" is different.

No matter what you see on this two-hour scenic cruise down the Kennebunk River, you'll be watching the mysteries of the deep come to life. And if you tire of what's going on underwater, check out the sights above sea level, like Walker's Point (former President Bush's summer home) or Goat Island Lighthouse.

First/Second Chance, Inc. (all ages)

4 Western Avenue; (207) 967–5507 or (800) 767–2628; www.firstchancewhalewatch.com. Cruises depart 10:00 A.M. Memorial Day weekend through Columbus Day. There is an additional 4:00 P.M. cruise in July and August. $$$$. Children under 3 are free.

Hey, mates, is that a seal? Is it a dolphin? No, it's a whale! Enjoy a four-and-a-half-hour whale watch aboard *Nick's Chance*, to Jeffrey's Ledge. This ledge, about 20 miles offshore, is the seasonal feeding grounds of these giant mammals. Species seen include finbacks, minkes, rights, and humpbacks. Experience the thrill of seeing one of these beautiful creatures up close and personal or your next trip is free.

The ship offers upper- and lower-deck viewing, with a fully equipped galley. Binoculars and film are also available on board. All cruises are fully narrated, teaching you about whales and other sea life you might encounter on your journey. Remember to dress in layers, as it can be 10 to 15 degrees cooler on the open ocean. Rubber-soled shoes, hats, and sunscreen are also good ideas for making your whale-watching adventure more enjoyable.

This cruise line also offers narrated scenic cruises aboard *Kylie's Chance*.

Where to Eat

All Day Breakfast. 55 Western Avenue; (207) 967–5132. Ever have a hankering for bacon and eggs in the afternoon? This is the place for you. $

Atlantic Pizza. 8 Western Avenue #21; (207) 967–0033. A great place for pizza, sandwiches, or salads. Great for a late-night snack. They'll even deliver to your hotel. $–$$

Federal Jack's Restaurant & Brewpub. 8 Western Avenue #6; (207) 967–4903; www.federaljacks.com. Dine on the deck or indoors. Kids get their own menu. Afterward, visit the game room or the gift shop. $$

Other Things to **See** and **Do**

There's more to do in Kennebunk than look at old buildings. Talk to the people at **Lady J Sportfishing Charters Inc.** (207–985–7304), and take the kids on a two-hour discovery trip. They can fish for mackerel or haul lobster traps. Catch up on your reading at **Kennebunk Free Library** at 112 Main Street. Enjoy a picnic or canoe ride at **Roger Pond.**

Windows on the Water. 12 Chase Hill Road; (207) 967–3313; www.windowsonthe water.com. Hailed "one of five best in Maine" by *Down East* magazine and "A must visit" by *Portland Magazine,* this place won't disappoint you. In fact there's a 100 percent satisfaction guarantee. This award-winning restaurant offers gourmet meals, including lobster ravioli and salmon nicoise. Aptly named, the dining room is lined with arched windows overlooking the port. You can also eat on a screened terrace or alfresco. Open for lunch and dinner, reservations are recommended for evening dining. An elegant choice for families with older children. $$–$$$$

Where to Stay

The Beach House Inn. 48 Beach Avenue, Kennebunk Beach; (207) 967–3850. The Victorian charm of the late 1800s lives on at this inn overlooking Kennebunk Beach. All thirty-four rooms offer a private bath, and the cost includes a hearty continental breakfast. Open year-round, you'll pay a little more to stay at this cozy bed-and-breakfast. However, off-season packages make such elegance more affordable. $–$$$

The Kennebunker Cottages. 195 Sea Road; (207) 967–3708; www.kennebunker. com. These cozy cottages are strategically located within walking distance of the beaches and Kennebunkport's Dock Square.

Open May through October, the cottages with kitchenettes are a great choice for families. $–$$

The Lodge at Kennebunk. 95 Alewive Road; (207) 985–9010 or (877) 918–3701; www.lodgeatkennebunk.com. This is another year-round option that's more basic and affordable. Enjoy a continental breakfast or cook outside at one of the picnic areas. Play lawn games or take your pet for a walk. Yes, even your four-legged friends are welcome here. A 10 percent AAA discount makes the savings even better. $–$$

The Ocean View. 171 Beach Avenue, Kennebunk Beach; (207) 967–2750; www.the oceanview.com. Enjoy the luxury of breakfast in bed when you stay in one of the inn's junior suites. This intimate B&B offers lots of little extras. An oceanfront porch with rocking chairs, a lending library with books and magazines, complimentary breakfast, early morning coffee, and afternoon refreshments are just some of the subtle amenities. All rooms are furnished with a mini refrigerator, cable TV, radio and CD player, and plush bathrobes. Rates are steep, but you should treat yourself to a few luxuries during your trip. $$$–$$$$

For More Information

Kennebunk-Kennebunkport Chamber of Commerce. (207) 967–0857; www.visit thekennebunks.com.

Kennebunkport

A small New England town, Kennebunkport is best known as the summer home of former president George Bush. He often vacationed here during his time in the White House—both as vice-president and president. His son, President George W. Bush, spent many summers here as well. Built in 1903, by George W.'s great-grandfather, George Herbert Walker, the Bush estate is at Walker's Point off Ocean Avenue. Surrounded by water on three sides, the home is still clearly visible from designated pull-offs along the avenue and perfectly positioned for picture taking.

Dock Square is the hot spot of Kennebunkport. Pulitzer Prize-winning author Booth Tarkington used to spend his summers here writing. Tarkington and others have written books about this lively slice of Maine, and to this day, people come from all around to celebrate summer at Dock Square.

Seashore Trolley Museum (all ages)

195 Log Cabin Road; (207) 967–2712; www.trolleymuseum.org. Museum and gift shop open weekends only in early May 10:00 A.M. to 5:00 P.M. Open daily late May to October. Admission includes unlimited trolley rides, access to the museum, and use of sheltered picnic areas. $$. Free for children under 6.

In 1939 a group of young men pooled their resources and bought trolley car #31 from the Biddeford & Saco Railroad for $150. The purchase saved the trolley from destruction, making it instead the first exhibit of the Seashore Trolley Museum. From such meager beginnings the museum has grown into the oldest and largest electric railway

Surf's **Up** in Kennebunkport

Kennebunkport beaches are for those looking for cozy and quiet places to enjoy the sea. White sand and salt marshes make Goose Rocks Beach and Colony Beach nice settings for family fun. However, no facilities and limited parking keep crowds to a minimum.

Goose Rocks Beach, made up of two crescents, offers calm shallows for little ones to enjoy. Older kids will like the adventure of walking to Timber Island at low tide. Windsurfers are attracted to this beach, and just watching them can be entertaining. Colony Beach, across from The Colony Hotel, is a great place for rock climbing. Both beaches are suitable for swimming, but the water is cold until well into the summer season.

Amazing
Maine Facts

President George W. Bush only summered in Maine. Over the years, however, many powerful players in Washington have called Maine home: Margaret Chase Smith was the first woman elected to Congress, Edmund Muskie was Secretary of State under President Carter, George Mitchell is a former Senate majority leader, and William Cohen is a former Secretary of Defense.

museum in the world. Today you can see more than 250 transit vehicles from around the world, and even hop aboard trolley car #31 for a 4-mile ride through woods and fields.

The museum also sponsors special events like the trolley parade on July 4. Wear red, white, and blue and get in **free.** Sunset and ice cream trolley rides are especially fun (offered in July and August with reduced admission).

If creating lasting memories is more important than saving money, inquire about the **Motorman Program**. After appropriate instruction you take the controls, operating the trolley yourself. Family and friends can ride while you drive. The program lasts about an hour and costs $50.

Where to Eat

Alisson's Restaurant. 11 Dock Square; (207) 697–4841; www.alissons.com. Known for its casual excellence, the menu is varied and the atmosphere inviting. Thursday night concerts on the River Green, right behind the restaurant, spotlight jazz, blues, and local artists. Grab an early dinner and enjoy the show at 7:00 P.M., or have a late supper afterward. $$–$$$

The Green Heron Inn. 126 Ocean Avenue; (207) 967–3315; www.greenheroninn.com. This is the best place for breakfast. Specialties include homemade granola, eggs Florentine, and blueberry pancakes. Staples for the little ones like cold cereal and chocolate milk are also available. Savor the great tastes as you enjoy the view afforded from the glassed-in, waterfront porch. Breakfast is **free** for guests and more than reasonable for everyone else. $

Mabel's Lobster Claw. P.O. Box 656A, Ocean Avenue; (207) 967–2562. A favorite of locals, including George Bush. Lobster is the specialty, of course—get it straight, on a roll, or smothered with a creamy Newburg sauce. $$–$$$$

Pier 77. 77 Pier Road, Cape Porpoise; (207) 967–8500; www.pier77restaurant.com. The name has changed and so has the decor, but the food and service are still top-notch. This is a great place to eat because of its location. You and your family will dine on a working fishing pier while enjoying seafood at prices that won't fry you. $$$

The Wayfarer. 1 Pier Road, Cape Porpoise; (207) 967–8961. Open March to late December, the atmosphere is casual, the food superb, and the prices attractive. Order seafood or a burger. Some meals come in smaller portions for the kids. Meals include salad, potato, and rolls. $$

Where to Stay

Cabot Cove Cottages. 7 South Main Street; (800) 962–5424; www.cabotcove cottages.com. White wicker and natural pine give these one- and two-bedroom units a cozy, country feel. All cottages include cable TV, kitchenette, and bathroom with shower. Cooking utensils in the kitchen and laundry facilities on the premises make it easy to keep your stomach full and your clothes clean. Open mid-May through mid-October. $$–$$$

The Nonantum. 95 Ocean Avenue; (800) 552–5651; www.nonantumresort.com. The Nonantum is actually two buildings: the Carriage House Inn and the Portside Lodge (117 rooms total). Portside is a good bet for families, as these rooms have refrigerators and coffeemakers. Rooms with kitchenettes are also available. Enjoy sandwiches poolside, casual fare in the Portside Pub, and fine dining in the River Room. Children under 12 stay for **free.** $$$$

Rhumb Line Motor Lodge. Ocean Avenue; (800) 337–4862; www.rhumbline maine.com. Conveniently located on the trolley line, this motel offers year-round accommodations, including continental breakfast. Kids will enjoy the pools (indoor and outdoor). Parents will appreciate the hot tub and fitness center. Kids 12 and under stay **free.** $–$$$

Village Cove Inn. 29 South Main Street; (800) 879–5778; www.villagecoveinn.com. Popular for romantic getaways, this inn is great for families as well. Kids 12 and under stay for $10 per night. An indoor and outdoor pool and a four-star restaurant are some of the extras. Special events like magic shows, movie nights, and pool parties are staged just for the kids. Rates vary according to season and day of the week. Packages available year-round. $$–$$$$

For More Information

Kennebunk-Kennebunkport Chamber of Commerce. (207) 967–0857; www.visit thekennebunks.com.

Tee Time

Some serious golf can be played in and around Kennebunkport. The **Cape Arundel Golf Club** (207–967–3494) accommodates the golfing requirements of former President Bush. Edmund Muskie reportedly preferred the slightly more difficult links at **Webhannet Golf Club** (207–967–2061; www.kennebunk golf.com). Both 18-hole courses are open to the public at various times throughout the day. **Dutch Elm Golf Course** (207–282–9850; www.dutchelm golf.com), located in Arundel, offers a pro shop, snack bar, and putting greens.

Other Things to **See** and **Do**

When the weather forces you indoors, visit the Kennebunkport Maritime Museum, the Louis T. Graves Memorial Library, the Nott House, and the School House. If the sun is out and you're up for a walk, check out Parsons Way, an oceanfront walk to Walker's Point. Another option is St. Anthony's Franciscan Monastery, where you can walk the beautiful grounds adorned with shrines and gardens.

Newfield

A forty-five-minute drive inland from the Kennebunks, the mammoth restoration village you'll find here is worth it.

Willowbrook at Newfield Restoration Village (all ages)
68 Elm Street; (207) 793–2784; www.willowbrookmuseum.org. Open daily mid-May through the end of September 10:00 A.M. to 5:00 P.M. $$. Free for children under 6.

History comes to life here, and children love it. Touring this restoration village, they'll learn how people lived more than one hundred years ago. The carpenter and print shops and the old schoolhouse are just some of the twenty-seven buildings waiting to be explored. Simply walking the beautiful grounds, complete with millpond and an 1894 carousel, is an adventure. However, the real thrill for youngsters is choosing penny candy from the Amos Straw Country Store.

Biddeford/Saco

Often referred to as the "twin cities," Biddeford and Saco, although closely linked, couldn't be more different. Biddeford is spotted with idle brick textile mills. Saco is dotted with white-clapboard mansions. French-Canadian roots run deep in Biddeford. The good old Yankee spirit is alive and well in Saco. Biddeford is worth visiting for the La Kermesse Festival, held in late June. This three-day extravaganza of parades, food, concerts, and special events celebrates the town's strong heritage. Saco's big drawing card is family-oriented amusement parks.

Amazing
Maine Facts

Saco was originally called Pepperellboro.

Saco Heath (all ages)

Off Route 112 (Buxton Road), Saco. Open from dawn to dusk. Free.

If you and your family are nature lovers, this is a must-see. Five hundred acres of lush grasses, sedges, and reeds make up the heath. In technical terms, the heath is a coalesced domed peatland. It is said that the area was made up of shallow ponds with clay bottoms some 12,000 years ago. As layers of reeds and sphagnum mosses have grown in the depressions, a spongy dome has been created.

You and your children will enjoy the walk through the woods at the beginning of the trail, then along the boardwalk through the heath. Some of the plants on the heath are pitcher plants, sundews, mountain laurel, huckleberry clusters, white cedar, and even cotton grass, which is an arctic species. Erected signs explaining the various types of vegetation and the ecosystem will help you answer questions your little ones are bound to ask.

Parking is not a problem here, but dogs are. They tend to frighten away the wildlife that naturally inhabits the heath, so leave your pooch at home.

Aquaboggan Water Park (all ages)

980 Portland Road, Saco; (207) 282–3112; www.aquaboggan.com. Open daily June through Labor Day from 10:00 A.M. to 6:00 P.M., weather permitting. $$–$$$$. General admission prices vary depending on age and area of the park to be visited. A super pass includes a day pass for all water rides plus eight tokens for nonwater rides. Free parking.

A funny name for a fun-filled place, Aquaboggan boasts torrents of water and tons of rides. There's no better way for kids of all ages to have a blast on a warm day. What can you and your family do at this fun-park in Saco? Well, grab your bathing suit and hold on . . . here we go.

Totally Tubular is designed for two people to enjoy the fun at once. Mount an inflated tube and ride down this slide with a friend. You'll make a big splash at the end, but what

Par for the Course

When you have only an hour or two to spare, golfing is a great way to pass the time. At the **Cascade Golf Range** (207–282–3524) you can drive a bucket of balls or putt for holes-in-one on the miniature golf course. The **Biddeford-Saco Country Club** (207–282–9892) offers you a full game with eighteen holes of lush course.

could be more refreshing on a hot summer day? Water slides are abundant in this amusement facility, and you have your choice: Go down on tubes or on your bottom.

The Aquasaucer is like a water version of "king of the mountain." A spewing fountain of water maintains a slippery surface as children use ropes to climb the giant, bouncy face of the Aquasaucer. Once the pinnacle is claimed, the successful climbers slide down and splash into a pool of water about 3 feet deep. Restricted to kids 16 and younger, it's common for two lifeguards to monitor activities at this attraction. Due to mass appeal, time limits may be enforced to ensure that everyone gets a chance to be king.

If you'd rather be king of the sea but don't care for salt water, visit the wave pool. Mechanically produced waves allow you and your older children to enjoy the simulated surf in a fun, safe environment. Regular swimming pools also dot the landscape at Aquaboggan.

Toddlers can frolic in their own splash-and-play section of the park. They can wade in kiddie pools or slide down kiddie slides. Float tubes are allowed in the water, but big kids aren't. Your youngsters will be playing in the company of their peers, but it is your responsibility to supervise your children. No lifeguards are on duty.

Aquaboggan also offers dry activities for those who prefer their water in glasses. Kiddie and adult bumper boats allow family members to bounce around and into each other's vessel. Skid cars provide the same type of fun on dry land. If Grand Prix racing is more your speed, take a spin around the track in a miniature race car.

Too much excitement for one day? Relax. Enjoy a leisurely round of putt-putt golf or rack up some points on the shuffleboard court to counter the calories racked up at the snack bar or ice-cream parlor. A gift shop is open to souvenir shoppers, and lockers are provided to visitors who wish to store their change of clothes and other articles.

You can bring your own food to the park's picnic grounds, but leave your grill in the car. Fires are not allowed. Lounge chairs are available, and the park is wheelchair accessible. A first-aid station is on the premises, in the unlikely event someone is injured.

Myths and **Legends:** Haunted Light

At night, out in the harbor off Biddeford Pool, the green-and-white beacon of Wood Island Light flashes, casting an eerie glow. It's a perfect place for ghosts—at least according to legend. In 1896 the deputy sheriff was murdered on the island by a local lobsterman, who then killed himself. It is the ghost of the deputy that supposedly lingers on the island.

Check It Out: Movies Old Style

If you loved going to the drive-in as a kid, think how much your kids will love the **Saco Drive-In** (207–284–1016). You'll enjoy a double-feature while sitting in your car. The movies are new releases broadcast over your car radio. Sorry, the speaker boxes didn't stand the test of time. However, you can still walk to the concession stand to buy popcorn.

Funtown/Splashtown USA (all ages)

774 Portland Road, Saco; (800) 878–2900; www.funtownsplashtownusa.com. Hours vary between the parks. Funtown is open weekends only May through mid-June, then daily 10:00 A.M. to 10:00 P.M. through Labor Day. Splashtown is open daily mid-June through Labor Day, 10:00 A.M. to 6:00 P.M. $$$$. A combination pass good for both parks is available as well as other ticket options.

Funtown/Splashtown USA resurrected the past, in 1998, with the opening of Excalibur, a four-and-a-half-acre wooden roller coaster. It had been more than fifty years since Maine's last wooden coaster burned down in Old Orchard Beach. Surrounded by a medieval motif, complete with a castlelike entrance, Excalibur is a thriller, topping out at 100 feet. Brave an 82-foot first drop and speeds up to 55 mph. Water slides are also a main attraction here, and swimming pools appear in all shapes and sizes. Loop-de-loop slides provide a new twist to traditional slides. You can drive miniature race cars, sit with a partner and swing yourself around with the power of a massive water hose, or just putt about on the miniature golf course. Young children will get plenty of exercise in the Noah Zark playground. Picnic spots are available.

Thunder Falls, the longest, tallest log flume ride in all of New England, is also found in this park. Kiddie rides include a merry-go-round, an umbrella ride, swings, helicopters, a Ferris wheel, a Red Baron ride, a kiddie train, and kiddie bumper boats. Rides for older people include, in addition to the log flume, a Tilt-A-Whirl, an antique car ride, a casino, bumper cars, a roller coaster, and an Astrosphere. It's not over yet—there are also Sea Dragon, Thunderbolt, Flying Trapeze, a teacup ride, Grand Prix race cars, bumper boats, a carousel, and a balloon race. A shooting gallery, an arcade, a gift shop, all sorts of eating places, and other surprises also await you.

Some of the newer additions to the park include Dragon's Descent and the Frog Hopper. After enjoying the panoramic view as you rise to the top of Dragon's Descent you will be turbo dropped 200 feet. The sudden downward rush gives passengers a negative "G" experience—better than a free fall. The Frog Hopper offers kids the thrill of hopping straight up to heights of 18.5 feet.

The AquaPlay Family Activity Area, new in 2003, is called Pirate's Paradise. You'll get soaked barreling down eight different water slides, one with a huge bucket that dumps water on those below. If the water doesn't cool you down, enjoy a cold drink from the Tiki Juice and Smoothie Bar. Need to dry off? Visit the gift shop. Funtown/Splashtown is one place you should definitely explore. It can provide hours of fun for the entire family.

Vacationland Bowling Center (ages 4 and up)

812 Portland Road, Saco; (207) 284–7386; www.vacationlandbowling.com. Open daily year-round. $–$$

Bowling is a little different in Maine. Here you will find candlepin bowling as opposed to tenpin. The pins are long and thin, and you bowl using a 2½-pound ball (about the size of a grapefruit). Also, dead wood is left on the lane for you to use in knocking down more pins. You get three chances to knock them all down. While this game is easier for kids (because of the low-weight ball), I still prefer tenpin (which is nearly extinct here).

This recreation center offers thirty-two lanes for candlepin bowling. Automatic scoring makes keeping track of who's winning easier. Gutter balls are nonexistent when you bowl on one of the twelve lanes that feature bumpers. Although this is designed to make playing more fun for the kids, grown-ups trying candlepin for the first time will also appreciate the help.

Once you tire of throwing a ball, why not try shooting one? Billiards can be enjoyed at any of six regulation tables. (You'll be happy to know that pool is the same in Maine as it is anywhere else.) There is also an arcade with video games to help kids dealing with Mario withdrawal and a snack bar to fuel up your little athletes.

Saco Museum (ages 4 and up)

371 Main Street, Route 1, Saco; (207) 282–3031. Open Monday through Friday noon to 4:00 P.M., Thursday noon to 8:00 P.M. $ suggested donation.

The history of York County is traced in this museum. The growth of the region is chronicled from its earliest settlement to its position as Maine's first industrial center. Furniture, decorative arts, and original paintings also fill the museum. Lectures, tours, and special exhibits are often offered. True history buffs will enjoy the institute's Dyer Library, located next door, which houses a remarkable Maine history collection. Craft and historical workshops for all ages are also offered here.

Surf's **Up** in Saco

If you tire of the water parks and long for the real thing, Saco has that too. Two of the best beaches for families are Camp Ellis Beach and Ferry Beach State Park.

Camp Ellis Beach, at the end of Route 9, is where the Saco River meets the sea. Warm shallows stretch along this beach, offering the little ones a fun place to swim. Besides a beautiful sandy beach, **Ferry Beach State Park** (207–283–0067) has a bathhouse, nature trails, and a picnic area. There is a charge to enter the park. Buying a family pass is a good idea if you plan on traveling throughout Maine—it gives you admittance to all state parks.

A Little **Culture**

While visiting the "twin cities," enjoy the cultural experiences of the City Theater (207–282–0849; www.citytheater.org) in Biddeford and the Saco Art Festival. A registered historic site, **City Theater** is regarded as one of the finest Victorian opera houses in the United States. First opened in 1896, the theater was designed by John Calvin Stevens to accommodate more than 500 patrons. Today you can enjoy productions such as *Carousel* in the grand elegance of a theater that has provided top entertainment for more than one hundred years.

The Saco Sidewalk Art Festival in late June, while offering performances by magicians and musicians, concentrates on fine arts and crafts. Oil paintings, pen-and-ink drawings, sculptures, and photography are on display. Clowns, balloons, and concession stands will keep the kids occupied so you can browse.

East Point Sanctuary (all ages)

Maine Route 208, Biddeford Pool; (207) 729–5181. Open dawn to dusk. Free.

Operated by the Maine Audubon Society, this thirty-acre bird sanctuary offers you leisurely strolls, beautiful views, and some of the best bird-watching in southern Maine. Trails take you through meadows and along the rocky coast. While you walk, you'll see many species of shore- and seabirds, including red-winged blackbirds, killdeer, and piping plovers. You might even spy an arctic tern or a snowy egret. Bikes and pets are not allowed in the sanctuary, and parking is limited.

Where to Eat

Buffleheads. 122 Hills Beach Road, Biddeford; (207) 284–6000. Frequented by locals, this is the place for dessert—especially if you love chocolate. But you'll need to eat all your dinner first. Open year-round; you can get breakfast and lunch here as well. $$

Wormwood's Restaurant. 16 Bay Avenue, Camp Ellis Beach, Saco; (207) 282–9679. Top off lunch or dinner at this wonderful seafood restaurant with a walk along the stone breakwater. The menu includes steak, chicken, pasta, and stir-fries. Daily specials are offered year-round. $$–$$$

Where to Stay

The Classic Motel. 21 Ocean Park Road, Saco; (800) 290–3909; www.classicmotel. com. All units have kitchenettes with microwaves—a family necessity. An indoor heated pool and complimentary beach parking are other amenities offered at this year-round motel. There is a $5.00 additional charge per child. $–$$

D'Allaire's Motel & Cottages. 528 Elm Street, Route 1, Biddeford; (207) 284–4100. This motel features something most don't—a miniature golf course. While that sounds nice, play is not free for guests. However, a game room, a large heated pool, lawn games, laundry facilities, and a billiards room almost make up for it. Kids stay for **free.** $–$$

Saco/Portland South KOA. 814A Portland Road, Saco; (207) 282–0502; www.koakamp grounds.com. KOAs are wonderful places for family camping. Clean and attractively landscaped, this campground offers tent sites, RV sites, and one-room "kabins." A pool, blueberry pancake breakfast, nightly dessert delight, **free** movies, and marshmallow roasts will keep your family happily occupied. $

For More Information

Biddeford/Saco Chamber of Commerce. (207) 282–1567; www.biddefordsaco chamber.org.

Old Orchard Beach

Old Orchard Beach is 12 miles south of Portland. A small town, with a population of only 7,789, it caters to tourists. Canadians flock to this resort area, as do people from all parts of the United States. As you move about the streets and shops in Old Orchard Beach, you are as likely to hear French being spoken as you are to hear English. Both languages are common in this fun-filled slice of Maine.

The beach runs for 7 miles and has a large pier, which houses dozens of shops, restaurants, and other establishments. Spending the night at Old Orchard Beach can be done in a campground, a motel, a hotel, a bed-and-breakfast inn, or even a condominium.

A special treat on this beach is the low surf, which welcomes swimmers. The pier, which has been a fixture of the beach since 1898, was 1,800 feet long at the time of its construction. Big bands once played at a casino on the pier, but a fire and several storms ravaged the long walk out over the ocean. Today's pier is 475 feet long, and the casino is gone.

Palace Playland (all ages)
1 Old Orchard Street; (207) 934–2001; www.palaceplayland.com. Open daily from the end of June through September. The arcade opens at 10:00 A.M. daily. During the week rides open at noon, on weekends at 11:00 A.M. Closing hours vary. Admission is **free.** Various

Batter Up

After you've hit the rides, try batting a ball at the Village Park Family Entertainment Center (207–934–7666).

Amazing
Maine Facts

In the early 1600s Captain John Smith sent a sketch of "the most beautiful beach" he'd ever seen to Sir Ferdinando Gorges in England. The sketch was of Old Orchard Beach.

ride passes are available, or you may purchase individual tickets. Rides require two to four tickets per person. $$$

This four-acre summer playground is located right on the shores of the Atlantic and is one of the country's few remaining beachfront amusement parks that still has an open entrance. You can enjoy the exciting atmosphere of the park whether you choose to ride any of twenty-five rides or not. Odds are you will.

Go up, up, and away in the 70-foot gondola-style Ferris wheel. The view alone is worth the trip. Like going in circles? The Terminator offers 360 vertical degrees of heart-pounding excitement. This ride will force your eyes closed when it appears you'll hit head on. For those looking to rise to new challenges, splash down the largest water slide in New England. On the calmer side, you might enjoy riding the hand-carved carousel that was made in 1906. A magnet for children is the giant pinball and video arcade.

Kiddie-land offers plenty of rides for the little ones. They can climb inside Giant Bears and spin off to fantasy land. The Gator Coaster, Rio Grande Train, and Wet Boats are all rides especially for children. Kids love Sheik Abdulla's fun house and the Space Cross play area. Fireworks every Thursday night is added fun for all.

Newer attractions include a log flume ride guaranteed to make a splash and the Orient Express. This family roller coaster allows you to take in some beautiful scenery as it takes your breath away. The Power Surge, new in 2003, is not for those weak in the stomach. Riders reach heights of more than fifty feet while turning 360 degrees in three different directions! Moby Dick, also brand-new to the park, will have you spinning as well—from a whale's tale.

Reminiscent of boardwalk carnivals from long ago, this is a great place to create lasting family memories.

Tee Time

You can play championship miniature golf at **Pirate's Cove Adventure Golf** (207–934–5086), or take a swing at the real thing at **Old Orchard Beach Country Club at Dunegrass** (207–934–4513 or 800–521–1029).

Where to Eat

If you visit the main attraction in Old Orchard Beach, Palace Playland, there are tons of take-out places offering pizza, burgers, and the like. You can also get fried dough or an order of famous pier fries. But if you want a place to sit down and eat, try one of these.

Barefoot Boy Restaurant. 44 East Grand Avenue; (207) 934–9587. If your mouth is watering for some down-home cooking that will make your morning special, try this restaurant. Open for breakfast, lunch, and dinner. $–$$

Joseph's By The Sea. 55 West Grand Avenue; (207) 934–5044. This four-star restaurant offers fine dining in a sophisticated setting. If your kids are younger, you might want to make another choice. But by all means try to dine here if you can. The pepper-crusted filet mignon is wonderful, and creative seafood dishes are the specialty. $$$

The Village Inn. 213 Saco Avenue; (207) 934–7370. More conducive to family dining, this restaurant is open year-round. The menu is vast and varied, everything from chicken and pasta to steak and seafood. There is a full children's menu, as well as daily lunch and dinner specials. $–$$

Where to Stay

Atlantic Birches Inn. 20 Portland Avenue; (888) 934–5295; www.atlanticbirches.com. This early-twentieth-century inn is graced with a wraparound porch. Begin the day with a fresh continental breakfast. Relax poolside in the afternoon. Rooms in the main house are furnished with canopied beds, and cottage house suites are great choices for families. $–$$$

Normandie Motor Inn. 1 York Street; (207) 934–2533; www.normandieinn.com. This oceanfront motel offers a heated indoor pool and Jacuzzi. Besides regular units, two- and three-bedroom condominium apartments with living room and full kitchen are available at weekly rates. Open year-round. $–$$$$

Old Colonial Motel. 61 West Grand Avenue; (888) 225–5989; www.oldcolonial motel.com. Located right on the beach, this motel offers oceanview rooms with refrigerators. Suites with separate bedrooms and units with private decks or full kitchens are also available. **Free** movies and boogie board rentals will impress the kids. There is a $7.00 charge for children over 6. $–$$$$

Paradise Park Resort. 50 Adelaide Road; (207) 934–4633; www.paradiseparkresort.com. Calling all campers. This resort provides a swimming pool, video arcade, paddleboat rentals, and pond fishing. $

For More Information

Old Orchard Beach Chamber of Commerce. (207) 934–2500 or (800) FMLY–FUN (365–9386); www.oldorchardbeach maine.com.

Scarborough

The town of Scarborough is just north of Old Orchard Beach, where Route 207 (Black Point Road) meets Route 77. The great American painter Winslow Homer called this part of Maine home. Within the 49 square miles known as Scarborough, the communities of Scarborough, Pine Point, and Prouts Neck can be found. More than 12,500 people live in this region, with Prouts Neck being known for its exclusive homes.

Pine Point provides a beach, accommodations, sportfishing, and restaurants. Prouts Neck claims the oldest home in the area—the Hunniwell House, built in 1673. Here is where you'll also find Winslow Homer's Studio. Beaches include Prouts Neck, Pine Point Beach, Higgins Beach, Scarborough Beach, and Western Beach. Parking is not a problem for most of these beaches, even during peak tourist season.

Len Libby Candies (all ages)
419 U.S. Route 1; (207) 883–4897; www.lenlibby.com.

The sweet aroma of handmade chocolates and candies has greeted patrons of this store for nearly eighty years. Chocolate creams, nut clusters, and caramels can surely satisfy your sweet tooth.

Even if you're on a diet, you'll want to stop in and see Lenny—the world's only life-size chocolate moose. Weighing 1,700 pounds and made of pure chocolate, Lenny stands in the Maine room in a scenic diorama. What's even more amazing than seeing him is watching a video of how he was made.

Scarborough Marsh Nature Center (all ages)
Route 9, Pine Point Road; (207) 781–2330 or (207) 883–5100. The Nature Center is open Saturday mid-May through mid-June, then daily throughout the summer. Admission to the center and walking trails is free.

Take a guided tour by foot or canoe at this 3,100-acre preserve. Canoe rentals are also available for the adventurous types who want to paddle the marsh themselves. Whether on land or in the water, you are certain to see an abundance of wildlife. A detailed map that helps identify exceptional plants, birds, and animals is offered to explorers.

Many special programs are offered by the center. Enjoy a full moon or sunrise canoe tour, or take a wildflower walk. There are tiny tot tours, story hour, and the great bug hunt to keep kids busy while learning about nature. A nature store offers books, gifts, and snacks.

Amazing
Maine Facts

Maine became the twenty-third state on March 15, 1820.

Scarborough Downs (ages 8 and up)

Route 1 and Payne Road; (207) 883–4331; www.scarboroughdowns.com. The clubhouse is open 11:00 A.M. to midnight, year-round. Live races are held from April to November, Wednesday through Sunday. Post time is 7:30 P.M., except for Sunday, when racing begins at 1:00 P.M. Entrance to the grandstand is $2.00, the clubhouse an additional 50 cents. Minimum wager is $2.00.

Betting or not, pick your favorite horse and see if you come out a winner. Even if you don't place first, the action of live harness racing will thrill you.

Watch the races from the 1950s grandstand or from the clubhouse. If you'd like to watch and dine, The Downs Club Restaurant, on the clubhouse's upper level, will meet your needs. The dining room is directly across from the finish line, and each table has its own television monitor for close-up viewing of the horses and sulkies. Mutuel windows are close by for your convenience in making wagers.

Smiling Hill Farm (all ages)

781 County Road (Route 22), Westbrook; (800) 743–7463; www.smilinghill.com. The barnyard is open May through September 10:00 A.M. to 5:00 P.M. Pony rides are offered Saturday and Sunday noon to 3:00 P.M. Wagon rides are offered daily at noon. $$

This 500-acre farm, located on the Scarborough/Westbrook line and just 3 miles from the Maine Mall, has been in operation since the 1600s. Currently it is a working farm of black-and-white Holstein dairy cows. That makes for great ice cream and fresh cold milk, which they sell right on the premises.

Kids will love the barnyard with all the animals to pet and feed. Grown-ups will enjoy hearing the history of the farm as they take a wagon ride over the hills and through the woods. Pony rides, a giant slide, and a picnic area make this an enjoyable place to spend the afternoon. Special events like Wow Wednesday, offering 99 cent ice-cream treats for kids, and Free Fridays, when each admission gets a free surprise (barnyard toy, stickers, milk samples) just add to the fun.

Portland

Portland is Maine's largest city and the state's first capital. The mammoth Mariner's Church, built of granite and glass in 1820, was designed as the capital's biggest structure. However, Portland's character and charm are found in more than its beautiful buildings.

The city's motto, *Resurgam* (I shall rise again), is fitting. The early settlement was wiped out more than once. In 1690 and again in 1775 it was burned to the ground. Each time it rose again. After the American Revolution it thrived as a lumbering port and railroad terminus. Then disaster struck yet again. On July 4, 1866, a fire erupted that leveled half the city. The fire started when a firecracker was accidentally thrown into a Commercial Street boatyard. Today, the redbrick buildings and the narrow granite streets of Old Port are a result of the rebuilding of the 1870s.

Children's Museum of Maine (all ages)

142 Free Street; (207) 828–1234; www.childrensmuseumofme.org. Open daily; hours vary. Free for children under 1. The first Friday of every month from 5:00 to 8:00 P.M. the museum is free for all. There is a parking garage 1½ blocks from the museum. Keep your ticket stubs for two hours of free parking. $

This is not some boring building that your kids will have to be dragged through. In fact, you will probably have trouble keeping up with your children in this fun-filled learning center. What can you expect to find?

One section of the building is set aside for toddlers only. They can slide down a small slide, play peek-a-boo from a plastic fort, or be fascinated by carnival-type mirrors. This is a small area of the facility, but it is a safe haven for little tykes.

Other areas offer fascinating activities in many subjects of interest. Let your children stick their heads into the center of an ant colony, for instance. A large ant farm is on display with provisions for children to rise up among the ants, protected by plexiglass, for a close-up view. In another area, energetic kids can scale a spider's web (a rope climbing net). A trip down on the farm will allow your kids to milk a plastic cow and see other farm items.

Finding a food basket at the grocery store here can be difficult. Children love to assume roles as cashiers while their peers collect plastic groceries. Just outside the grocery store is a boat that rocks to and fro on a wood platform. Kids get to use an automatic teller machine to learn the mechanics of money. If your family is into spelunking, you will enjoy the cave tunnel that you can walk through. A fire truck is always filled with children, and we haven't left the first floor yet.

A spaceship awaits your children on the second floor. Ride the stationary bike and watch the skeleton in front of you demonstrate how your bones are moving. A huge globe of the world rotates on a base and allows children to turn it until their arms get tired. Balls

A Merrill Family Adventure:
The Power of Imagination

My girls love the Children's Museum of Maine. We try to visit several times a year. They have many exciting exhibits, but when my youngest daughter, Jaclyn, was six, she especially enjoyed playing vet. She donned a lab coat, placed a stethoscope around her neck, and went to work (they have giant stuffed animals for the kids to "work" on). She chose a German shepherd as her patient. He was bathed, examined, suffered through a shot, got fed, and then was able to rest in a kennel. Jaclyn talked about the experience for days and decided then and there she wanted to be a veterinarian. Although she's added to her list of career options for when she grows up, a vet is still in the top three. It's amazing what a little imagination will do.

hovering over a shaft of air captivate children; other exhibits are equally fun. There is a lot to do, and most of it adds to the learning experience that children need.

In the new L.L. Bear Discovery Woods exhibit, kids will learn a lot about the great outdoors. The eager explorers can climb Mt. Kid-ta-din, fill their own backpack, and construct their own shelter. They can splash around in Cascade Stream and check in at the Ranger Station. They can test their knowledge of the wilderness by trying to identify leaves and animals indigenous to the Maine woods.

A gift shop is located on the first floor. Parents enjoy taking breaks in the vending-machine cafe downstairs. Special activities that kids enjoy are offered on a regular basis. What are you waiting for? Let's go!

Portland Museum of Art (all ages)

7 Congress Square; (207) 775–6148; www.portlandmuseum.org. Open Tuesday, Wednesday, Thursday, Saturday, and Sunday 10:00 A.M. to 5:00 P.M., Friday 10:00 A.M. to 9:00 P.M. From Memorial Day through Columbus Day the museum is also open on Monday 10:00 A.M. to 5:00 P.M. Admission is free for children under 6 and free for everyone on Friday from 5:00 to 9:00 P.M. $$

Maine's largest art museum, the Portland Museum is itself a work of art. Constructed in 1983, the award-winning architecture features dramatic use of open space and beautiful grand staircases. Housed in this breathtaking building is an extensive collection by American artists. See Maine captured in the works of Andrew Wyeth, Winslow Homer, and Rockwell Kent. Works by Renoir, Degas, and Picasso also adorn the gallery walls. Exhibits change frequently, so call to see what will be on display while you're in town.

Tours are given daily at 2:00 P.M. in July and August. A cafe and gift store are both open to the public with no admission. If you're visiting in October or November, you'll enjoy Concerts in the Cafe, featuring a jazz breakfast.

Maine Narrow Gauge Railroad Co. and Museum (all ages)

58 Fore Street; (207) 828–0814; www.mngrr.org. Open daily 10:00 A.M. to 4:00 P.M. Museum and gift shop admission is free. Rates for train rides vary according to age. $$. Children under 4 ride free.

Railroad enthusiasts will enjoy a stop at this museum, where a collection of narrow-gauge railcars and equipment is on display.

Kids of all ages will be pleased by the small railcars that saw regular use from the 1870s to the 1940s. Among the collection is a 2-foot parlor car said to be the only one in the world, Rangeley locomotives, a railbus, and a Model T inspection car. Once you have seen all you want to see, hop aboard one of the running trains for a ride of about 2 miles.

Rides are given on weekends only until about the middle of May. If you like trains, this depot is for you.

Portland Head Light, Museum at Portland Head Light, Fort Williams State Park (all ages)

1000 Shore Road, Cape Elizabeth; Lighthouse (207) 799–2661, State Park (207) 799–5251; www.portlandheadlight.com. The park is open dawn to dusk, and admission is free. The lighthouse museum is open daily from June to October 10:00 A.M. to 4:00 P.M. In November, December, April, and May the museum is open weekends only, same hours. Admission to the museum is free for children under 6. $

Located in Fort Williams State Park, Portland Head Light is the oldest lighthouse in Maine and perhaps the most photographed lighthouse in the world. It was brought into service in 1791 under the order of George Washington. Poet Henry Wadsworth Longfellow often visited the light. A plaque inscribed with some of his most famous lines can be found to the right of the lighthouse, as you face the sea. You can get up close to this magnificent lighthouse. In fact, you can walk all the way around it.

The Portland Head Light Museum is located in the former lighthouse keeper's quarters. Kids will enjoy learning about the interesting facets of life in a lighthouse. Exhibits tell the history of the light and of Fort Williams. There is also a gift shop in case you want to take home a souvenir.

Although the light is the centerpiece, the park itself has a lot to offer. There are trails along the cliffs, a small crescent beach, a playground, and picnic tables. Kids will have fun exploring the remains of Fort Williams and watching locals fly kites.

Portland Sea Dogs (all ages)

271 Park Avenue; ticket office (207) 879–9500 or (800) 936–3647; www.portlandseadogs. com. Ticket office is open 9:00 A.M. to 5:00 P.M. Monday through Friday and 11:00 A.M. to 4:00 P.M. Saturday. $$

Take the family out to Hadlock Park to watch the Portland Sea Dogs, class AA affiliate of the Boston Red Sox, play some serious baseball. "Slugger," the team's mascot, will be on hand to add to your family's entertainment.

Inspired by the skill of the players and the thrill of the game, you might want to test your arm at Dunkin Donuts Speed Pitch. Better at batting than pitching? Take a turn at the Home Run Derby, a "virtual" batting cage. Both are located behind the left field stands in the Q97.9 Games Area.

Loving the support of fans, the Sea Dogs offer various promotions that make an afternoon or evening at the ballpark even more fun. If you come to a Sunday game, all kids in attendance get to run the bases after the game. Stop by C.N. Brown or a Big Apple store and pick up a Family Night coupon. Then redeem it at the Hadlock ticket window on a Tuesday night and get your entire family general admission seating for only $10.

Portland Pirates (all ages)

531 Congress Street; (207) 828–4665; box office (207) 775–3458; www.portlandpirates.com. $$–$$$

Join the Portland Pirates as they take to the ice at the Portland Civic Center for a thrilling game of hockey. It's a great way to spend a fall or winter evening.

The Pirates, AHL affiliate of the Washington Capitals, offer many promotions through-out the season to add to the excitement of the game. Jokers Kid's Opening Night, Puck Day, Poster Night, Photo Day, and the popular "Shirt Off Their Backs" day, where a lucky winner gets a Pirate player's jersey, are just a sample.

Scotia Prince Cruises (all ages)

Portland; (800) 845–4073; www.scotiaprince.com. Sailing nightly from Portland at 8:00 P.M. and daily from Yarmouth, Nova Scotia, at 9:00 A.M. Children under 5 cruise free. $$$$

While vacationing in Maine, why not take a day or three to visit another country? The *Scotia Prince* sails nightly from Portland to Yarmouth, Nova Scotia, making this vacation within a vacation a practical option. You'll cruise the Atlantic for eleven hours port to port.

Riding aboard the *Scotia Prince* for nearly a day round-trip can be a mini vacation in itself. Enjoy great food, live entertainment, casino action, or tax- and duty-free shopping. Whale watch, catch some rays, or take a dip in one of the hot tubs on the SkyDeck. If you're sailing during a school holiday, there are even children's activities and entertainment especially for your little ones.

Simply curious about Nova Scotia? Take the twenty-three-hour overnight Cruise Sensation trip, giving you one hour to sample what Canada has to offer. Need more time to explore? Take the three-day getaway, which gives you a full day and night in Yarmouth with hotel and transportation as part of the package. The Royal Getaway adds an upgraded cabin on the *Prince,* a welcome basket, express check-in, a two-hour tour of Yarmouth, dinner, and a full breakfast to the three-day deal.

The *Prince* is more than just a cruise ship. It's a cruise ferry—so you can drive right on board.

Casco Bay Islands

Islands dot Casco Bay and invite visitors to their shores. Long Island boasts a general store, a restaurant, several beaches, and about one hundred year-round residents. Peaks Island is a quick ferry ride from Portland and a favorite summering spot. A fun way to see the island is on bike. Rentals are available from Peaks Island Mercantile (207–766–5631).

Amazing
Maine Facts

Portland native Henry Wadsworth Longfellow based his poem "The Wreck of the Hesperus" on the wreck of the *Helen Eliza,* which sank off the coast of Peaks Island in 1869.

Cruisin' to Eagle Island

The Atlantic Seal (207–865–6112 or 877–ATL–SEAL) offers three-hour cruises to Eagle Island, the former summer home of Admiral Robert E. Peary, the first explorer to reach the North Pole. Seals and osprey are the subject of summer trips; foliage is the main interest of fall excursions. Lobstering demonstrations are usually included on these cruises, except on Sunday, when lobstering is prohibited.

The largest, Great Chebeague Island, is home to a classic summer resort. You'll find food and lodging on Great Diamond Island, but neither on Cliff Island. It's a long ride (about ninety minutes), but you're greeted with sandy beaches once you arrive, and hot dogs and lobster rolls are available on the ferry landing.

The cottages, wildflowers, and quiet inlets of the various islands bid you to come, and there are several ferries available to get you there.

Casco Bay Lines (207–774–7871) can get you to any of the islands. Rates vary, depending on where you're going. If you want to ride the daily mail boat, you will be out for close to three hours. The boat puts in at all the islands in the morning and again in the afternoon. Other seasonal cruises are offered by Eagle Tours, Inc. (207–774–6498) and Bay View Cruises (207–761–0496).

Eagle Island State Historic Site (all ages)
Three miles off the coast of Harpswell; (207) 624–6075. Open June 15 through Labor Day from dawn to dusk. Admission is free for children under 5. $

North Pole explorer Admiral Robert E. Peary once called Eagle Island home. History buffs will enjoy touring the Peary family home. Nature lovers can pleasantly explore the island along a hiking trail.

An island pier makes visitation possible during the summer. The Bureau of Parks and Lands can provide you with island transportation information.

Where to Eat

Anthony's Italian Kitchen. 151 Middle Street, Portland; (207) 774–8668. Some days are just made for pizza, and this is a great place to get it. $$

DiMillo's Floating Restaurant. 25 Long Wharf, Portland; (207) 772–2216; www.dimillos.com. Open for lunch and dinner, this is Maine's only floating eatery. Menu items include seafood, steak, Italian cuisine, and little meals for children. The water views are wonderful. $$–$$$

Porthole Restaurant. 20 Customs Wharf, Portland; (207) 780–6533. The accommodations aren't fancy, but the food is good and inexpensive. Open for breakfast, lunch, and dinner. An all-you-can-eat fish fry at lunch is more than reasonable. $

Other Things to **See** and **Do**

Whether you like culture, history, or adventure, there's plenty to keep you busy in Portland. Take in a play at the Portland Performing Arts Center. Listen to the Portland Symphony Orchestra at the elegant Merrill Auditorium at City Hall. Browse the galleries in the Old Port.

Historic sites abound in this timeless city. Here are just a few worth visiting: the George Tate House, the Victoria Mansion, the Morse-Libby House, and the Wadsworth-Longfellow House.

Thrill seekers can lift off in a hot air balloon courtesy of Balloon Rides (800–952–2076; www.hotairballoons.com) or learn to paddle a sea kayak with the help of folks at Maine Island Kayak Co. (207–766–2373).

Ruby's Choice. 127 Commercial Street, Portland; (207) 773–9099. Burgers, burgers, and more burgers are what you'll find here. A great, affordable place to take the kids. $

Where to Stay

Bayley's Camping Resort. 275 Pine Point Road, Scarborough; (207) 883–6043; www.bayleys-camping.com. This campground with more than 400 sites accommodates everything from pup tents to 50-foot motor homes. Bayley's is worthy of resort billing because of all it has to offer: miniature golf, entertainment, three playgrounds, three heated pools, three ponds, four Jacuzzis, nature trails, a game room, and bike and paddleboat rentals. Should you want to leave this fun-filled place, the camp's double-decker bus will shuttle you to the beach at no charge. $

Chebeague Island Inn. R.R. 1 Box 492, Chebeague Island 04017; (207) 846–5155. A classic summer resort. You and the kids can swim at Hamilton Beach, maybe play a round of golf on a private course below the hotel, or go exploring on bikes. If it rains, snuggle in next to the massive stone fireplace and play a variety of board games. $$–$$$

Holiday Inn By the Bay. 88 Spring Street, Portland; (800) 345–5050; www.innbythebay.com. This modern, eleven-story hotel is right in the middle of everything. Portland's Art District and the Old Port are just a short stroll away. Amenities include a large indoor pool, saunas, a fitness center, a restaurant, and a lounge. **Free** parking and Portland Jetport courtesy vans are also part of the package. $$$

Keller's. Peaks Island; (207) 766–4406. This guest house, which used to be a general store and restaurant, is open year-round and located close to the ferry landing. A beach is on the property. Credit cards aren't accepted, but personal checks are fine. $–$$

For More Information

Chamber of Commerce of the Greater Portland Region. (207) 772–2811; www.portlandregion.com.

Convention and Visitors Bureau of Greater Portland. (207) 772–5800; www.visitportland.com.

Yarmouth

Yarmouth is famous for its annual Clam Festival, but there's more than one reason to visit.

The Teddy Bear Factory (all ages)
294 Route 1, South Yarmouth; (207) 865–0600. Open Monday through Saturday 10:00 A.M. to 5:30 P.M., Sunday noon to 5:00 P.M. $$$–$$$$

One of the last makers of stuffed animals in the United States, the Teddy Bear Factory will show you how teddy bears are designed, cut, and sewn. Better yet, make your very own bear. You choose the fur, the eyes, the nose, and the amount of stuffing. You even get to stuff the bear on the stuffing machine. Then your bear will be sewn and groomed right before your eyes. After a "bear bath," add the finishing touches of clothes and accessories. It's expensive, but it's a lot of fun.

Yarmouth Clam Festival (all ages)
(207) 846–3984; www.clamfestival.com. $$

This fun-filled festival is held for three days in July. Centered around delicious Maine clams, you'll enjoy mouthwatering food, **free** entertainment, and, if you choose, lively competition.

Kids will love the carnival, face painting, and horsedrawn wagon rides. Adults can peruse the Craft and Art Shows, find a treasure at the Pink Elephant Sale, compete in a tennis tournament, or relax at Railroad Park.

Those with a really competitive spirit can run a 5-mile road race, enter the Clam Shucking Contest, paddle their way across the finish line in the Great Royal River Canoe Race, or pedal into first place in the Festival Bike Race. Kids can participate in the Fun Run or the Diaper Derby. If you prefer, just be a spectator of all the fun, including the Festival Parade.

A great way to spend the day. Visit on bracelet day and cruise the entire festival plus get unlimited carnival rides at one low price.

Where to Eat

Muddy Rudder. 1335 Route 1; (207) 846–3082; www.muddyrudder.com. Lousy name, wonderful restaurant. The atmosphere is casual but fun. If you go at the right time, as we did, someone will be tickling the ivories. There is a special children's menu and specials for grown-ups as well. Ladies' Night entitles women to a **free** entree from a selected menu. Look for candlelight dinner specials. $$–$$$

For More Information

Yarmouth Chamber of Commerce. (207) 846–3984.

Freeport

Put on the map by the presence of L. L. Bean, Freeport draws thousands of visitors each day. L. L. Bean is surely one of the main attractions in Freeport, but it is far from the only one. Outlet stores for shoes, clothes, skis, and other items are plentiful in Freeport, as are gift shops, restaurants, hot dog stands, ice-cream parlors, and inns. Another big pull to this area is the Desert of Maine. Allow plenty of time for your visit to Freeport, and bring some good walking shoes.

Shopping is very big business in Freeport. At last count, there were more than 125 outlet stores. L. L. Bean alone attracts about two and a half million customers each year. When you consider that this is probably twice the total population of Maine, you can understand why Freeport seems so crazy in the tourist season. You can buy anything in Freeport, from herbs to brass buttons. Only a handful of the shops concentrate on items of interest to children, though, so you may have to split parental duties for shopping and entertaining. Kids can be kept busy at many locations ranging from restaurants to shops, but their patience may run out before you peruse all of the buying opportunities.

Desert of Maine (all ages)

95 Desert Road; (207) 865–6962; www.desertofmaine.com. Open May through October. $$. **Free** for children 5 and under. Narrated coach tours are included in the price and provide a good explanation of the formation of the desert.

Few people would expect to find a desert in Maine, but this one is for real. Geologists have determined that a glacier slid through the area some 8,000 years ago and began to create the desert.

If you and your family want to venture off on your own, go right ahead. There are about forty acres of sand to see that was once farmland. The Tuttle Farm, as the desert was once known, was heavily farmed, then logged off to feed the railroad's need for timber. In the process, glacial sand deposits began to rise. They now cover old farm buildings and trees. It's an amazing sight. The sand is rich in mineral deposits that make it unstable for commercial use, but local rockhounds love it, as do children.

When you come back from your tour of the desert, check out the 1783 barn that is full of exhibits. Your kids can see old farm implements and push buttons to put displays into motion. Another good attraction is the sand-art area. Kids can make their own sand art or watch other artists at work. You can even buy colored sand to take home with you. The desert is less than 3 miles from the hub of Freeport. If you like to camp, you can even stay here (see Where to Stay).

L. L. Bean (all ages)

95 Main Street; (800) 341–4341 ext. 17801; www.llbean.com. Open twenty-four hours a day, 365 days a year.

This landmark is a Maine tradition, and there's plenty under its roof to keep your kids busy while you shop. Children can marvel at the live trout swimming in the indoor pool or contemplate the porcupine and bears (both stuffed) that stand guard around the camping

FYI: Bean Counter

In the early 1900s Leon Leonwood Bean sold one hundred "guaranteed" pairs of his hand-stitched boots, mail order. Ninety were sent back. He refunded his customers' money and worked on making a better boot. The rest, as they say, is history.

section. Taxidermists have created a virtual wildlife show throughout this store, with moose heads, bears, foxes, ducks, birds, fish, and other animals represented.

Some kids just enjoy riding the elevator between floors. Others are fascinated by the on-screen demonstrations that are given in various departments on everything from canoeing to turkey hunting. If you think that L. L. Bean is only for people who enjoy hunting, fishing, and camping, you're wrong. These areas are covered nicely, but other attractions include clothes, travel bags, housewares, books, dog accessories, footwear, and canoes.

In the new Kid's Department within the main store, you'll find everything your outdoor lovin' kids could ever want, from clothes to equipment. Interactive exhibits let them try out mountain biking and rock climbing. There's even a trout pond with glass windows to satisfy youthful curiosity.

Winslow Memorial Park (all ages)
Staples Point Road; (207) 865–4198. Open Memorial Day through October. $

This ninety-acre municipal park has a sandy beach and a large, grassy picnic area. Boating and camping are also available, as are rest rooms and showers.

Wolfe's Neck Woods State Park (all ages)
425 Wolfe's Neck Road; (207) 865–4465 or (207) 624–6080. Open to vehicles Memorial Day through Labor Day. Kids under 5 get in free. **$**

This 244-acre park offers opportunities for shoreline hiking along Casco Bay, the Harraseeket River, and salt marshes. There are 5 miles of hiking trails, picnic areas with charcoal grills, and rest rooms. Guided walks and lectures are also available. In the past, a children's program called "Ready, Set, Sleep" was a big hit. The program taught how animals and plants prepare for winter. Call to find out about current programs.

Mast Landing Sanctuary (all ages)
Upper Mast Landing Road; (207) 865–9090. Open year-round from dawn to dusk. Admission is free.

Maintained by the Maine Audubon Society, this one-hundred-acre preserve has self-guided trails through apple orchards, woods, meadows, and along a millstream. The sanctuary is so named because, in the past, pines from the area were used as masts for the British Navy.

Where to Eat

Blue Onion. 193 Lower Main Street; (207) 865–9396. Located at the southern end of town, the Blue Onion offers good food at a fair price. You can get anything from lobster to soup at this indoor-outdoor eatery that is happy to have your children as guests. $–$$

China Rose. 10 School Street; (207) 865–6886. This intimate restaurant offers Szechuan-Mandarin and Hunan dishes at reasonable prices. There is also a popular sushi bar. $$

Crickets Restaurant. 175 Lower Main Street; (207) 865–4005. Crickets is popular with the locals for its wide variety of menu items. Seafood, steak, pasta, burgers, sandwiches, and fajitas are some of the choices. There's also a kids' menu. Open daily for lunch and dinner, breakfast on the weekends. $

Lobster Cooker. 39 Main Street; (207) 865–4349; www.lobstercooker.com. A pleasant place to take a break from shopping, conveniently located just 1 block from L. L. Bean. It's even fast, as the lobster is quick-steamed in just ten minutes. Dine in the 1860 barn or the garden patio. $

Where to Stay

Desert Dunes of Maine Campground. 95 Desert Road; (207) 865–6962; www. desertofmaine.com. The campsites are inexpensive and include hookups, hot showers, laundry facilities, a convenience store, propane, fire rings, picnic tables, horseshoe pits, and nature trails. And, of course, the desert. $

Freeport Inn and Cafe. 31 U.S. Route 1, South Freeport; (800) 998–2583; www. freeportinn.com. An affordable choice for families is the Freeport Inn. All rooms have a refrigerator, coffeemaker, hairdryer, and river view. A swimming pool and play area will help keep the kids entertained. $–$$$$

Harraseeket Inn. 162 Main Street; (800) 342–6423; www.stayfreeport.com. One of the most popular, but expensive, places to stay and dine in Freeport is the Harraseeket Inn. This luxury hotel is just 2 blocks from L. L. Bean and the downtown shopping area. Antiques, canopy beds, and whirlpool tubs are all found in this charming setting. A drawing room, a library, a ballroom, a formal dining room, and an informal tavern are part of its appeal. $$–$$$$

For More Information

Freeport Merchants Association. (800) 865–1994; www.freeportusa.com.

Other Things to **See** and **Do**

Try canoeing the Harraseeket River. Ring's Marine Service (866–865–6143; www.ringsmarineservice.com) can outfit you with all you'll need for the trip. Top the adventure off with ice cream from Ben and Jerry's.

Mid-Coast Maine

The Mid-Coast region of Maine is full of family fun. There are islands to visit, lighthouses to see, and plenty of good restaurants to tempt your taste buds. Drive along the coast to see working fishing villages, visit historical sites, or spend a few days on any of the numerous beaches this region has to offer. Whether you're swimming at Coffin Pond in Brunswick, searching the tidal pools at Reid State Park, checking out the ships in Boothbay Harbor, hiking up Mount Battie in Camden, or watching an aerial show in Owls Head, you and your children are sure to enjoy your time in Mid-Coast Maine.

Brunswick

Brunswick is a charming college town, with Bowdoin College, founded in 1794, at its hub. One of the oldest colleges in the country, Bowdoin is the alma mater of many famous Americans, including Civil War hero General Joshua L. Chamberlain. Today, besides being an excellent liberal arts college, Bowdoin, with its museums and theater, is also a source of cultural entertainment. Tours of the campus, which covers 110 acres and includes more than fifty buildings, can be arranged by appointment (207–725–3100).

Besides the college, the town is also home to the Brunswick Naval Air Station, which is open for drivers' self-guided tours. After you've seen the base and the campus, you might be in the mood to do some shopping or eating. No problem. Brunswick's main street (actually called Maine Street) is one of the widest in the country and brimming with distinct shops and ethnic restaurants.

Maine State Music Theatre (ages 7 and up)
14 Maine Street, Suite 109; (207) 725–8769; www.msmt.org. Performances from early June through the end of August. Tickets $$$$

Maine's only professional music theater offers performances at Bowdoin College's 610-seat Pickard Theatre. For more than forty years, a cast of Broadway talent has presented a

MID-COAST MAINE

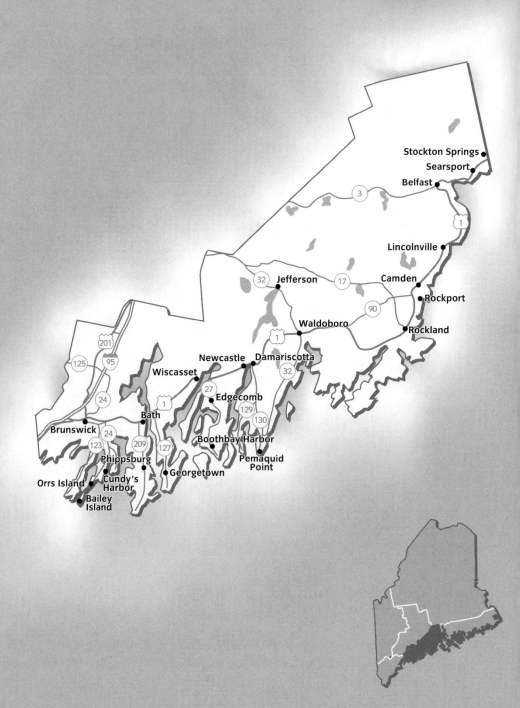

Stockton Springs
Searsport
Belfast
3
1
Lincolnville
32 Jefferson
17
Camden
90
Rockport
Waldoboro
1
Rockland
201
Newcastle Damariscotta
125
95
Wiscasset
32
24
27 Edgecomb
1
129
Bath
130
Brunswick
24
Boothbay Harbor
123
209
Pemaquid
Phippsburg
127
Point
Orrs Island
Georgetown
Cundy's
Harbor
Bailey
Island

diverse summer repertoire, including such musicals as *Man of La Mancha, Grease,* and *Show Boat.* Two productions targeted especially to children are also showcased each year.

Bowdoin College Museum of Art (ages 5 and up)

Walker Art Building, Bowdoin College, 9400 College Station, Maine Street; (207) 725–3275; www.academic.bowdoin.edu/artmuseum. Open 10:00 A.M. to 5:00 P.M. Tuesday through Saturday and 2:00 to 5:00 P.M. Sunday. Admission is free.

Outstanding art collections and various special exhibits await visitors. Past exhibits have included European and Mediterranean works, as well as American art. Paintings by Winslow Homer are periodically on display, but it's a good idea to call ahead to see if a Homer exhibit is planned during your visit.

Bonnie's Top Ten Picks for Mid-Coast Maine

1. Traveling to Land's End on Bailey Island; (207) 833–2313.
2. Splashing around at Popham Beach State Park, Phippsburg; (207) 389–1335.
3. Putting around at Dolphin Mini Golf, Boothbay; (207) 633–4828.
4. Petting sharks at the Maine Resources Aquarium, Boothbay Harbor; (207) 633–9559.
5. Rock climbing at Pemaquid Point Lighthouse, Pemaquid; (207) 677–2494.
6. Enjoying a piece of pie at Moody's Diner, Waldoboro; (207) 832–7785.
7. Watching the aerial show at Owls Head Transportation Museum, Owls Head; (207) 594–4418.
8. Taking a lobster boat cruise aboard the *Lively Lady Too*, Camden; (207) 236–6672.
9. Savoring the view from Mount Battie at Camden Hills State Park, Camden; (207) 236–3109.
10. Surviving the attempted train robbery on the Belfast and Moosehead Lake Railroad, Unity; (800) 392–5500.

Penny **Pinching**

You can purchase combination tickets for the Skolfield-Whittier House and the Joshua L. Chamberlain Civil War Museum at $8.00 for adults, $4.00 for kids 6 to 12. These are multiday tickets, so you can enjoy the museums at your leisure and on different days, if you wish.

The Peary-MacMillan Arctic Museum (ages 5 and up)

Hubbard Hall, Bowdoin College; (207) 725–3416; www.academic.bowdoin.edu/arcticmuseum. Open 10:00 A.M. to 5:00 P.M. Tuesday through Saturday and 2:00 to 5:00 P.M. Sunday. Admission is **free.**

It is fitting that Bowdoin would honor alumni Robert Edwin Peary (class of 1877) and Donald Baxter MacMillan (class of 1898), the first explorers to reach the North Pole. Clothing, trophies, and other mementos from their first and subsequent Arctic expeditions are on display.

Pejepscot Museum (ages 7 and up)

159 Park Row; (207) 729–6606; www.curtislibrary.com/pejepscot.htm. Open year-round Tuesday through Friday 9:00 A.M. to 5:00 P.M., Thursday till 8:00 P.M. Also open Saturday from 9:00 A.M. to 4:00 P.M. during the summer. Admission is **free.**

This facility exhibits materials that show the history of Brunswick, Topsham, and Harpswell.

Skolfield-Whittier House (all ages)

161 Park Row; (207) 729–6606; www.curtislibrary.com/pejepscot.htm. Summer and fall tours are given Tuesday through Saturday at 10:00 A.M., 11:30 A.M., 1:00 P.M., and 2:30 P.M. Closed in winter and spring. $$

This seventeen-room mid-nineteenth-century home was sealed for fifty years, preserving its original furnishings and decor. This is an excellent opportunity for your children to see how people of the past lived.

Joshua L. Chamberlain Civil War Museum (ages 5 and up)

226 Maine Street; (207) 729–6606; www.curtislibrary.com/pejepscot.htm. Open during summer and fall, Tuesday through Saturday 10:00 A.M. to 4:00 P.M. Guided tours twice an hour, 10:00 A.M. to 3:15 P.M. Closed in winter and spring. $$

Joshua Chamberlain was a college professor who became known for his Civil War heroics on Little Round Top during the Battle of Gettysburg. He also served four terms as the governor of Maine and was the president of Bowdoin College. The museum occupies five restored rooms of Chamberlain's house. Displays include Civil War artifacts and memorabilia of General Chamberlain. Said to be one of Brunswick's most unusual homes, the structure started out as a typical Cape Cod in the mid-1820s. When Chamberlain bought it in 1871, he had the house raised vertically by 11 feet and inserted a new ground floor of living space.

Surf's Up in **Brunswick**

If you're ready for active adventure, consider taking a dip in one of the local swimming holes. **White's Beach** (207–729–0415) is a campground with a swimming area, a sandy beach, and a small water slide. It's a little out of town, on the Durham Road, and it can be crowded during prime season.

Thomas Point Beach (877–TPB–4321; www.thomaspointbeach.com) is off Route 24 near the section of town known as Cook's Corner. This is a good picnic spot, and there's lots of room for kids to roam. The sandy beach is on tidal water, so low tide presents swimmers with mudflats. This is a nice place to let kids explore and discover unusual creatures like horseshoe crabs. Sixty-four acres of lawns and groves, a playground for kids, and a snack bar and arcade round out the areas of exploration and entertainment. In addition, special events are staged here throughout the summer season. Admission is $3.50 for adults, $2.00 for children.

Coffin Pond (207–725–6656) on River Road near Pleasant Street is a fine spot for swimming. A sandy beach surrounds a town-owned pond/pool, where a large water slide has kids standing in line for a chance to splash down. Lifeguards are on duty, and the swimming is safe for kids of all ages with reasonable supervision. Picnic tables are scattered among trees, and a playground is open to children. The food from the snack bar is good and not as expensive as you might expect.

Brunswick Fishway (all ages)

Brunswick-Topsham Hydro Station, Maine Street. Open May and June, Saturday and Sunday from 10:00 A.M. to 2:00 P.M. and Wednesday from 7:00 to 9:00 P.M. Admission is free.

Kids will get a kick out of watching fish climb a ladder. An underwater, forty-step fish ladder allows Atlantic salmon, alewives, and shad to migrate over the Androscoggin dam to spawn upstream. As the fish move upriver, they pass the counting and viewing area for all to see.

Amazing Maine Facts

Did the Civil War really begin in Brunswick, Maine? In a matter of speaking, yes. For it was here, just a few blocks from Bowdoin College, that Harriet Beecher Stowe penned *Uncle Tom's Cabin*. President Abraham Lincoln later credited the book for arousing sentiments that spurred the Civil War.

Where to Eat

Cook's Corner has plenty of franchise places to eat: Denny's (good breakfast), Applebee's (try the tequila lime chicken), Friendly's (delicious ice cream), as well as a couple of drive-ins (just for fun). However, if you prefer something more authentic, downtown Brunswick offers food of all types and for all budgets.

Fat Boy Drive-In. 111 Bath Road; (207) 729–9431. Open from mid-March through October. Just park your car and flash your headlights, and a waitperson will come and take your order. The burgers are great; you'll want to try the onion rings too. $

MacMillan & Company. 94 Maine Street; (207) 721–9662; www.mainerestaurants.com/macmillans. This family-style restaurant serves a variety of foods at moderate prices. $

Narcissa Stone Restaurant. 10 Water Street, Captain Daniel Stone Inn; (207) 725–9898; www.someplacesdifferent.com/cdsi-cal.htm. Dress casually or dress up as you dine in elegance at this award-winning restaurant. $$–$$$

Richard's Restaurant. 115 Maine Street; (207) 729–9673. Enjoy bauernwurst, wienerschnitzel, and strudel at this authentic German restaurant. There are also fish, steak, and chicken dishes. $

Rosita's Mexican Food. 212 Maine Street; (207) 729–7118. Serves authentic Mexican food at family prices. $

Stick To Your Ribs Barbecue. 18 Bath Road; (207) 729–9439. Reminiscent of the "good ol' days," this authentic drive-in has a large awning to park under, complete with speaker phones. Place your order and your food will be brought to you. The slogan here is "Fine Swine by the Bowdoin Pines." Not the most appetizing of slogans, but those ribs are good. Besides regular fast-food fare, there are chowders and seafood. $

Where to Stay

Brunswick Atrium. 21 Gurnet Road, Cook's Corner; (207) 729–5555. Added amenities such as a small indoor pool and a health club are nice, but rates can be high. $$–$$$

Brunswick Bed & Breakfast. 165 Park Row; (800) 299–4914; www.brunswickbnb.com. Eight spacious guest rooms with private baths await visitors. Sleep in antique beds and awake to a delicious breakfast prepared by the innkeepers. Children are welcome, staying for **free**, and a third-floor suite is perfect for families. $$–$$$

Captain Daniel Stone Inn. 10 Water Street; (207) 725–9898; www.captaindanielstoneinn.com. Rates at this elegantly restored Federal-style home include a large continental breakfast. There are thirty-four rooms, ranging from standard rooms to large suites. $$–$$$$

Comfort Inn. 199 Pleasant Street; (207) 729–1129. A very nice place to stay. Rates include a deluxe continental breakfast. $–$$

For More Information

Bath-Brunswick Chamber of Commerce. (800) 725–8797 or (207) 725–8797; www.midcoastmaine.com.

Other Things to **See** and **Do**

Visit the Long Shot Golf Center (207–725–6377) if your children enjoy playing miniature golf or driving a bucket of balls on a range. Yankee Lanes of Brunswick (207–725–2963) offers tenpin bowling. Movie buffs can take in a first-run film at Hoyts Brunswick Cinema Ten (207–798–3996). Bookworms will want to visit the area's largest bookstore: Greater Bookland & Cafe (207–725–2313; www.booklandcafe.com). Last but not least, kids will enjoy a shopping spree at KB Toys (207–725–8741).

Cundy's Harbor, Orrs Island, and Bailey Island

Before you leave the Brunswick area, you owe it to yourself and your kids to take a ride down Route 24 to explore Cundy's Harbor, Orrs Island, and Bailey Island. This is a trip that you should plan to take when the weather is good and you're in no hurry. There are not a lot of commercial attractions on this tour, but the scenery and the salt air will do wonders for you. Plus, there are enough diversions along the way to keep your kids satisfied.

Start your journey on Route 24 at Cook's Corner. Follow the signs out of town to the islands. If you want a chance to see some seals, follow Cundy's Harbor Road after crossing the first bridge. There is a sign at the intersection. Stay on this road until you run out of dry land—it won't take very long. You'll be in picturesque **Cundy's Harbo**r in just a few minutes, where lobstermen will be mending their traps and seals may be swimming playfully or resting on shore. This side trip will give you a taste of how real Mainers live and work in a harbor area.

Back on Route 24, head for **Orrs Island.** You'll know that you're on Orrs Island when you dip down into a low spot and cross over some of the most beautiful green water you've ever seen. As you reach the top of the hill, there will be a small pull-off with picnic tables on your left. This is a pleasant place to take a break, but keep an eye on your kids. The road is a busy one in season, and the picnic area is steep and leads to deep water.

You will see many side roads worth exploring as you continue along on Route 24. Lowell Cove Road, on your left, leads to a small cove, Lowell Cove, where a whale came in for a visit a few years ago. This is a good place to stop and let the kids run around on the natural beach. They should wear shoes; this is not a sandy area. Shells and glass may cut bare feet. Once you're back on the road, you will see a number of tourist stops selling everything from art to old buoys.

Amazing
Maine Facts

When you cross from Orrs Island to Bailey Island, you will do so on the only remaining cribstone bridge in the world. The bridge is made with granite blocks that are laid in a honeycomb pattern, without cement, to allow tidal flows to pass. The bridge is narrow but sturdy.

On **Bailey Island** you will see Mackerel Cove on your right and down low, filled with a variety of boats. This is a colorful place to take some pictures and to explore the water's edge. When you continue down Route 24, you won't have much farther to go. The road will cease at **Land's End,** where a fascinating gift shop, a small beach, and terrific views will capture your attention.

Where to Eat

Food on the islands naturally focuses on seafood specialties, but you and your kids can get some land-lover's dishes if seafood is not your favorite.

Cook's Lobster House. 68 Garrison Cove Road, Bailey Island; (207) 833–2818; www.cookslobster.com. This is a good place to eat, but service can be slow due to the large number of customers this waterfront spot can accommodate. Voted the #1 seafood restaurant in the mid-coast since 1995, the food is worth the wait. After enjoying a steaming lobster, stroll along the dock and let the kids watch as lobsters and crabs are hauled in from boats. $$–$$$

Jack Baker's Ocean View Restaurant. Route 24, Bailey Island; (207) 833–5366. You'll find the restaurant on the left just after crossing the bridge onto Bailey Island. Views are good, and the kids can play around in the rocky tidal pools after eating. $$

Lobster Village. Mackerel Cove, Route 24, Bailey Island; (207) 833–6656. Offers both a coffee shop and a restaurant. This is a working pier, and the language can get pretty salty. If you have impressionable children, this probably isn't a great place to stop for lunch. Otherwise, the service is usually fast and the prices are fair. $$

Where to Stay

Bailey Island Motel. P.O. Box 4, Route 24, Bailey Island 04003; (207) 833–2886; www.baileyislandmotel.com. This small two-story motel is located directly across from the world's only cribstone bridge (see sidebar above). Besides regular rooms, an efficiency unit with a kitchen is available. A continental breakfast of freshly baked muffins, juice, and coffee is included. Open May to October. Kids under 10 stay for **free.** $–$$

Driftwood Inn and Cottages. P.O. Box 16, Washington Street, Bailey Island 04003; (207) 833–5461. Open from mid-May through mid-

October, this facility has been in the same family for more than fifty years. Kids will get a kick out of the small saltwater swimming pool that is set into the rocky shore. You and your family can enjoy the dining room from late June through Labor Day. Almost all of the rooms and cottages have views of the ocean, and the personal attention from your hosts will not be forgotten. $–$$

Little Island Motel. 44 Little Island Road, Orrs Island; (207) 833–2392; www.littleisland motel.com. This intimate resort offers only nine units. However, a buffet breakfast including freshly baked muffins, along with bacon and smoked salmon, is part of the package. Bicycles and boats are available to guests, so you can pedal around the island or enjoy some great fishing. $$–$$$

Log Cabin. P.O. Box 41, Route 24, Bailey Island 04003; (207) 833–5546; www.logcabin-maine.com. Eight elegant rooms are available in this rustic retreat, open from April to October. You can relax in a hot tub on your own private deck while enjoying views of Casco Bay, the White Mountains, and Mount Washington. The restaurant features seafood and home-baked desserts. Reservations are required for dinner. $$–$$$$

For More Information

Bath-Brunswick Chamber of Commerce. (800) 725–8797; www.midcoast maine.com.

Bath and Phippsburg

Bath is a strategic Maine town due to its proximity to the Kennebec River. Some 5,000 vessels have been built in Bath shipyards. Today Bath Iron Works (BIW) is the shipbuilder in the area and it's American naval ships, not wooden schooners, that you see docked near the drawbridge. However, before you spot the ships you're likely to see a red-and-white crane reaching approximately 400 feet into the air at BIW. This is the largest crane on the East Coast. Bath is built around the shipyard, but there is more to this town than just tugboats and welders.

Downriver from Bath is Phippsburg, a peninsula where the Kennebec River flows into the Atlantic. It was here, in 1607, that the English first attempted to colonize New England. The Popham Colony, established thirteen years before the Pilgrims landed at Plymouth Rock, lasted only through one bitter winter. Those who did not die headed home on a thirty-ton pinnace christened *Virginia*. It was the first wooden ship built in the New World.

Maine Maritime Museum (all ages)

243 Washington Street, Bath; (207) 443–1316; www.bathmaine.com. Open daily from 9:30 A.M. to 5:00 P.M., except Thanksgiving, Christmas, and New Year's Day. Admission is free for children under 6. $$

Maritime artifacts and archives of the state can be found in this museum, which includes the Percy & Small Shipyard, the country's only surviving wooden shipbuilding yard. Most of the exhibits are post–Civil War, when about 80 percent of the country's full-rigged ships

Amazing **Wooden** Ships

The 3,730-ton *Wyoming*, built in 1909 at the Percy & Small Shipyard, is the largest wooden schooner ever built—a modern missile cruiser is smaller.

were built in Maine. Nearly half of them were built in Bath. The museum now holds about one million pieces of art, artifacts, and documents.

A gift shop offers a wonderful selection of nautical gifts and books. You'll also find a picnic area and a playground with a giant ship-shaped sandbox. Summer and winter camp programs are available for children 6 and under—something to look into if you plan to be in town for a while. There is something here for everyone to enjoy, and it's worth the time and price of admission.

The museum also offers cruises along the Kennebec River aboard the excursion boat *Summertime.* You can take a lighthouse cruise, visit an island game preserve, or venture to Georgetown, listening to seafaring stories along the way and enjoying a seafood dinner right on the dock. The cruises are extra, and reservations are highly recommended. Call or check the museum's Web site for the latest schedule.

Chocolate Church Arts Center (ages 5 and up)

798 Washington Street, Bath; (207) 442–8455; www.chocolatechurcharts.org. Office and art gallery open Tuesday through Saturday noon to 4:00 P.M. The gallery is **free.** Performances, times, and ticket prices vary widely. Call for a current schedule.

A renovated, historic 1847 Gothic church now houses art in the annex and offers performances, classes, and lectures in the one-hundred-seat Curtis Little Theater. Gallery shows range from juried competitions to individual and group shows. Productions featured at the center are even more varied. Everything from quality performances by traveling groups and sellout performers to **free** singalongs are staged here. Special programs for children are offered during the summer.

Popham Beach State Park (all ages)

10 Perkins Farm Lane, Phippsburg; (207) 389–1335. Open from dawn to dusk April 15 through October 30. Admission is **free** for children under 5. $

As you wind your way into Popham Beach, you should enjoy the country atmosphere. The entrance to the beach will be on your right, and it's well marked. This recreational area includes 3 miles of sandy beach to play on. Sandbars, tidal pools, and smooth rocks attract children just like bread crumbs pull in seagulls. But watch your young ones carefully; the undertow can be strong. Also, the water can be quite cold, so don't expect to swim except during the warmer summer months. This beach is not crowded, but it does attract most of the tourists in the area. A bathhouse provides freshwater showers, and picnic tables and charcoal pits are available in the wooded area of the park.

Fort Popham (all ages)

10 Perkins Farm Lane, Phippsburg; park season (207) 389–1335, off-season (207) 624–6080. Open Memorial Day to Labor Day. Admission is free.

If you want a secret place to enjoy as a native, this is it. The fort is located just a mile or so beyond the state park. When you reach the end of Route 209, you will see lobster boats to your left and a sign pointing to Percy's Store on your right. Park at Percy's. A fee is charged for all-day parking, but it's cheap and this is the best place to leave your vehicle while you explore the fort and the hidden beach. This beach is not known by many tourists. Locals spend their time fishing the surf for bluefish, and children love to chase after the thousands of bait fish that the blues chase to shore. You and your kids can kick back and relax here without all the roar of a typical tourist beach.

Once you've felt the sand between your toes, take the short stroll up the rocks to Fort Popham. The structure is semicircular in design and was never finished. The granite fort was built in 1861. Kids like to climb on the ramparts and explore the dark (and often mosquito-filled) rooms that make up this waterfront fort. Spiral staircases made of granite allow access to some good lookout points. Except for some campgrounds, the fort and the beach are about all there is to this little hidden haven, but the trip is worthwhile.

Fort Baldwin (all ages)

At the end of Route 209, Phippsburg. Admission is free.

Across the cove from Fort Popham and part of Popham Beach State Park, this fort is hidden atop Sabino Hill. Take the road to the top or park at Fort Popham and walk. Three batteries, built in the early 1900s, await exploration. There's also a fire control tower to climb for outstanding views of the Atlantic.

Where to Eat

The Cabin. 552 Washington Street, Bath; (207) 443–6224. Located across from BIW, The Cabin features great pizza. Some say it's the best in Maine. $

Front Street Deli and Club. 128 Front Street, Bath; (207) 443–9815. This is a little-known but fabulous place for a quick, delicious lunch. If you enter this hideout through the main entrance, you'll find booths and a family setting. Go downstairs, and you have ambience like you wouldn't believe, complete with the club cat, who may take a nap on your feet as you sit in overstuffed couches and chairs. Not only is the setting of this place unique, so is the food. A favorite is the chicken salad BLT. That's right—you get a chicken salad sandwich and a BLT all packed into one double-decker. It's great! This is the place for interesting food, calm eating conditions, and a setting you won't want to leave. $–$$

J. R. Maxwell & Co. 122 Front Street, Bath; (207) 443–2014; www.midcoastrestaurants. com. A renovated 1840s hotel with exposed brick walls and hanging plants provides a great atmosphere in which to enjoy great food. The large menu specializes in seafood but offers steak, chicken, and pasta as well. There's even steak and seafood on the children's menu. A two-for-one deal is featured every Wednesday night. $$

Kristina's Restaurant & Bakery. 160 Centre Street, Bath; (207) 442–8577. You'll want to try this one, if only for the dessert. Rated one of the top ten restaurants in Maine, it has been frequented by Cher, Maury Povich, and Connie Chung. It's open for breakfast, lunch, and dinner. $–$$

New Meadows Inn. 412 State Road, West Bath; (207) 443–3921; www.newmeadow inn.com. Here you can just eat or spend the night in a room or a cottage. Buffets are common at this restaurant, and you and the kids can sit at a water-view window while enjoying an all-you-can-eat meal at down-home prices. $$–$$$$

Where to Stay

Fairhaven Inn. 118 North Bath Road, Bath; (888) 443–4391; www.mainecoast.com/fair haveninn. This 1790 colonial inn has nine guest rooms that are wallpapered in various flower prints and furnished with antiques and comfy quilts. Rates include a three-course breakfast prepared by innkeepers Susie and Dave Reed, who formerly owned and operated a pastry shop in Washing-

ton, D.C. Special fall and winter packages are available. $–$$

Holiday Inn. 139 Richardson Street, Bath; (207) 443–9741; www.holiday-inn.com/ bathme. In plain view of Route 1 as you enter town, the Holiday Inn offers a super breakfast menu in the dining room, along with lunches and dinners. Its Bounty Lounge is a nightspot for area residents, and a sauna and hot tub are available to guests. $–$$

Inn at Bath. 969 Washington Street, Bath; (800) 423–0964; www.innatbath.com. Children 6 and over are welcome at this inn, where you can stay in a suite with a sitting room that had been a hayloft. $$–$$$$

For More Information

Bath-Brunswick Chamber of Commerce. (800) 725–8797; www.midcoast maine.com.

Other Things to **See** and **Do**

Enjoy nature at the Morse Mountain Sanctuary in Phippsburg. If you're visiting Bath in early July, don't miss **Bath Heritage Days** (207–443–9751). It's a three-day festival filled with everything from parades and craft shows to musical entertainment and the Fireman's Follies. The grand finale is fireworks over the Kennebec River.

Amazing Maine Facts

Sequin Light is the highest lighthouse on the Maine coast, at 180 feet above sea level. It is also the second oldest, and a bit obscure, as it can only be seen by boat. For information on tours contact Maine Maritime Museum (207–443–1316, www.bathmaine.com), Captain Nick Sewall of Hermit Island Campground (207–443–2101), or Atlantic Seal Cruises of South Freeport (207–865–6112).

Georgetown

The mid-coast is known for its rocky shores. That's why the nice expanse of sand you'll find at Reid State Park in Georgetown is a rare surprise.

Reid State Park (all ages)
375 Seguinland Road; (207) 371–2303. Open year-round from 9:00 A.M. to sunset. $

Just over the bridge from Bath you'll see signs for the park. It's about 14 miles to the beach, but the drive is pleasant and offers good views.

Reid State Park has so much for families. Two sandy beaches provide a choice of swimming areas. The surf can be rough, but it is rarely dangerous. Rock outcroppings allow for plenty of climbing, and coin-operated binoculars provide long views. A special lagoon is situated below the sand dunes to give younger children a wave-free place to splash and play in warmer water. Don't turn the kids loose—the lagoon is not overly shallow, but it can be waded by adults in most areas without ever going in over your head.

Picnic tables are placed throughout the park, and endless tidal pools and other areas of exploration will keep the kids happy. A snack bar cranks out good food for a fair price, but watch out for the gulls. They love to steal french fries or any other food left lying around. Changing rooms and rest rooms are on the premises.

Parking is rarely a problem, although you may have to walk a bit in prime season. This park offers what feels like a commercial beach area, but it also gives visitors a taste of the wild Maine waterfront.

After a day of sun and sand dine outdoors at the Five Island wharf. Here the Georgetown Fisherman's Co-op serves up fresh and fabulous seafood. Order a lobster and watch the cooks pull the traps from the water and catch your dinner.

Where to Eat

The Robinhood Free Meetinghouse.
210 Robinhood Road; (207) 371–2188;
www.robinhood-meetinghouse.com. Enjoy
five-star dining in a fully restored 1855 meetinghouse. A menu offering thirty-six entrees
ranging from pork Roquefort to grilled
Jamaican jerk shrimp promises to satisfy the
most discriminating taste. Special events
such as wine tasting, theme night, and old-
fashioned Maine lobster bakes are also a big
draw. Open year-round. $$$$

Where to Stay

Sagadahoc Bay Campground. P.O. Box
171, Georgetown 04548; (207) 371–2014;
www.sagbaycamping.com. In business for
five years, they offer forty-five sites: twenty-
two for tents and twenty-three for RVs.
Oceanfront camping let's you enjoy beautiful
views of Seguin Lighthouse. At Molly Point
Park you'll find a boat launch, picnic tables,
grills, and a large field for lawn games. $

For More Information

**Bath-Brunswick Chamber of Com-
merce.** (800) 725–8797; www.midcoast
maine.com.

Wiscasset

When you enter the town of Wiscasset, you'll be greeted by a number of antiques shops. In the summer, traffic along the main street is
stopped by a crossing officer to allow pedestrians, of which there
are many, to browse through a variety of shops and stores. The
Sheepscot River creates a beautiful backdrop for this delightful
town, known as the "Prettiest Little Village in Maine."

The Musical Wonder House (all ages)

18 High Street; (800) 336–3725; www.musicalwonderhouse.com. Open for daily guided
tours May through October 1, from 10:00 A.M. to 5:00 P.M. Thirty-minute, hour, and three-
hour tours are offered. Three-hour tours must be reserved in advance. $$–$$$$

This house, due to its content, holds more interest for children than most house tours. An
unusual collection featuring music boxes, reed organs, pump organs, and other music
makers is housed here. When you take one of the daily guided tours, the many musical
wonders are played and demonstrated. A tour of the entire house takes about three
hours. Boasting thirty-two rooms, this gorgeous Greek Revival home was built in 1852 as a
sea captain's mansion.

Nickels-Sortwell House (ages 5 and up)

121 Main Street; (207) 882–6218. Guided tours given daily June through October, from
11:00 A.M. to 4:00 P.M. $$

This beautiful mansion, built by Captain William Nickels in the early 1800s, is reminiscent of
the wealth and prosperity of Wiscasset when it was Maine's chief port. However, the

Day Tripping: **All Aboard!**

If you plan to ride the Maine Coast Railroad, I recommend taking a morning train to Bath. When you arrive, get off and stretch your legs with a walk into town for some shopping and a bite to eat. A stop at the Chocolate Church is always fun. Just hold onto your ticket stub and you can catch an afternoon train back to Wiscasset.

Embargo Act of 1807 crushed the town's sea trade and eventually robbed Nickels of his fortune. The mansion was sold and used as a hotel until it was bought by Foye Sortwell, the mayor of Cambridge, Massachusetts, in 1895. The house became his summer residence.

Castle Tucker (ages 5 and up)

2 Lee Street; (207) 882–7364; www.spnea.org/visit/homes/castle.htm. Open June 1 to October 15, Friday through Sunday, from 11:00 A.M. to 4:00 P.M. Tours on the hour. Children under 6 admitted free. **$$**

This Victorian mansion was originally built by Judge Silas Lee in 1807. Captain Richard Tucker purchased the home in 1958, and his heir, Jane Tucker, continues to live in the house—though it is maintained by the Society for the Preservation of New England Antiquities. The mansion features original furnishings and wallpaper. The elliptical, freestanding staircase is breathtaking, as is the wall of glass overlooking the Sheepscot River.

The Lincoln County Museum and Jail (all ages)

133 Federal Street; (207) 882–6817; www.lincolncountyhistory.org. Open Saturday only in June and September 10:00 A.M. to 4:00 P.M., Tuesday through Saturday 10:00 A.M. to 4:00 P.M. in July and August. $

The main attraction here is the old jail. It was built with 41-inch-thick granite walls in 1811 and used until 1953. Tools and alternating exhibits are displayed, and the jailer's house can be toured, but the kids will probably find the jail itself more interesting.

Morris Farm (all ages)

156 Gardiner Road; (207) 882–4080; www.morrisfarm.org. Open year-round during daylight hours. Admission is free.

When the Morris family sold their farm in 1994, caring residents formed a trust in order to buy the farm and preserve it for public use. Since then the farmstand, offering certified organic fruits and vegetables, has been the gateway welcoming visitors to explore the farm. Kids will enjoy walking the pastures, visiting the animals, and investigating the woods.

Winter and summer day camps are offered for the children. Special events throughout the year, such as the Spring Contra Dance in April, a Wine and Cheese Tasting and Art Auction in October, and the "Tour de Farms" Bicycle Tour and Barbecue in August, give adults plenty to do as well.

Wiscasset Raceway (ages 5 and up)

West Alna Road; (207) 882–4271; www.wiscassetraceway.com. Weekly racing Friday at 7:30 P.M. and Sunday at 6:00 P.M. Admission is **free** for children under 6 for Friday and Sunday races and **free** for children under 10 for Slam Series races. $$

Gentlemen, start your engines! A night of live stock car racing awaits you at the Wiscasset Raceway. Pick a winner before the race starts and cheer them on. Loud engines and noisy crowds are all part of the excitement.

Where to Eat

Le Garage. 15 Water Street; (207) 882–5409. Antique tools are displayed like art at this restaurant, which was once an automotive repair shop. Set above the Sheepscot River, Le Garage offers a view that is nearly as good as the food. Seafood, pasta, and vegetarian selections are just part of the menu. You can enjoy breakfast, lunch, or dinner. Dinner is served by candlelight (only the entryway lights remain on). The food and service are good, and children are welcome. $–$$

Red's Eats. At the corner of Main Street and Water Street; (207) 882–6128. Serving Wiscasset for more than sixty years, this landmark eatery is famous for the "best lobster rolls in the state." I would have to agree. Each sandwich is made with the meat of an entire lobster. Open April through September, Red's also serves up hot dogs, crab rolls, and shrimp. Dine at picnic tables or across the street at the public deck over the river. $

Sarah's Cafe. 100 Water Street; (207) 882–7504. Open daily. Sarah's serves what is probably the best pizza around. Mexican meals and lobster are also available. The triple soup buffet with your choice of stuffed breads is a favorite. Kids will enjoy the balloons and coloring contests. $–$$

Where to Stay

Snow Squall Bed and Breakfast. 5 Bradford Road; (800) 775–7245; www.snowsquall inn.com. This renovated 1850s New England home offers accommodations with private baths, fireplaces, and suites for large families. Savor a full breakfast in the morning or a chocolate chip cookie from a jar on the front desk anytime. Kids can roam around the sprawling backyard while adults relax on the porch or in the gazebo. $$$–$$$$

Edgecomb

Edgecomb is not a town where you are likely to spend a lot of time, but it's a nice place to pass through. Horse lovers might want to stop off at **Ledgewood Riding Stables** (207–882–6346) at the intersection of Route 27 and Old County Road; there's trail riding at hourly rates. Shoppers won't want to miss **Edgecomb Potters** (207–882–9493; www.edgecomb potters.com), the state's largest American craft gallery. The pottery is nationally acclaimed for its vibrant color. Located just over the bridge from Wiscasset, Edgecomb offers additional dining and lodging options at competitive rates.

Penny **Pinching**

Iron sculptures punctuate the outside deck at Edgecomb Potters. My 7-year-old daughter, Kaitlyn, was particularly taken with one of a 10-foot horse—so taken, she wanted to buy it. She asked a clerk how much it cost, stating that she was saving her allowance and would save until she had enough. "That sculpture costs $50,000, my dear," the clerk replied. "I'm afraid you'd have to save for a very long time." But don't be fooled; the deck is where you'll find the best deals on pottery, with seconds selling at up to 70 percent off.

Fort Edgecomb (all ages)
66 Fort Road Davis Island; (207) 882–7777 in summer, (207) 624–6080 off-season. Open Memorial Day through Labor Day. $

Originally built to protect Wiscasset, Fort Edgecomb boasts an 1808 octagonal blockhouse and restored fortifications. Today the musket ports and rectangular openings on all eight sides of the blockhouse provide visitors beautiful views of the Sheepscot River and the surrounding area.

The fort has a large picnic area where you can enjoy a leisurely lunch, and the chance of spying harbor seals or nesting osprey are very good.

Where to Eat

Sheepscot River Restaurant. 306 Eddy Road; (207) 882–7748; www.sheepscotriverinn.com. Enjoy a relaxed ambience, river views, and piano tunes. Although the setting is a little formal, casual clothing is fine. Specializing in steak and seafood, the restaurant is open daily from 11:00 A.M. to 10:00 P.M. $$

Where to Stay

Cod Cove Inn. 22 Cross Road; (800) 882–9586; www.codcoveinn.com. All rooms have a private balcony or patio, cable TV, refrigerator, and private bath. Suites have a fireplace, sunken Jacuzzi, and wet bar. The grounds feature gardens, along with a gazebo, heated pool, and hot tub. An expanded continental breakfast is part of the package. $$–$$$$

Sheepscot River Inn. 306 Eddy Road; (800) 437–5503; www.sheepscotriverinn.com. Open year-round, the inn offers a choice of guest rooms, motor lodge suites, or cottages. Rates include a continental breakfast; pets are welcome. $–$$

The Boothbay Region

If you love water, boats, and a variety of shops, Boothbay is a good place to go. The Boothbay region is a major tourist attraction. You should allow several hours for this visit.

Boothbay Railway Village (all ages)

586 Wiscasset Road, Route 27, Boothbay; (207) 633–4727; www.railwayvillage.org. Open daily from 9:30 A.M. to 5:00 P.M. from June through Columbus Day. **Free** for children under 3. $–$$

Narrow-gauge trains, both as exhibits and as rides, are the main attraction here. Twenty-seven exhibit buildings show all aspects of small-town life, antique cars, and trains. Your children might enjoy seeing the one-room schoolhouse and the blacksmith shop. They will certainly like the twenty-minute ride on *Boothbay Central,* a coal-fired narrow-gauge train that treks around 1.5 miles of track. Children's Day, held in mid-August, features **free** admission for children 12 and under.

> ## Myths and Legends: Finders Keepers
>
> A large bundle adrift at sea after a shipwreck was once recovered by a lighthouse keeper at Hendrick's Headlight (built in 1829). The bundle, a box sandwiched between two feather beds, held a baby girl. The sole survivor of the wreck, she was adopted by the lighthouse innkeepers.

Marine Resources Aquarium (all ages)

194 McKown Point Road, West Boothbay Harbor; (207) 633–9559; www.maine.gov/dmr/rm/aquarium/index.html. Open daily Memorial Day through September 30, from 10:00 A.M. to 5:00 P.M. **Free** for children 4 and under. $

Completed in 1995, the aquarium is small but fun. A 20-foot touch tank lets kids hold lobsters, crabs, and sea urchins. They might even get squirted by a sea cucumber or scallop. The biggest thrill is petting a live shark or skate as it swims around an open 850-gallon tank. The exhibits of albino, blue, and calico lobster are both colorful and fascinating. Bring along a picnic lunch and enjoy the harbor view. A great way to get here during the summer is by the Rocktide Trolley.

The Carousel Music Theatre (ages 8 and up)

196 Townsend Avenue, Boothbay Harbor; (207) 633–5297 or (800) 757–5297; www.booth baydinnertheatre.com. Open mid-May through mid-October. Prices include dinner and show. $$$$

You'll be served dinner by cast members in a turn-of-the-twentieth-century atmosphere. While dining on chicken, fish, or steak perfectly prepared, you'll be entertained with a cabaret performance of America's classic popular music. Top off dinner with some apple pie or cheesecake and then sit back, relax, and enjoy the show.

Cruisin' Boothbay Harbor

As you might imagine, boating is the theme of Boothbay Harbor. **Boothbay Whale Watch** (888–942–5363; www.boothbayharborwhalewatch.com) at Pier 6, Fisherman's Wharf, runs cruises May through October. Whale watching is the main attraction with this line. **Cap'n Fish Boat Cruises** (800–636–3244; www.capnfishsboats.com) at Pier 1 operates from mid-May to mid-October, seven days a week. You can schedule a cruise for one, two, or three hours and hope to see seals, puffins, whales, and other aquatic attractions. Families who would rather catch fish than photograph them can go sportfishing for mackerel, tuna, shark, bluefish, or striped bass. Call **Blackjack Sportfishing and Charters** (207–633–6445) at Pier 7, Fisherman's Wharf, to arrange a fishing trip.

Vaudeville, Broadway, and good old show biz come to life as a talented cast of actors, in full costume, perform musical hits from the past. The dancing, acting, singing, and dining all work together for an enjoyable evening.

Balmy Days Cruises (all ages)
42 Commercial Street, Pier 8, Boothbay Harbor; (207) 633–2284; balmydayscruises.com. $$–$$$$

This cruise line offers a little bit of everything. Step aboard the *Balmy Days II* and you're on your way to Monhegan Island, 12 miles off the coast. One of Maine's most famous islands, Monhegan offers hours of fun exploration. The lighthouse, fishing village, and nature trails will capture you. The cliffs, the highest in Maine, will take your breath away.

The *Novelty* takes you on an hour harbor tour, past Burnt Island Lighthouse. Man the deck of the *Bay Lady* and you might be helping sail this 31-foot Friendship Sloop on an hour-and-a-half cruise. Or if you prefer, set sail on *Miss. Boothbay* for two hours of Mackerel fishing.

Dolphin Mini Golf (ages 5 and up)
510 Wiscasset Road, Boothbay; (207) 633–4828. $$

A pro mini-golf course and so much more. A Merrill family favorite, this is a great, inexpensive place to spend a couple of hours. Begin with a game of golf on eighteen well-maintained, beautifully landscaped holes with names like Lobster Traps, Bobbin Buoys, and Cliff Hanger. Finish up at hole 19—Pilings—where a hole in one gets you a free game. Next spend some time in the arcade, where there are oldies but goodies like Ms. Pac Man and Galaga. You might be able to impress the kids with your high score. Pinball machines and more up-to-date video games round out the arcade.

On your way over to the Ice Cream Hut, stroll through the Shell Museum inside the covered bridge. Shells of all shapes and sizes from all kinds of places can be found here. Finally, enjoy your ice cream at one of the picnic tables overlooking the fish pond. You can do all of this for the same price you'd pay to go to the movies. Great time. Good deal.

Boothbay Region Land Trust Preserves (all ages)

1 Oak Street, Boothbay Harbor; (207) 633–4818; www.gwi.net/~brlt. Open dawn to dusk. **Free.**

Hikers will enjoy the eighteen miles of coastal and woodland trails offered here. Pick trails that are right for you and your little ones, as difficulty levels vary from trail to trail. This is a more relaxing, less crowded way to take in the beauty of Boothbay.

Coastal Maine Botanical Gardens (all ages)

Barters Island Road, Boothbay; (207) 633–4333; www.mainegardens.org. Open dawn to dusk. Admission is **free.**

Walking is a breeze on the nicely groomed, well-marked trails you'll find here. The gardens, which are in development, cover 128 acres, with a generous amount of shore frontage. Various special events and programs, suitable for young and old, are hosted here throughout the year.

Mackerel Sky Studio (ages 3 and up)

18 Todd Avenue, Boothbay Harbor; (207) 633–7678; wwwlmackerelskystudio.com. Open studio hours are Monday through Saturday noon to 4:00 P.M. during the summer and Saturday 10:00 A.M. to 5:00 P.M. off-season. $$

Kids will love the single-shot workshops held at this retail/public art studio. They'll impress their friends with totes and T-shirts they make themselves.

Where to Eat

Brud's Hotdogs. 13 Atlantic Avenue, Boothbay Harbor; (207) 633–2135. Brud's cart is motorized, but you will usually find him in the center of town or on the east side of the harbor. A Boothbay Harbor fixture for more than fifty years, this is still a delicious quick fix for a growling stomach. $

The Downeast Ice Cream Factory. On the Byway, Pier One, P.O. Box 795, Boothbay Harbor; (207) 633–3016. Enjoy a make-your-own-sundae buffet. $

Ebb Tide. 43 Commercial Street, Boothbay Harbor; (207) 633–5692. Follow your nose until you see the red-striped awning. This establishment may bring back memories. It is

Extended **Menu**

There are tons of places to eat in the Boothbay Region. Here's just a sampling: Daffy Taffy Factory, Lobstermen's Co-Op, Pier Pizza, Lobster Dock, Daily Catch, not to mention those listed in Where to Eat. Go to the Chamber Web site (www.boothbayharbor.com) and get a free brochure.

decked out with knotty pine walls and booths that many adults may remember from their younger days. Breakfast is served here all day, along with other meals, such as lobster, club sandwiches, and seafood platters. The homemade desserts are all the reason you need to come here. $$

Fisherman's Wharf Inn. 22 Commercial Street, Boothbay Harbor; (800) 628–6872; www.fishermanswharfinn.com. A family favorite, we enjoy eating lunch on the deck overlooking the harbor. At dinner enjoy baked lemon-honey sea scallops, broiled sesame-garlic salmon, or a filet mignon in the casual elegance of the panoramic dining room. $$–$$$

Orne's Candy Store. 11 Commercial Street, Boothbay Harbor; (207) 633–2695; www.ornes candystore.com. Since 1885 this candy store has been offering passersby something sweet to eat. The shop looks very much like it did more than a century ago, with chocolates displayed in fancy dishes inside antique glass and wooden cases. Almond butter crunch (buttery toffee in a thin layer of chocolate dipped in crushed almonds) is a favorite. You can also enjoy crystallized ginger, an Asian treat brought to the coast by Down East skippers. Orne's smooth and creamy fudge is popular among those with less exotic tastes. $

Where to Stay

Lodging opportunities in the Boothbay region are abundant. The local chamber of commerce lists about fifty facilities, including Shore Hills Campground, Ship Ahoy Motel, Flag Ship Inn, Rocktide Inn, Spruce Point Inn, and Smuggler's Cove. Don't just come for the day. Stay awhile.

Emma's Guest House and Cottages. 110 Atlantic Avenue, Boothbay Harbor; (207) 633–5287. This establishment offers water views and proximity to all the action in town, at about the best rates. $–$$

The Lion d'Or. 106 Townsend Avenue, Boothbay Harbor; (207) 633–7367 or (800) 887–7367; www.liondorboothbay.com. Five spacious rooms are available in this comfortable Victorian home built in 1857. The rates are extremely reasonable for the area, and a full gourmet breakfast is included. Afternoon treats of fruited iced tea and cookies are an added delight. There is an additional charge of $5.00 for children 12 and under. $–$$

For More Information

Boothbay Chamber of Commerce. (207) 633–4743.

Boothbay Harbor Region Chamber of Commerce. (800) 266–8422 or (207) 633–2353; www.boothbayharbor.com.

Year-round **Festivities**

If you're visiting in the spring, don't miss the Fisherman's Festival, with its pageant, blessing of the fleet, and competitions. Bring in summer celebrating Windjammer Days, with activities including concerts and fireworks. Finally, party in color at the Fall Foliage Festival in October. Crafts, artwork, entertainment, and food guarantee fun.

Newcastle and Damariscotta

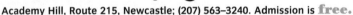

Maine has a long and beautiful coastline. You could spend weeks exploring it and never come close to seeing all there is to see. Families often have their favorite places, and Camden often appears on lists of preferred destinations. Rockland and Belfast also rate highly, and although Damariscotta is not as well known as the other towns, it too has a lot to offer adults and children.

Separated by the Damariscotta River, neither Newcastle nor Damariscotta is a flashy tourist attraction, yet people come through these towns in incredible numbers. Primarily attractive as the logical jumping-off points to many other desirable locations, such as Down East and the Pemaquid region, Newcastle and Damariscotta also offer attractions of their own.

St. Patrick's Church (all ages)
Academy Hill, Route 215, Newcastle; (207) 563–3240. Admission is free.

This is New England's oldest surviving Catholic church. Built in 1808 and listed on the National Register of Historic Places, the building has been restored and maintains its original Revere bell.

Chapman-Hall House (all ages) 🏛
At the corner of Main and Church Streets, Damariscotta; (207) 563–3175. Tours are offered from mid-June to early September. $

During the nineteenth century, Damariscotta was a major source of clay for brick making. Kilns were set up along the Damariscotta River, and the product was shipped out by boat. The Chapman-Hall House, built in 1754, is one of the oldest remaining historic homes in Maine.

Where to Eat

Andrews Pine View Restaurant. Route 1, Damariscotta; (207) 563–2899. The prices are a little high, but the quiet ambience, friendly service, and delicious food is worth it. Open for breakfast, lunch, and dinner. $$–$$$

Backstreet Restaurant. 17 Elm Street Plaza, Damariscotta; (207) 563–5666. Seafood here is mouthwatering. Homemade soup is always a big hit, and chowders are a frequent favorite. Prices are reasonable, and the service is good. $$

Paco's Tacos. Main Street, in the alley below Sheepscot River Pottery, Damariscotta; (207) 563–5355. You might have to look for this little joint, but it's worth the search—especially for the chicken soft taco. Come in on Friday and enjoy their enchilada specials. $

Paige's Deli. Main Street, Damariscotta; (207) 563–1999. A good place to get a hearty sandwich, a hot bowl of chili, or a salad. $

Rogue River Cafe. 155 Main Street, Damariscotta; (207) 563–2992; www.roguerivercafe.com. You can get dinner, lunch, or brunch here year-round. Enjoy homemade pastries, espresso, and live entertainment. $–$$

Other Things to **See** and **Do**

If you stop by Round Top for some delicious ice cream, you might want to wander over to the Round Top Center for the Arts (207–563–1507). Various plays, concerts, and gallery exhibits are showcased here throughout the year.

Round Top Ice Cream. 526 Business Route 1, Damariscotta; (207) 563–5307. Open 11:30 A.M. to 10:00 P.M. seven days a week from April to Columbus Day. You can't find a better place to please your palate with ice cream. $

Salt Bay Cafe. 88 Main Street, Damariscotta; (207) 563–3302. This establishment serves local seafood, steak, burgers, and many fried dishes. $$

Where to Stay

Lake Pemaquid Camping. P.O. Box 967, Twin Cove Lane, Damariscotta; (207) 563–5202; www.lakepemaquid.com. Rent a cabin or a cottage, bring your RV, or pitch a tent. Whichever you decide, you're bound to enjoy your stay. Swim in the shallow waters here or in the swimming pool. Relax in a Jacuzzi or sauna. Rent a boat, play tennis, or go fishing. During the summer there are kids' workshops featuring a variety of activities, from movie matinees to chalk art. $–$$$

Oyster Shell Motel. Box 267, Business Route 1, Damariscotta; (800) 874–3747; lincoln.midcoast.com/~oystrshl. This low-key "resort" motel has a swimming pool and features one- and two-bedroom suites that overlook the salt bay. $$

For More Information

Damariscotta Region Chamber of Commerce. (207) 563–8340; www.damariscottaregion.com.

Damariscotta Region Information Bureau. (207) 563–3175.

Pemaquid Point

On your drive from Damariscotta to Pemaquid Point along Route 130, you'll travel through the town of Bristol, in the vicinity of Round Pond, through the town of New Harbor, and eventually to the end of land. Pemaquid Lighthouse sits majestically on the point.

Home to Pemaquid Beach, New Harbor is perhaps one of the most photogenic working harbor towns in Maine. This inlet area was once a major shipbuilding location, and it remains an active fishing spot for lobstermen and commercial fishermen.

Thompson Ice House (all ages)

Route 129, Bristol; (207) 644–8551 in summer, (207) 729–1956 in winter. Open year-round during daylight hours. Museum open three days a week in July and August. Admission is free but donations are suggested.

Here you can see slide shows and videos that explain how this 150-year-old family business continues to harvest ice the old-fashioned way. You can also see the tools of the ice trade.

Watch ice harvesting in February and enjoy ice cream in July made with harvested ice.

Myths and Legends: Buried Treasure

The fishing village of Round Pond has the reputation of once being home to pirates. Rumor has it that the infamous Captain Kidd may have buried treasure in the Devil's Oven, near New Harbor.

Pemaquid Beach (all ages)

Route 130, New Harbor; (207) 677–2754. Open Memorial Day to Labor Day from 9:00 A.M. to sunset. Children under 12 are admitted free, but adults pay a use fee of $1.00 each.

You will find rest rooms, picnic areas, a bathhouse, and a concession stand at the beach. This is a good swimming beach, but sea breezes are often strong here, so consider bringing jackets with you.

Hardy Boat Cruises (all ages)

P.O. Box 326, New Harbor 04554; (800) 278–3346; www.hardyboat.com. Sailing May through October. Ticket prices vary depending on destination and length of cruise. $$–$$$

You can depart New Harbor in search of puffins on Eastern Egg Rock or take a sunset cruise to Pemaquid Point. Seals and other marine life are often sighted on the trips. You may also want to ask about the clambakes that are held on Monhegan Island. Daily cruises to the island offer you and your family a full day's adventure. Explore the island's seaside cliffs, hiking trails, and art galleries.

Colonial Pemaquid State Historic Site (all ages)

Route 130, Pemaquid ; (207) 677–2423 park in season; (207) 624–6080 off-season. Open Memorial Day to Labor Day, from 9:30 A.M. to 5:00 P.M. Admission is free for children under 5 and adults over 65. $

This is an interesting place to spend some time with your kids. A settlement was built here in the early 1600s, and you can still see an old burial ground dating to 1695. Children can see the artifacts from years gone by in this in-the-field museum.

Other Things to See and Do

The Rachel Carson Salt Pond Reserve, neighboring New Harbor, covers seventy-eight acres. It features a small cove, a tidal salt pond, many trees, and granite outcroppings. Parking is provided at a scenic lookout.

Fort William Henry (all ages)

Off Route 130, Pemaquid; (207) 677–2423; www.state.me.us/doc/parks/. Open from Memorial Day to Labor Day. Admission to the fort is included in your fee to the Historic Site.

This replica fort (the original was built in 1698) is typical of a series of English fortifications used to defend against pirates and

Amazing
Maine Facts

The beauty of Monhegan Island has been drawing artists for centuries. Today, you might spy Jamie Wyeth, who still summers here, painting inside an upended wooden crate. (He uses the crate to prevent curious observers from looking over his shoulder while he works.)

the French. A stockade was erected in 1630, but Dixie Bull, the pirate, destroyed it promptly. In 1689 Baron Castine captured the fortification, which was manned by fifty men.

The Pemaquid Point Lighthouse, Art Gallery, and Museum (all ages) 🏛 🍴
At the end of Route 130, Pemaquid; (207) 677–2494; www.lighthouse.cc/pemaquid. The museum is open Memorial Day to Columbus Day, from 10:00 A.M. to 5:00 P.M. Monday through Saturday, 11:00 A.M. to 5:00 P.M. Sunday. $. Admission is free for children under 12.

The lighthouse was built in 1824. Keep your children away from the waves, which can be rough along the rocks, but let them dabble in the numerous tidal pools. This fascinating activity can occupy children for hours as they discover the small marine creatures that inhabit the pools.

At low tide, rock climbing is a fun activity (even my 73-year-old mother enjoyed it).

You will also want to visit the Fishermen's Museum, where you'll find model ships, photographs, and artifacts of the Maine fishing industry. If you enjoy local art, check out the Pemaquid Art Gallery. While you're here, you can picnic on the museum grounds or eat at the nearby Sea Gull Shop and Restaurant.

Where to Eat

Anchor Inn Restaurant. Anchor Inn Road, Round Pond; (207) 529–5584. Open Memorial Day through Columbus Day for lunch and dinner. As you sit in the tiered dining room, you will have a commanding view of the harbor and village. The view alone is worth the trip, but you won't be disappointed by the food or service. $$–$$$

Captain's Catch Seafood. Pemaquid Beach Road, New Harbor; (207) 677–2396.

Known for its picnic-style dining on seafood and homemade desserts. Open 11:00 A.M. to 8:00 P.M. daily during the summer; you can eat indoors or out. There's a fish fry on Fridays. $$

Shaw's. Route 32, New Harbor; (207) 677–2200; www.shawsfishandlobster wharf.com. A local lobster pound and favorite feeding spot, Shaw's is a wonderful place to take the kids for fresh seafood on a dock. Lobster and steamed clams are specialties, but you can get meat loaf, turkey, and

A Merrill Family Adventure:
Young at Heart

When my mother came for a visit from Virginia she wanted to see as many lighthouses as possible. She got to see several but her favorite was Pemaquid Point Lighthouse. We spent a wonderful day in the Pemaquid area. We began at the beach, strolling along the water's edge in the cool wet sand. Beautiful pebbles washed smooth by the waves and various seashells filled my daughters' pockets, their shoes, and their beach hats before we left.

At the lighthouse the horizon was adorned with sailboats. However, what caught my mother's eye were the waves crashing on the rocks just below the lighthouse and the narrow path that led to them. Despite arthritis and her age, we made our way down, getting as close as safety would permit. This is a beautiful place to get a picture of the lighthouse, after which you can climb the mammoth slatelike rocks back up to the lighthouse—which we did. We toured the Fisherman's Museum and the Art Gallery, then had lunch at the Sea Gull Restaurant.

A picture of Pemaquid Lighthouse and the rocks leading up to it from the sea now hangs in my mother's living room. It's a reminder that the natural beauty of Maine empowers you to do things you haven't done in a while. It makes you feel like a kid again.

assorted stews and sandwiches if you're not in the mood for seafood. Choose between the dining room and the picnic tables on the dock. Watch out for the seagulls if you eat outside: They'll steal your food if you're not careful. Open late May to mid-October. $$

Where to Stay

Bradley Inn. 3063 Bristol Road, New Harbor; (207) 677–2105 or (800) 942–5560; www.bradleyinn.com. Open April through January 2. A dozen guest rooms, each with a private bath, are available in this century-old inn. You and your kids can rent bicycles to pedal down to the lighthouse. Upper-level rooms have a view of John's Bay. $$–$$$$

The Gosnold Arms. 146 Route 32, New Harbor; (207) 677–3727. Stay at the inn or in one of twenty cottage units. Established in 1925 and located on the historic Pemaquid Peninsula, the Gosnold Arms has simple elegance. Have breakfast on the porch overlooking the harbor, or curl up with a good book in front of one of the stone fireplaces in the library. $$–$$$$

The Hotel Pemaquid. 3098 Bristol Road, New Harbor; (207) 677–2312; www.hotel pemaquid.com. The hotel sits less than 200 feet from Pemaquid Point, although there are no water views from the rooms. The interior views are pretty, though; a Victorian theme is played out well in this inn. Many rooms have private baths, but some don't. The inn has a no-smoking policy. $–$$$

Waldoboro and Jefferson

Neither town is far out of your way, and each has something special to offer. Damariscotta Lake in Jefferson offers some good warm-water fishing opportunities, while Waldoboro offers some of the best pie around.

Damariscotta Lake State Park (all ages)
8 State Park Road, Route 32, Jefferson; (207) 549–7600 (in season), (207) 941–4014 (off-season). Open Memorial Day to Labor Day. Admission is free for children under 5. $

This park offers a sand beach on the lake. You can swim, picnic, fish, or hike at the beach and park.

Spruce Bush Farm/Blueberry Hill Farm Bed and Breakfast
(all ages)
101 Old Madden Road, Jefferson; (207) 549–7448. Maple syrup sugarhouse tours are held in late winter and early spring. Open year-round for accommodations.

This farm is one of many in the local area that participate in Maple Sugar Sunday (in late March). They tap their own maple sugar trees, collect the sap, and boil it down into pure Maine maple syrup. Come for a tour and you can watch a syrup-making demonstration as well as sample some maple syrup products.

While staying in the area, this restored 1774 farmhouse can be your home away from home. A full breakfast (featuring pure Maine maple syrup) is included in the package.

Waldo Theatre (ages 3 and up)
916 Main Street, Waldoboro; (207) 832–6060; www.waldotheatre.com. $$

The Waldo Theatre, built in 1936, was originally a movie house. Shows ran daily, twice on Saturday, and tickets were only 35 cents. Called "Maine's Little Radio City," it was a bustling place with crowds lined up around the block. But by 1957, with the growth of television, the death of Carroll T. Cooney—Waldo Theatre's visionary—and the drop in ticket sales, the doors to the theater were chained shut. It stayed that way for almost twenty-five years.

In 1981 the theater was renovated and restored to its former glory, the doors reopened, and crowds began to return. Today the theater hosts plays, bands, and stand-up comedians. See productions of *Cinderella*, *Oliver Twist*, or *Anne of Green*

Amazing
Maine Facts

It takes forty gallons of sap to produce one gallon of pure Maine maple syrup.

How **Sweet** It is

Every year, in early spring, dozens of Maine sugarhouses open their doors to the public. Tours give visitors a glimpse of one of Maine's oldest traditions, refining maple sugar into syrup. You can log onto www.mainefoodandfarms.com/fairs/maplestuff.html for a listing of sugarhouses.

Gables. Participate in Open Mike Night or Family Night Open House. Laugh at Tim Sample's Maine humor. Tap your foot at the annual Fiddling Festival. It may not be Radio City Music Hall, but it's worth a visit.

Where to Eat

Moody's Diner. At the intersection of Route 1 and Route 220, Waldoboro; (207) 832–7785. This classic diner is a landmark famous for its cream pies. (The coconut cream is my personal favorite.) Open for breakfast, lunch, and dinner, it's worth a stop. The gift shop is worth a look as well. $

Where to Stay

Town Line Campsites. 483 East Pond Road, Jefferson; (207) 832–7055. A family tradition since 1960, this 160-acre camping area offers a rustic camping experience in a noncommercial atmosphere. Located along Damariscotta Lake, the campground offers lawn sports, canoe and paddleboat rentals, a game room, a camp store and snack bar, complete laundry facilities, and free hot showers. The prices, even for the two-bedroom cottage with kitchen and bath, are the best you'll find. $

For More Information

Waldoboro Town Office. (207) 832–5369.

Rockland

Rockland is a good-size town with a very busy waterfront. It is said to be one of the busiest lobster distribution points in the world. Many activities will keep the kids happy in Rockland and its surrounding towns.

Farnsworth Art Museum, Victorian Homestead, Library, and Wyeth Center (ages 5 and up) 🏛

352 Main Street; (207) 596–6457; www.farnsworthmuseum.org. Summer hours are daily from 9:00 A.M. to 5:00 P.M. Winter hours are Tuesday through Saturday 10:00 A.M. to 5:00 P.M., Sunday 1:00 to 5:00 P.M. $$. Admission is **free** for children 17 and under.

Maine art from the eighteenth century onward is on display at the museum. The Wyeth Center, which opened in 1998, houses the world's largest collection of works by N. C., Andrew, and Jamie Wyeth.

Amazing
Maine Facts

Rockland gets its name from the limestone that was mined here for years.

Shore Village Museum (all ages)

104 Limerock Street; (207) 594–0311; www.lighthouse.cc/shorevillage. Open daily, June to mid-October, from 10:00 A.M. to 4:00 P.M. and by appointment. Admission is free, but donations are accepted.

This museum has something for everyone. Children with an interest in the United States Coast Guard can see a variety of old artifacts. All sorts of lighthouse paraphernalia can be found here—foghorns, flashing lights, bells, boats, and buoys are all part of the collection. Civil War memorabilia may not be expected in such a place, but it's here. Anyone with an interest in dolls will love the large collection on display. The dolls are dressed in period costumes right up to the Gay Nineties.

Rockland Breakwater Light (all ages)

End of Samoset Road, Jameson Point, Rockland Harbor; www.lighthouse.cc/rocklandbreak water. Free.

A visit to this lighthouse is a great idea for kids needing to burn off some energy in a hurry. Built in 1888, the lighthouse sits at the end of a granite pier. Parking is free, and there is plenty of space for walking and stretching cramped muscles.

Maine Lobster Festival (all ages)

Call 800–LOB–CLAW for a free brochure or log on to www.mainelobsterfestival.com. Admission is free for children under 12. $–$$

After more than fifty years of guaranteed good food and great fun, this festival, held along the waterfront in Rockland, has become a New England tradition. One taste of succulent lobster dripping with melted butter and you'll know why people return year after year. The largest lobster feed anywhere begins with King Neptune's arrival from the sea. Festivities include a parade, carnival rides, arts and crafts, waterfront activities, and concerts.

You can take a harbor cruise, tour a Navy or Coast Guard ship, or watch a lobster trap-hauling demonstration. If you like to get really involved, enter the lobster crate race, in which participants run across a string of lobster crates floating in the water.

Cruisin': **Sailing in Style**

■ **Long Excursions:** This is an expensive vacation amusement (rates range from $350 to $850 for three- to six-day cruises), but when you consider the cost of lodging and food elsewhere, it may not be such a bad deal. Most of the boats are not fancy, but they provide the essentials. If you want a once-in-a-lifetime memory for your kids, this might be just the ticket.

The *Isaac H. Evans* (877–238–1325) is 65 feet with eleven double cabins and a total guest capacity of twenty-two. The *Timberwind* (800–759–9250), a 70-foot schooner, offers three-, four-, and six-day cruises. The *Victory Chimes* (800–745–5651) is the only original three-masted schooner in the windjammer trade. At 132 feet, it is also the largest.

For more information, contact the Maine Windjammer Association at P.O. Box 317P, Augusta, ME 04332; (800) 807–WIND; www.sailmaine coast.com.

■ **Sailing Galore:** If you want to ride the waves, Rockland offers everything from day trips to weeklong excursions. Sailing possibilities are too numerous to mention, but here are a few.

■ **Short Trips:** Monhegan Boat Line (207–372–8848; www.monheganboat. com) offers lighthouse tours and nature and puffin cruises aboard the *Elizabeth Ann*. The schooner *Simplicity* (207–596–0108) offers a day of mackerel fishing. The 55-foot ketch *Morning in Maine* (207–563–8834; www.amorninginmaine.com) will take up to twenty-one passengers out for day trips. *Wendameen* (207–594–1751; www.www.schooneryachet.com), a 67-foot schooner, will take you out for an overnight trip. M/V *Monhegan* (207–596–5660; www.mvmon-hegan. com) runs lunch and dinner cruises as well as harbor tours.

Owls Head Light (all ages) 🏛

At the end of Lighthouse Road, Owls Head; www.lighthouse.cc/owls. Free.

Worth the short side trip, Owls Head Light commands attention from its rocky perch. Built in 1825, the white brick conical tower stands 87 feet above sea level. There are sheer cliffs here, so watch your kids. There are, however, safe trails down one side to the rocks below.

Amazing Maine Facts

Maine has sixty-three lighthouses, more than any other coastal state. The Rockland-Thomaston area is home to fourteen of them.

Owls Head Transportation Museum (all ages)

P.O. Box 277, Route 73, adjacent to Knox County Airport, Owls Head 04854; (207) 594–4418; www.ohtm.org. Open daily, except Thanksgiving, Christmas, and New Year's Day. Open April through October from 10:00 A.M. to 5:00 P.M., November through March from 10:00 A.M. to 4:00 P.M. $$. Admission is **free** for children under 5. A family ticket for two adults and any number of children is $18 on nonevent days.

Founded in 1974, this museum specializes in old planes and automobiles. What makes it different from most museums is that all of the displays still function. On some weekends you might see a 1918 plane in the air or a 1901 car on the road. Rides are occasionally offered. If it has wheels, you will probably find it here.

Downeast Air Inc. (ages 8 and up)

P.O. Box 966; (888) 594–2171; www.midcoast.com/~dea. Flights average $170 per hour.

Get an aerial view of the mid-coast region as you fly high above the sights in single- and twin-engine aircraft. You can take fifteen-minute, thirty-minute, or hour-long flights. The planes accommodate up to three passengers.

Other Things to **See** and **Do**

If the kids need to burn off some energy in a hurry, take them to the Community Playground at Merritt Park on Limerock Street. If you feel like taking in a movie, see what's showing at the Flagship Cinemas (207–594–2100) in the neighboring town of Thomaston. Dozens of antiques shops for you to browse through are in the Rockland area, as are numerous other stores of interest. Plan on spending a little time poking around the local shops for fun and souvenirs.

Where to Eat

The Brown Bag. 606 Main Street; (800) 287–6372 or (207) 596–6372. A casual and affordable place. The food is good, and there's an extensive menu. $

Cafe Miranda. 15 Oak Street; (207) 594–2034; www.cafemiranda.com. You'll need dinner reservations here, because area residents fill this fine food establishment quickly. International dishes, ranging from Italian and Thai entrees to Southwestern and Chinese dinners, are the specialty. $–$$

Landings Restaurant and Marina. 1 Commercial Street; (207) 596–6563. You can get hot dogs, steak, lobster, or almost anything else you might want. A kids' menu is available. Open May through October; indoor or outdoor waterfront dining. $–$$

Park Street Grill. 279 Main Street; (207) 594–4944. Open for lunch and dinner, this newly renovated restaurant offers casual family dining and an extensive menu. Southwestern fare, lobster shore dinners, steaks, burgers, and salads are just some of the choices. Kids get their own menu, and nightly specials are available. $–$$

Wasses Wagon. Usually at 2 North Main Street or at the corner of Park Street and Broadway; (207) 594–7472. Hot dog lovers will want to track this one down. $

Where to Stay

The LimeRock Inn. 96 Limerock Street; (800) 546–3762; www.limerockinn.com. This beautiful bed-and-breakfast offers eight guest rooms, all with private baths. Open April through November; children are welcome. $$–$$$$

The Navigator. 520 Main Street; (207) 594–2131; www.navigatorinn.com. Located across from the ferry terminal and within walking distance to shops. Prices here are a little cheaper, but there's no pool. $–$$

Trade Winds. 2 Park View Drive; (800) 834–3130; www.tradewindsmaine.com. This 142-room motel offers ocean views, a heated indoor pool, a fitness center, and a seafood restaurant. $–$$$

For More Information

Rockland–Thomaston Area Chamber of Commerce. (800) 562–2529; www.thereal maine.com.

Camden, Rockport, and Lincolnville

Before you reach Camden on Route 1, you'll pass through the town of Rockport. Although Camden is probably the most popular tourist attraction in this area, places like Rockport and Lincolnville (farther down Route 1) all have something to offer. If you plan to spend some time in this area, Camden is a good place to call home for a while. Make reservations early, however; this town fills up fast.

Seal of **Honor**

What child hasn't seen the movie *Andre*, the true tale of a playful seal who helps a shy little girl come out of her shell? The small harbor town of Rockport is where the story actually took place. Visit the Rockport Marine Park to view a life-size bronze statue of Andre. You can also enjoy a stroll among the gardens at the Vesper Hill Children's Chapel.

The Old Conway House Complex (all ages)

P.O. Box 747, Rockport 04856; (207) 236–2257; www.crmuseum.org. Open during July and August, Tuesday through Friday 10:00 A.M. to 4:00 P.M. Free for kids 5 and under. $

This eighteenth-century farmhouse is furnished to represent many periods. Kids can see carriages, sleighs, and early farm tools. A blacksmith shop on the property is often the most intriguing exhibit for children.

Camden Snow Bowl (all ages)

P.O. Box 1207, Hosmer's Pond Road, Camden 04843; (207) 236–3438; www.camdensnow bowl.com. Toboggan Chute/Tube Sliding Hill is open from 9:00 A.M. to 4:00 P.M. weekends and holidays. Ski rates vary depending on time and day. $–$$$$. Children under 5 ski free.

A short drive from Camden Harbor, you can thrill to a 950-foot vertical drop on Ragged Mountain, while enjoying a breathtaking view of the Atlantic. Trails suitable for beginners and experts are available. Night skiing is offered. The facilities include a lodge, a cafeteria, and a rental and repair shop.

If your kids are younger, you might opt for a fast ride down the toboggan chute or the tube-sliding hill. The Camden Snow Bowl is the only area in the state with a public toboggan chute. The National Toboggan Championships are held here each year. Ice-skating is also available on Hosmer Pond.

Camden Hills State Park (all ages)

280 Belfast Road, Route 1, Camden; (207) 236–3109 in season, (207) 236–0849 off-season. Open May 15 to October 15. Admission is free for children under 6. $

This park provides cross-country skiing on marked and maintained trails in winter. In warmer weather, you can enjoy other activities at the park. This 6,500-acre area includes Mount Megunticook, one of the highest points on the Atlantic seaboard. More than one hundred campsites provide accommodation for tenters in the park, and hiking is the number one attraction. Excellent trails suitable for the whole family take you to the park's most scenic spots.

A Merrill Family Adventure:
Happy Birthday

Camden is "where the mountains meet the sea," and that makes for fun and adventure. It's a great place to spend the day. One family outing began with a trek up Mount Battie. The view from the top is breathtaking. We shot tons of film and had a picnic lunch. Back in town for the afternoon, we put on our deck shoes and went out on the *Lively Lady Too* for a great lobster fishing and nature cruise (207–236–6672). Because it was my oldest daughter's birthday, she got to cruise for free. She also got a birthday gift of a seal pup coming right up to the boat. My youngest daughter enjoyed steering the boat for a while on the way back to shore. Afterward we spent some time shopping and finished the day with a great meal at the Village Restaurant, overlooking the harbor.

The park is still worth a visit, even if hiking isn't your thing. Mount Battie is the only peak in the park accessible by car. At the top you are rewarded with spectacular views of Penobscot Bay.

Kelmscott Rare Breeds Foundation (all ages)
Van Cycle Road, Lincolnville; (207) 763–4088; www.kelmscott.org. Open May through September 10:00 A.M. to 5:00 P.M., October through April 10:00 A.M. to 3:00 P.M.; closed Sunday and Monday. Admission is free for children under 4. $

This conservation learning center consists of a working farm with nearly 200 animals and more than twenty breeds of rare livestock. Founded in 1995, the purpose of the foundation is to conserve and protect rare and endangered livestock. That's right! Lions, tigers, and whales are not the only kinds of animals facing extinction. Gloucestershire Old Spot pigs, Kerry cattle, and Cotswold sheep are also in danger—but not at Kelmscott.

Come for a visit and you're sure to learn something about sustainable agriculture, farming, animal husbandry, and conservation breeding. Tour the livestock barns, browse the Wool Shed Museum and Gift Shop, stroll around Waterfowl Pond. Before you leave you might decide to adopt an animal. That's right, you can look into taking one of Kelmscott's rare and wonderful animals home with you.

Barret's Cove Megunticook Lake
Beaucaire Road, off Route 52 northwest of Camden. Free.

You'll know when you're close because of Barret's Cove cliffs on the right. This hidden cove is quiet (especially on weekdays), small, and beautiful. There is a large shallow area for little ones to play safely and a dock in the deep water for diving. Picnic tables, bathrooms, a playground, and a short sandy beach make this a convenient and fun place to spend the day.

Besides swimming it's a good spot to take out a canoe or kayak. If you like, just lie on the sand and enjoy the gorgeous view of Lake Megunticook reflecting the sky and the rocky mountains surrounding it. Your eyes will be drawn upward by the breathtaking cliffs of Mount Megunticook. Near the summit, Maiden's Cliff is marked by a large white cross. There a young girl, reaching to grab for her windblown hat, fell to her death.

The Camden Civic Theatre (ages 7 and up)

P.O. Box 362, 29 Elm Street, Camden 04843; (207) 236–2281. Open April through December. Ticket prices vary per event.

This community theater has offered a wide variety of productions for more than thirty years. Performances are held in the renovated Camden Opera House (207–236–7963; www.camdenoperahouse.com).

Bay Chamber Concerts (ages 7 and up)

10 Summer Street, Suite 102, Rockport; (888) 707–2770; www.baychamberconcerts.org. Performances are held Thursday and Friday evenings in July and August, and monthly September through June. $$–$$$

Classical music and jazz concerts performed by internationally acclaimed musicians are held in the renovated Rockport Opera House (207–236–2514).

Where to Eat

Camden Deli. 37 Main Street, Camden; (207) 236–8343; www.camdendeli.com. You can choose from about thirty-five different New York-style sandwiches. There's a children's menu and a view of the harbor falls. Grown-ups will enjoy the gourmet coffee. $

Cappy's Chowder House. 1 Main Street, Camden; (207) 236–2254; www.capps chowder.com. Cappy's likes kids. Your children will get their own menu, a souvenir carrying box, a place mat with puzzles, and crayons for coloring. Sometimes balloons round out the kiddie package. From eggs to burgers to granola and, of course, chowder,

Surf's **Up**

If you prefer to swim outside the confines of a pool, you're in luck. Laite Memorial Park and Beach at upper Bayview Street offers saltwater swimming. You can also swim at Shirttail Beach on Route 105 outside Camden and the Willis Hodson Park on the Megunticook River at the Molyneaux Road.

On the **Green**

Golfers can go to **Goose River Golf Club** (207–236–8488) at 50 Park Street, Rockport, for a quick nine holes. Cart rentals are available. An eighteen-hole course that has gained much publicity is the **Samoset Golf Course** (207–594–1431) at 220 Warrenton Street in Rockport. Many of the fairways run along the water, and the views are outstanding. Carts are available. This same facility offers tennis courts for both indoor and outdoor play.

you can enjoy a good meal at a fair price here. $–$$

Capt'n Andy's. 156 Washington Street, Camden; (800) 437–5398 or (207) 236–2312. Would you like to have a lobster picnic delivered to you at the harbor park or town landing? Call the captain and your dream will come true. There's **free** delivery in Camden, and live lobster can be shipped anywhere in the world. $$–$$$

Scott's Place. 85 Elm Street, Camden; (207) 236–8751. It's easy to miss, but you really shouldn't pass it by. For quality food and very low prices, this is the place to be. Kids can have hot dogs, while adults can enjoy succulent lobster rolls. Marinated chicken, burgers, and other yummy stuff dot the menu. It's a take-out stand in the parking lot of a shopping center, but don't let the appearance fool you. $

Village Restaurant. 5-7 Main Street, Camden; (207) 236–3232. Overlooking Camden Harbor, the Village Restaurant offers casual elegance. A family favorite, the broiled scallops are perfection. The service is excellent, and kids can order from their own menu. $–$$

Where to Stay

At last count there were more than twenty bed-and-breakfasts in Camden. However, the number of rooms offered is minimal and usually not enough, especially on summer weekends. If you'd like to stay here, you'll need to call well in advance.

The Blackberry Inn. 82 Elm Street, Camden; (800) 388–6000; www.blackberry inn.com. Enjoy a delightful stay in this Italianate Victorian inn. Feast on a full breakfast in the dining room, still adorned with the original tin ceiling and plaster moldings.

Cruisin' in **Camden**

In Camden you don't have to look far to find a boat for hire. Even kayaks and canoes are available. The *Lewis R. French* (800–469–4635) is the oldest windjammer in the fleet, launched in 1871. A National Historic Landmark, this 64-foot schooner takes passengers on four- to six-day voyages. The *Surprise* (800–241–8439; www.friendshipsloop.com), out of Tenants Harbor, offers two- to three-hour trips. Climb aboard the classic yacht *Shantih II* (800–599–8605; www.midcoast.com/~shantih) out of Rockport for a half-day sunset cruise. The *Olad* (207–236–2323; www.mainschooners.com) also gives two-hour trips. The *Betselma* (207–236–4446; www.betselma.com) offers one-hour sight-seeing tours. *Lively Lady Too* (207–236–6672; www3. sympatico.ca/lively.lady) has a lobster fishing and sea life nature cruise that the kids will love. Windjammer cruises typically run for several days. If you're interested in an extended cruise, contact the Maine Windjammer Association (800–807–WIND) for a complete listing of opportunities.

Bette Davis stayed in the inn back in the 1950s after a cast party for the movie *Peyton Place* was hosted here. A room, reminiscent of that era, bears her name. $$–$$$$

Glenmoor by the Sea. P.O. Box 1389, Route 1, Camden 04843; (800) 439–3541; www.glenmoorbythesea.com. This is the only oceanfront complex in Camden, and it's a little more practical than the Norumbega. A stay here treats you to an in-room continental breakfast, a private shoreline, tennis courts, and a pool. $$–$$$$

Norumbega. 63 High Street, Camden; (207) 236–4646; www.norumbegainn.com. Okay, this is a little extravagant, but after all, it is a castle. Overlooking the Penobscot Bay, this Victorian inn is sure to catch your eye. You'll be pampered with award-winning luxury accommodations and a full country breakfast. Prices are steep, and only children over 7 are allowed, but sometimes extravagance is a good thing. $$$$

Samoset Resort. 220 Warrenton Street, Rockport; (800) 341–1650; www.samoset. com. This resort has more than 200 water-view rooms, some standard, some suites, and some efficiencies. Play tennis, tee off, take a dip in the pool, or relax in the Jacuzzi. If that's not enough, there's a fitness room, a restaurant, and kids' activities. $$$–$$$$

Strawberry Hill Motor Inn. 886 Commercial Street, Rockport; (800) 589–4009; www. strawberrymotorinn.com. Open year-round, this nice inn sits atop cliffs overlooking the Atlantic. More affordable than most lodging in the area, it also has much to offer: a pool, continental breakfast, access to the shore, and sea views from every room. $–$$$

For More Information

Camden–Rockport-Lincolnville Chamber of Commerce. (800) 223–5459; www.visitcamden.com.

Other Things to **See** and **Do**

A good way to see the town is on bike. You can rent one at Fred's Bikes (207–236–6664). If you feel the need for some time in the gym, you can go to the YMCA (207–236–3375). A small day-use fee gives you access to an Olympic-size pool, weight room, and basketball court. Art galleries are numerous in this area. The three to visit in Camden are Harbor Square Gallery (207–594–8700), Pine Tree Shop and Bay View Gallery (800–236–4534), and A Small Wonder Gallery (207–236–6005). Rockport offers the Maine Coast Artists Gallery (207–236–2875).

Belfast

Traveling to Belfast, you'll pass through Northport. Belfast doesn't get all the hype that Boothbay Harbor, Camden, and Bar Harbor get, but don't let this fool you. Belfast may prove to be one of your favorite spots. Let me tell you why.

Perry's Tropical Nut House (all ages)
17 Searsport Avenue; (207) 338–1630 (call for hours).

This isn't what you might expect to find in Maine. In fact, you might not expect to find anything like this anywhere. Irving Perry started the place back in the 1920s. He wanted to sell pecans to passing tourists. In doing so, he collected every type of nut known. These nuts were put on display to pull in the pecan trade. Nuts were not the only items he collected and exhibited. Even today, long after Perry's passing, his stuffed alligators, monkeys, ostriches, gorillas, and similar exotic animals are still on view. This is a good place to stop for pictures with the kids.

Amazing
Maine Facts

In 1765 most of the founding fathers wanted to give the name Londonderry to the new settlement at the head of Penobscot Bay. However, John Miller of Belfast, Ireland, protested. To solve the dilemma they flipped a coin. Belfast won.

Belfast City Park (all ages)

High Street; (207) 338–5900; www.belfastmaine.com. **Free.**

This multi-acre park has a lot to offer and all **free** of charge. Practice your swing or your pitch at the baseball diamond. Improve your serve on the lighted tennis courts. Let the children loose at the playground. Dive into the outdoor swimming pool. There are lockers to store your stuff and showers to clean off afterward. All this activity will make you hungry. No problem if you brought a picnic lunch—picnic areas are spread throughout the park.

The Belfast Museum (ages 7 and up)

10 Market Street; (207) 338–1875. Open June through October, Thursday and Sunday, from 1:00 to 4:00 P.M. Admission is **free.**

A museum for real history buffs, this may not appeal to all children. However, it does offer exhibits of area artifacts, paintings, and similar works.

Belfast and Moosehead Lake R.R. Co. (all ages)

1 Depot Square, Unity; (800) 392–5500; www.belfastrailroad.com. Trains run June through October. Weekly trains from Belfast to Waldo depart at 1:00 P.M. On Saturday and Sunday trains depart at 11:00 A.M. Passengers should arrive one hour before departure. Special family rate available. $$$

Before you leave Belfast, consider a stop here. The train leaves for a two-and-a-half-hour excursion from the Belfast waterfront along the Passagassawakeag River. You'll travel to the village of Brooks and back. Along the way, the infamous "Waldo Station Gang" will attempt a train robbery. Kids love this, although some youngsters may be frightened by the authenticity of this staged event.

This railroad offers several fun-filled specials. You can charter a Murder Mystery Dinner Train—a unique and memorable way to experience this Classic GE seventy-ton locomotive. The Belfast Comfort Inn is a new hotel offering overnight packages. Ride the train and stay at the inn. In the morning enjoy a continental breakfast, then board the train for your return trip. The hotel offers a hot tub, sauna, oceanfront views, and a heated pool. Call (800) 303–5098 to make a reservation.

Common Ground Country Fair (all ages)

Fairgrounds, Crosby Brook Road, Unity; (207) 568–4141; www.mofga.org. Held the third weekend after Labor Day. Admission is **free** for children 12 and under. $

A longtime tradition, this is the fair my husband went to every year as a child. It created some wonderful childhood memories for his and it will for your young ones as well. Offering something for everyone, this festival celebrates the agricultural history of the area. Vendors display Maine made crafts and art. Farmers show off their livestock. You'll enjoy a variety of music and entertainment and feast on delicious, locally grown organic food.

Where to Eat

Weathervane Restaurant. Main Street, on the waterfront; (207) 338–1774; www.weathervaneseafoods.com. Remember the one in Kittery? There's another in Belfast. From burgers to lobster, you won't be disappointed. $$

Young's Lobster Pound. Box 4, Mitchell Avenue; (207) 338–1160. Young's has 30,000 lobsters on hand to take care of the most hearty eaters. There's a great view of the Passagassawakeag River that you can take in while you wait for your meal. $$

Where to Stay

Belfast Bay Meadows Inn. 192 Northport Avenue; (800) 335–2370; www.maineguide.com/belfast/baymeadows. You'll feel at home in this Down East shingled cottage. Built a century ago, it has provided rest for weary travelers for more than fifty years. Children are welcome. The complimentary breakfast includes lobster omelettes and strawberry pancakes. $–$$$$

Belfast Harbor Inn. 91 Searsport Avenue; (800) 545–8576; www.belfastharborinn.com. You can walk to the ocean, sit by the pool, savor a generous continental breakfast, and enjoy Down East hospitality. $$–$$$

For More Information

Belfast Area Chamber of Commerce. (207) 338–5900; www.belfastmaine.org.

While in **Belfast**

The Belfast City Park on Route 1 has a swimming pool, tennis courts, and a gravel beach. Picnic areas are also available. Along Main and High Streets you'll discover art galleries, bookstores, and other specialty shops.

Searsport

Searsport offers visitors nearly 8 miles of beautiful coastline. Such easy access to the sea once made this Penobscot Bay town the leader of Maine's maritime industry. During the 1800s eleven shipyards dotted the area, and many a sea captain called Searsport home. Today Searsport's strong maritime heritage lives on at the Penobscot Marine Museum and the old mansions that have been preserved as bed-and-breakfast inns.

The Penobscot Marine Museum (all ages)

Church Street, P.O. Box 498, Searsport 04974; (207) 548–2529; www.penobscotmarine museum.org. Open daily Memorial Day through mid-October, Monday through Saturday, from 10:00 A.M. to 5:00 P.M., Sunday from noon to 5:00 P.M. Free for children 6 and under. $$

Housed in the 1845 town hall, the museum attractions track the evolution of sailing vessels from the seventeenth century. Other exhibits show how local people made their livings around the bay. This includes working with granite, lime, ice, and fishing. A gift shop has souvenirs.

14 · Monday · January 2008

PURPLE-THROATED SUNANGEL

Heliangelus viola

A measure of the great diversity of hummingbirds, as well as their beauty, is the array of fanciful names they have been given in English (and Latin). This glittering midsize species is a good example. It is one of the most common hummingbirds seen in the Andean highlands and is more habituated to human settlement and open habitats than are its congeners.

Other Things to **See** and **Do**

For outdoor fun, you might try the **Mosman Beach Park** at the town dock. It offers a public boat ramp, and you can go fishing or swimming for **free.** A good picnic spot is Moose Point State Park on Route 1 just south of Searsport. Cookout facilities, fields, and an evergreen grove await you.

The **Waldo County Craft Co-Op** (207–548–6686) and **Silkweeds** (207–548–6501) offer crafts for sale. Dolls, needlepoint, quilts, pillows, jams, wooden items, and lots of ceramics provide great ideas for gifts and mementos of your trip. Antiques lovers can't pass up the Searsport Antiques Mall. This place is open daily year-round and represents the wares of seventy-some dealers. About thirty other antiques shops are in the area, as are flea markets to browse through for treasures. Just ride up Route 1, and you'll find them.

Where to Eat

Chocolate Grille. 1 East Main Street; (207) 548–2555; www.chocolategrille.com. This hopping place serves lunch and dinner. Zany creations like Fried Dill Pickle Chips, Hickory Charred Salmon with Pomegranate BBQ Sauce, and Fire Chicken Proscuitto Focaccia Sandwich make the menu fun. But chocolate, chocolate, and more chocolate makes their desserts heaven. You might want to order your desserts when you order dinner because many need to bake in the oven while you dine. The Chocolate Soufflé and Chocolate Chip Cookie Sensation are two that come to you fresh from the oven. $$

Jordan's Restaurant. Route 1; (207) 548–2555. Serves all three meals in classic style. You'll find everything from beef to seafood to a special menu for kids, and you can eat in or take it out. $–$$

Where to Stay

Captain Green Pendleton B&B. 428 East Main Street; (800) 949–4403. Eight acres of grounds, a cross-country ski trail, and a private pond make this option attractive to families. Special rates are available for families with children. $

Carriage House Inn. Route 1; (207) 548–2167. This was once the summer home and studio of Maine artist Waldo Pierce. $–$$

Homeport Inn. 121 East Main Street; (800) 742–5814; www.bnbcity.com/inns/20015. Open year-round, this 1861 captain's mansion overlooks the bay. Ten gorgeous rooms are available for rent. Some rooms share a bath; others have private baths. Children over 3 are welcome, but there is a $6.00 charge per night for each child. $–$$

The Thurston House B&B Inn. 8 Elm
Street; (207) 548–2213. This vintage 1830s
house can accommodate a family of five in
one of the guest rooms. There is an extra
charge of $10 per night per child. $

For More Information

**Searsport Economic Development
Committee.** (207) 548–7255; www.
searsportme.com.

Stockton Springs

It's not much to look at on a map, but Stockton Springs is a pretty place to spend some
time. Like many of the coastal areas in Maine, it's not big and flashy. It has some features,
however, that are worth your attention.

Fort Pownal and Fort Point State Park (all ages)

**Route 1; (207) 941–4014; www.lighthouse.cc/fortpoint/index.html. Open Memorial Day
through Labor Day. Admission is free for children 4 and under. $**

The forts and park are located less than 4 miles off Route 1 (just follow the signs). In 1759
the forts were built to defend Maine from the British. After being burned twice, only earth-
works remain. A park on the tip of the peninsula juts into Penobscot Bay. A favorite fishing
and picnic spot, it features a lighthouse and a pier. It's worth going a little out of your way
to reach this spot.

Fort Knox State Historic Site (all ages)

**RFD #1; (207) 469–7719; www.fortknox.maineguide.com/index.html. Open May through
October. $$**

The fort is actually located in Prospect on the banks of the Penobscot River. Built between
1844 and 1864, it was never completed. Though the fort never saw military action, it was
garrisoned during the Civil War and the Spanish-American War.

  This Fort Knox may not hold money, but it will hold your family's attention. (It is my
daughter Jaclyn's favorite place.) The first granite fort built in Maine, it is also the most vis-
ited historic site in the state. Massive in size, Fort Knox offers many hidden walkways to
explore, towers to climb, and fields to run. The kids will want to bring a flashlight as many
of the rooms, halls, and tunnels that call to them are cloaked in darkness.

  While exploring, you're bound to notice the Rodman cannons featured here. These
cannons took seven men to load and fire, with shells weighing 315 pounds each. Its firing
range was more than 2 miles.

Surf's Up at **Sandy Point Beach**

Sandy Point Beach is a great place to jump in the water on a hot day. To get here, turn off Route 1 and head for the water when you see the Rocky Ridge Motel. There are no facilities, but this place will bring back memories of the old swimming hole you knew (or dreamed about) as a child, and it will create new memories for your children.

Due to the efforts of the Friends of Fort Knox, parts of the fort that were in disrepair due to a leaking roof have been fixed. Construction of a visitor center and the staging of various cultural and historical events at the fort are coming soon.

Where to Eat

Just Barb's. Main Street; (207) 567–3886. Enjoy home cooking at this family-friendly restaurant seven days a week. Famous for its seafood stews and chowders, the prices are something to spotlight as well. All you can eat Fish 'N Chips costs only $4.99. When you stop by for a visit, you might want to congratulate the staff—Just Barb's was voted as the favorite restaurant among 62 restaurants participating in the statewide "Get Real. Get Maine" program. $–$$

Where to Stay

Hichborn Inn. Church Street; (800) 346–1522; www.hichborninn.com. If you're looking for atmosphere, you'll find it here. Dad will enjoy the "gent's parlor," where evening fires burn and men come to talk. This Victorian Italianate mansion is open year-round, except Christmas. Water views are standard, and the accommodations are quite comfortable. $$

Rocky Ridge Motel. R.R. 1; (207) 567–3456 or (800) 453–0754. Overlooking Penobscot Bay, this motel is directly across from Sand Beach. Open year-round. $–$$

For More Information

Searsport Economic Development Committee. (207) 548–7255; www.searsportme.com.

Down East Maine

Many people will tell you that you haven't been to Maine until you've been Down East. Certainly many sights and activities throughout the state deserve your attention, but Down East is a big part of Maine's reputation. Bar Harbor is probably the most famous town in the region, and Acadia is synonymous with Down East. They're just two of the places you will want to go.

Ellsworth

Ellsworth is the gateway to Down East and Acadia. When you arrive, you'll find attractions that are worth the drive. Along your way to Ellsworth, you will pass through the town of Orland. Your kids might enjoy a brief side trip here.

Craig Brook National Fish Hatchery (all ages)
306 Hatchery Road, East Orland; (207) 469–2803. Open daily 8:00 A.M. to 5:00 P.M. Admission is free.

This salmon hatchery, established in 1871, is something to see. Aquariums, nature trails, an old icehouse, and picnic tables make this a good place to take a short break from traveling.

The Grand Auditorium (ages 8 and up)
P.O. Box 941, Ellsworth 04605; (207) 363–9500 or (207) 667–5911; www.grandonline.org. Open year-round. Ticket prices vary.

When the lights go down in this auditorium, you can catch a first-run movie or a foreign film. Some nights the spotlight shines on ballet dancers; other times people come to enjoy live concerts. This theater offers a little bit of everything.

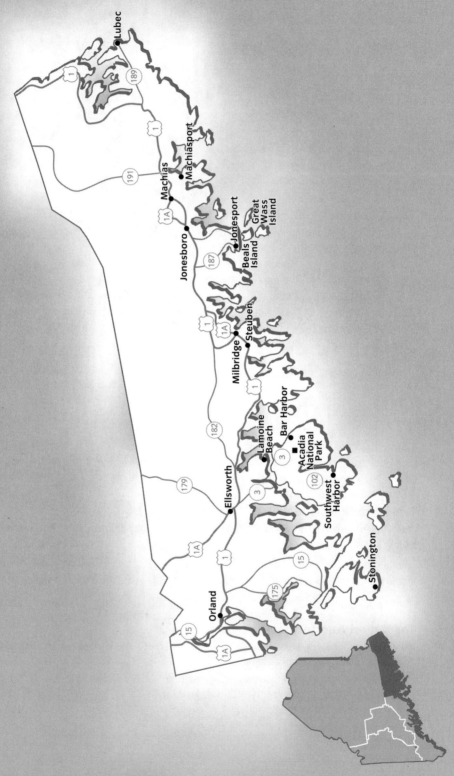

DOWN EAST MAINE

Lubec

189

1

Machiasport

191

1

Machias

1A

Jonesboro

187

Jonesport

Beals
Island

Great
Wass
Island

1

1A

Steuben

Milbridge

11

Bar Harbor

182

Lamoine
Beach

3

Acadia
National
Park

179

Ellsworth

3

102

Southwest
Harbor

1A

1

15

Stonington

15

Orland

175

1A

Woodlawn Museum—The Black House (all ages)

81 West Main Street; (207) 667–8671; www.ellsworthme.org/cbmm. Building open June through September, 10:00 A.M. to 5:00 P.M. Tuesday through Saturday, 1:00 to 4:00 P.M. Sunday. Open May to October Tuesday through Sunday 1:00 to 4:00 P.M. Grounds and gardens open year-round. $$

This Georgian-style home is richly furnished with authentic period furniture. Many of the pieces are one of a kind, including a miniature portrait of George Washington, which he gave to General Cobb (John Black's father-in-law) as a memento after the Revolutionary War. The property also features beautiful gardens and hiking trails.

Acadia Zoo (all ages)

Route 3 between Ellsworth and Bar Harbor; (207) 667–3244. Open daily from 9:30 A.M. to sunset from May through Christmas Eve. $$

Some forty-five species are on view at this fifteen-acre park. Included are native species, such as whitetail deer, foxes, porcupines, and moose, along with leopards, reindeer, and monkeys. An indoor rain forest exhibit features exotic mammals, reptiles, amphibians, and birds. Most children are drawn to the zoo's petting area, which allows them to watch and touch such domestic animals as goats, rabbits, and sheep.

Bonnie's Top Ten Picks for Down East Maine

1. Taking in a grand performance at the Grand Auditorium, Ellsworth; (207) 363–9500.
2. Visiting the Oceanarium Lobster Hatchery, Bar Harbor; (207) 288–5005.
3. Enjoying the view from Cadillac Mountain, Acadia National Park; (207) 288–3338.
4. Hearing the roar of the Atlantic at Thunder Hole, Acadia National Park; (207) 288–3338.
5. Biking along the carriage trails, Acadia National Park; (207) 288–3338.
6. Touching sea creatures at Mount Desert Oceanarium, Southwest Harbor; (207) 244–7330.
7. Whale watching, Bar Harbor; (207) 288–2386.
8. Observing the wildlife at Acadia Zoo, Trenton; (207) 667–3244.
9. Day tripping to Nova Scotia via Bay Ferries, Bar Harbor; (888) 249–7245.
10. Eating blueberry treats at the Machias Blueberry Festival, Machias; (207) 255–6665.

Columbia Air (ages 8 and up)

112 Caruso Drive; (207) 667–5534. Open daily 7:00 A.M. to 7:00 P.M. in April, 7:00 A.M. to 9:00 P.M. from May through October, and 7:00 A.M. to 6:00 P.M. from November through March. Scenic tours are twenty to thirty minutes. $$$$

Airplane rides can be arranged at the Trenton airport. You can rent a plane, take some flight instruction, or go on a sight-seeing or whale-watching expedition.

Where to Eat

China Hill. 301 High Street; (207) 667–5308. Chinese food in a fine-dining setting. $$

Ellsworth Giant Sub, Bar Harbor Road, Route 3; (207) 667–5585. The best subs in town can be found here. With more than sixty varieties, there's bound to be something for everyone. Hot dogs and hamburgers are offered, just in case. $

Larry's Pastry Shop. 241 East Main Street; (207) 667–2557. The perfect stop if you're craving something sweet to eat. $

The Mex. 191 Main Street; (207) 667–4494; www.themex.com. A good choice for Mexican fare. $$

The Riverside Cafe. 151 Main Street; (207) 667–7220. Open daily for breakfast and lunch. At lunch try munching on a burger or sipping some soup (the homemade fish chowder is a favorite). A vegetarian menu is available for those who prefer artichoke hearts to hamburger. Either way, top it off with a fresh fruit smoothie. Breakfast is served all day, with offerings of fresh baked muffins and omelettes. $

Union River Lobster Pot. 8 South Street; (207) 667–5077; www.lobsterpot.com. Ellsworth's only waterfront restaurant. Open for lunch and dinner. Dine on a Down East shore dinner, barbecue ribs, or steak. If you'd like something lighter, try the clam cakes or choose from sandwiches named after ships, such as the *Quindaro*. I know it's unusual, but so is the sandwich. $$

Where to Stay

Colonial Travelodge. 32 High Street; (888) 667–5548. Sixty-eight spacious rooms include family suites with kitchen facilities. Enjoy in-room tea and coffee year-round and a **free** continental breakfast from June through mid-October. Features an indoor heated pool and Jacuzzi; kids under 12 stay for **free**. $–$$

Holiday Inn. 215 High Street; Reservations (800) 401–9341; (207) 667-9341; www. holiday-inn.com. The wonderful thing about this place is that kids stay and eat for **free.** Killarney's Restaurant is located on the premises, and even room service offers a kids' menu. There's an indoor tennis court, an indoor pool, cable TV with Disney and Nickelodeon, and Nintendo. $–$$$

Jasper's Motel. 200 High Street; (207) 667–5318; www.jaspersmaine.com. Besides the thirty-three rooms, this motel also has a restaurant. There are single, double, king, and cottage rooms available. New family units have adjacent bunk rooms. $$

Twilite Motel. 147 Bucksport Road; (800) 395–5097; www.twilitemotel.com. Twenty-two cozy units nestled on six acres. Pets are welcome for a one-time fee, and kids under 12 stay for **free.** A continental breakfast is also part of the package. $

For More Information

Ellsworth Area Chamber of Commerce. (207) 667–5584; www.ellsworthchamber.org.

Other Things to **See** and **Do**

The YMCA invites you to work out at its facility on State Street. A pool, a gymnasium, and a fitness center offer plenty of opportunities for the whole family. Call (207) 667–3086 for more details.

Bar Harbor

Bar Harbor, located on Mount Desert Island, has been famous since the 1800s. Named L'Isles de Monts-Déserts in 1604 by Samuel de Champlain, Maine's second largest island offers plenty of natural recreation opportunities through its seventeen mountains and five large lakes. A bridge from the island to the mainland was built in 1836. Once access was made easy, artists began to come to Bar Harbor to fill their canvases with images that were distributed far and wide. The area was soon a popular stop for steamboat tourists; then trains brought visitors from as far away as New York and Philadelphia. By 1880, Bar Harbor was growing as a popular summer resort. Today, the harbor area remains a major tourist attraction.

George B. Door Museum of Natural History (all ages)
College of the Atlantic, 105 Eden Street; (207) 288–5015; www.coa.edu/nhm. Open mid-June to Labor Day, Monday through Saturday from 10:00 A.M. to 5:00 P.M., and from September to May, Friday through Sunday from 1:00 to 4:00 P.M. Closed Thanksgiving week through mid-January and the last two weeks in March. Admission is free for children under 3. $

Children can see numerous species of wildlife represented in the museum. The animals are mounted, as are skeletons of local species. Sea tanks show off the local marine life, and there is usually a special activity planned for the kids.

Oceanarium Lobster Hatchery and Maine Lobster Museum (all ages)
Head of the Island, Route 3, Thomas Bay; (207) 288–5005. Open Monday through Saturday from 9:00 A.M. to 5:00 P.M. mid-May through mid-October. Admission is free for children under 4. $$

This is a great treat for those interested in or just curious about lobster farming. You and your children will witness the daily routine of a working lobster hatchery, where thousands of lobsters are being farmed for future release.

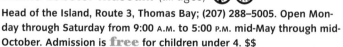

How about communing with harbor seals and taking a walk around a salt marsh? You can do it here. Visit the seal pavilion, where sick seals are rehabilitated and released. Kids love to get close to the seals and watch them play at feeding time. You can also take a fisherman-led tour of the Maine Lobster Museum and a guided trip around the Thomas Bay salt marsh.

Diver Ed Live Underwater Video Tours (all ages)

Bar Harbor Inn Pier; (207) 288–DIVE; www.divered.com. Open Memorial Day to Columbus Day. Offering two-and-a-half- hour trips Monday through Saturday at 9:30 A.M., 1:30 P.M., and 5:30 P.M. during peak season. Tours are **free** for children under 5. $$$$

This unique sight-seeing trip allows you to journey under the sea without ever getting off the boat. You stay nice and dry aboard the 50-foot motor vessel *Seal* while Diver Ed and others suit up. You even get to push them overboard! Then sit back, relax, and enjoy the show. Watch on a 4-foot screen as divers fill their catch bags with incredible sea creatures, all captured live on an underwater digital camera.

Back on board, the divers share their catch with you. Lobsters, starfish, scallops, and sea cucumbers are just some of the fascinating critters you'll get to hold and see up close. Once your curiosity is satisfied, the sea treasures are returned safely to the water and you are returned to shore. A great adventure for the whole family.

Robert Abbe Museum (all ages)

Sieur de Monts Spring; (207) 288–3519; www.abbemuseum.org. The museum and gardens are open May to October from 10:00 A.M. to 5:00 P.M. daily with extended hours Thursday through Saturday during the summer. Admission is **free** for children under 6. $

Native Americans lived, hunted, and fished on Mount Desert Island. Their activities are recorded in this museum. Children will love the authentic tepee and birch-bark canoe, as well as the jewelry, moccasins, baskets, and other artifacts on display. Dioramas show the living conditions of the region's tribes throughout the changing seasons. Exhibits change periodically to reflect recent archaeological excavations.

While you're here, step out to the adjacent Wild Gardens of Acadia, an easy stroll among some 300 species of native plants labeled and displayed along a self-guided trail.

Downeast Nature Tours (all ages)

3 Pines Bird Sanctuary, Knox Road; (207) 288–8128; www.mainebirding.net/downeast. Open year-round. Two-hour, four-hour, and all-day tours are available. $$$–$$$$

You can tour by bike, foot, or cross-country skis to see bald eagles, osprey, and other fauna and flora, as well as the natural features of the land and sea. Tours are available as half-day and full-day packages and leave sunrise to sunset. Overnight camping tours can be arranged.

Acadia National Park Tours (all ages)

Purchase tickets at Testa's, Bayside Landing, 53 Main Street; (207) 288–3327 in season, (207) 288–0300 off-season. Tours operate April through August. $$$

You'll enjoy a two-and-a-half-hour bus ride, complete with narration, through some of the most beautiful country in the world. There are three stops: Cadillac Mountain, Ocean Drive, and Thunder Hole. In business for nearly half a century, these tours are very popular. Reservations are highly recommended.

Biking Acadia

Bicycles are a favored mode of transportation around the island. To rent some two-wheel transportation, contact **Acadia Outfitters,** 106 Cottage Street (207–288–8118). They're open late May through September, 8:00 A.M. to 8:00 P.M. **Bar Harbor Bicycle Shop,** 141 Cottage Street (207–288–3886; www.bar harborbike.com), is open 8:00 A.M. to 8:00 P.M. seven days a week in season, 10:00 A.M. to 5:30 P.M. Monday through Saturday off-season. The **Acadia Bike & Canoe Company,** 48 Cottage Street (800–526–8615; www.acadiabike.com), rents all kinds of bikes plus trailers for young children. It's open 9:00 A.M. to 6:00 P.M. Tuesday through Saturday in the spring, 9:00 A.M. to 6:00 P.M. seven days a week in the summer.

Acadia and Island Tours (all ages)

Tickets may be purchased at One Harbor Place, 1 West Street, or aboard the trolley; (207) 288–9899; www.acadiaislandtours.com. Tours run from May through October and depart at 10:00 and 11:30 A.M., and 2:00, 3:30, and 6:00 P.M. $$-$$$

Hop a trolley and take a one-hour or two-and-a-half-hour tour of old mansions and mountains. Part of your trip will have you walking on, but not to, the summit of Cadillac Mountain, the highest peak in Acadia. This is an open-air ride, and the air, even in summer, can have a bite to it. Be sure to bring a jacket.

Acadia Bike and Canoe (ages 8 and up)

48 Cottage Street; (800) 526–8615 or (207) 288–9605; www.acadiabike.com. Open daily 9:00 A.M. to 6:00 P.M. during the summer. There are two-and-a-half-hour, four-hour, and full-day tours. Prices vary depending on length of tour. $$$$

If your kids are old enough and you have an adventuresome spirit, you can go out in a sea kayak. Acadia Bike and Canoe will fix you up with all the equipment needed and provide a registered Maine guide to lead your outing. These trips last anywhere from two and a half hours to a full day; romantic sunset trips are also offered. Reservations are recommended.

Acadia Outfitters (ages 8 and up)

106 Cottage Street; (207) 288–8118. Open 8:00 A.M. to 8:00 P.M. from late May through September. $$$$

An extension of Acadia Bike and Canoe, Acadia Outfitters offers the same tours at the same prices. Everything you need is included in the cost. Reservations are recommended.

Get a **Foothold**

You don't have to be an expert or even have any previous experience to enjoy an introduction to scaling granite cliffs. **Atlantic Climbing,** 24 Cottage Street (207–288–2521), will be happy to show you and your children what rock climbing is all about. Small, personalized courses are offered for all age and experience levels. You can choose half-day adventures that expose you to real climbs in Acadia or more advanced treks of several days. Instructors are professional guides with years of experience.

Another reputable rock-climbing outfitter is **Acadia Mountain Guides,** 198 Main Street (207–288–8186; www.acadiamountainguides.com). Here you get professional instruction for climbing even if you have never before found a foothold in rock. All safety equipment is provided, and you can arrange half-day, full-day, or multiday experiences. It's open from 8:00 A.M. to 8:00 P.M. mid-May through early October, 9:00 A.M. to 6:00 P.M. October through mid-May.

Bar Harbor Whale Watch Company (all ages)

1 West Street, Harbor Place; (207) 288–2386; www.whalesrus.com. Cruises sail from 8:30 A.M. to 4:45 P.M., May through October. $$$–$$$$

Ride Maine's only catamaran whale watcher. The *Friendship V* sails at 40 miles per hour in search of whales. The passenger list can number 140, all in a heated cabin. **Free** parking is provided during the trip. Also attractive is the 100 percent money-back guarantee—no whales, no charge.

Not into whales? Consider a ride aboard *Acadian*. This boat takes you on a two-hour nature cruise. With a little luck, you will see seals, eagles, and porpoises off the coast. Other attractions may include lighthouses, islands, and gorgeous sunsets.

New to the company's fleet of pleasure crafts is the *Angler*, a 65-foot fishing boat. Weekdays spend 4½ hours on the water deep-sea fishing. On weekends the trips are extended two hours. Bait and tackle are included in the trip. The catch, however, is up to you.

Along the **Shore**

One of the most popular activities in Bar Harbor and its immediate environs is enjoying the water. The best spot is along the Shore Path, which starts at Agamont Park near the Bar Harbor Town Pier and runs about 1 mile along the bay. This trail is also accessible from Grant Park, off Albert Meadow, at the corner of Main and Mount Desert Streets. Just remember that the water is inviting but cold.

What's in a **Name?**

Trenton has been called the gateway to Mount Desert Island. Over the years, however, it has acquired the nickname Lobsterville USA, because of the large number of lobster pounds along Route 3.

Downeast Windjammer and Lighthouse Cruises (all ages) ⚠

27 Main Street; departs from Bar Harbor Inn Pier; (207) 288–4585; www.downeastwindjammer.com. Sails May through October from 8:00 A.M. to sunset. $$$–$$$$

Check this one out if you want a slow, peaceful ride through the waters of Bar Harbor and surrounding areas. This family-style cruise will show you lighthouses and wildlife along the way. You can cruise for one and a half to two hours aboard the fishing boat *Seal* or aboard the four-masted schooner *Margaret Todd*. Some sunset tours are theater cruises, during which true tales of intrigue and horror from Maine's maritime past and present are performed. These cruises are not recommended for children under 6. Prices for the theater cruises are a little higher.

Bay Ferries, Inc. (all ages) ⚠

121 Eden Street; (888) 249–7245; www.catferry.com. The ferry sails from May to October, with cruises departing Bar Harbor at 8:00 A.M. and 4:00 P.M., departing Yarmouth, Nova Scotia, at 1:00, 4:00, and 8:45 P.M. Children under 5 travel **free.** There are also discounts for youth and seniors as well as special family rates. $$$$

How about a boat trip to Canada? Bay Ferries offers day trips as well as overnight trips from Bar Harbor to Yarmouth, Nova Scotia. The *Cat*, a high-speed catamaran, speeds across the Bay of Fundy at 55 mph. You simply drive on board and within two and a half hours you've turned your vacation into an international adventure. You'll enjoy buffet dining, bars, slot machines, duty-free shopping, and a kids' play area.

Boating Smarts: **Shiver Me Timbers**

If you're going out on a boat, take a sweatshirt, water, and snacks. Even if it's hot on land, the wind at sea is chilly. Also, some boats don't sell food items, and adventure makes the little ones hungry. Having your own snacks and water will prevent potential problems.

National Park Outdoor Recreation Center (ages 5 and up)

1 West Street; (207) 244–5854 or (877) 378–6907; www.nationalparkoutdoorrecreation center.com. Prices vary depending on activity. $$$

This center, located at the tip of Long Pond, offers you a variety of choices. You can take a guided sea kayak tour. If lakes and ponds are more your style, no problem. You can rent a canoe or kayak and explore on your own. If dry land is your pleasure, rent a mountain or hybrid bike and hit the Acadia National Park carriage roads. A lot of choices for a lot of fun.

LuLu Lobster Boat Ride (all ages)

Bar Harbor Regency Dock, 123 Eden Street; (207) 963–2341; www.lululobsterboat.com. Operating May through October. $$$

This is a great way to experience what lobster fishing is really like. Captain John will give you an up-close and personal lobster fishing demonstration. Traveling to Frenchman Bay aboard *LuLu*, a traditional wooden lobster boat, you're also bound to spot some seals and other water wildlife.

Your two-hour tour will undoubtedly be filled with beautiful scenery and some tales of local history and folklore from the captain. You'll have a great time and learn a thing or two.

Odyssey Park (all ages)

Route 3, Bar Harbor Road, Trenton; (207) 667–5841 in season, (207) 989–7670 in winter. Open mid-May through June 20, weekends only; late June through Labor Day, daily 10:00 A.M. to 9:00 P.M. Rides priced individually.

This is an amusement park—something you don't see a lot of in Down East Maine. Your kids can enjoy speedboats, aqua bikes, go-carts, bumper boats, and a variety of kiddie rides.

Where to Eat

When you're ready to eat, your only problem will be deciding where to go. Bar Harbor has no shortage of fine food. The following suggestions only scratch the surface of the eateries and restaurants that offer good choices and values for families.

Cottage Street Bakery & Deli Cafe. 59 Cottage Street; (207) 288–3010. Features gourmet pizza, burgers, salads, pancakes, and sandwiches. Open 6:30 A.M. to 10:00 P.M. May 15 to October 15. $

Epi Sub & Pizza. 8 Cottage Street; (207) 288–5853. There's not a lot of atmosphere

here, but the food and prices can't be beat. Crabmeat rolls, pasta, quiche, pizza, and hearty salads are just a few of the items on the menu. Hours are 10:00 A.M. to 8:00 P.M. $

The Fish House Grill. Intersection of Route 3 and Mount Desert Street; (207) 288–3070; www.fishhousegrill.com. A very family-oriented restaurant. There's abundant parking, and the prices are affordable. It's open seven days a week for breakfast and lunch. Seafood, chicken, and steak are part of the dinner menu, as is a special children's menu. $

Fisherman's Landing. 35 West Street; (207) 288–4632. They can fix you up with anything from hot dogs to boiled lobster. $–$$

The Island Chowder House. 38 Cottage Street; (207) 288–4905. This is tops when it comes to chowder. $

Log Cabin Restaurant. Route 3, Hulls Cove; (207) 288–3910. If you've just finished a game of miniature golf at Pirate's Cove, stop into this nearby eatery. Seafood and prime rib are the specialties. This family-style restaurant has plenty of parking and is open seven days a week, 7:00 A.M. to 9:00 P.M., from late May to October. $$

Maine Street Restaurant. 297 Main Street; (207) 288–3040; www.mainestreet restaurant.com. Great for family dining. You can enjoy burgers, sandwiches, and fried seafood. Choose to sit in the air-conditioned dining room or take in the fresh air on the outdoor deck. A large menu, a children's menu, and early-bird specials every day between 4:00 and 6:00 P.M. just add to this restaurant's family appeal. $–$$

Miguel's Mexican Restaurant. 51 Rodick Street; (207) 288–5117. Serves some of the best Mexican food found Down East. Open 5:00 to 10:00 P.M. Wednesday through Sunday. $$

124 Cottage Street Restaurant. 124 Cottage Street; (207) 288–4383. If you like vegetarian dishes, stop here. This place is also popular for its seafood, steak, and chicken dishes. Desserts here are heavenly. Call ahead for reservations to be sure you get a seat. Open from 5:00 to 9:30 P.M. $$

Poor Boy's Gourmet. 300 Main Street; (207) 288–4148; www.poorboysgourmet. com. Famous for homemade desserts, you'll also find the $7.95 early-bird special delightful. Dinner choices include steak, chicken, pasta, and seafood. In fact, you can get lobster prepared ten different ways. $–$$$

Testa's. Bayside Landing on Main and Cottage Streets; (207) 288–3327. Italian dishes, seafood, and steak are the specialties. Harbor views, good service, and plenty of good entrees are offered here. You can also buy tickets for the Acadia National Park tours and boat rides. $–$$

Where to Stay

Just as there are a host of good places to eat in Bar Harbor, so are there many magnificent places to spend the night. Considering all the fun, food, and entertainment in the region, you may plan to spend a few nights in town. Where will you stay? It's easy to find information on the more expensive lodgings and resorts in Bar Harbor, but you'll have to look harder for moderately priced and inexpensive accommodations. The following choices are especially affordable and welcoming to families.

Blackwoods Campground. Located in Acadia National Park off Route 3, 5 miles south of Bar Harbor; (207) 288–3274 or (800) 365–2267. Reservations are recommended between June 15 and September 15 (call eight weeks in advance). Camping is **free** from the end of November through early April. $

FYI: Taxes

All accommodations, including bed-and-breakfasts and inns, are subject to Maine's 7 percent lodging tax.

Edenbrook Motel. 96 Eden Street; (800) 323–7819. Four buildings with forty-seven rooms on a sloping hillside. $–$$

Emery's Cottages on the Shore. P.O. Box 172C, Bar Harbor 04609; (888) 240–3432 or (207) 288–3432; www.emeryscottages.com. Located just 2 miles from the main entrance to Acadia National Park, along the shores of Frenchman Bay, it offers cottages with both kitchenettes and complete kitchens. Cottages without kitchens have refrigerators. You can launch your own canoe or kayak from the pebbled beach. $–$$

Maine Street Motel. 315 Maine Street; (800) 333–3188 or (207) 288–3188; www.mainestreetmotel.com. Enjoy comfort and convenience at reasonable rates. All rooms have air-conditioning and free HBO. Children under 15 stay for **free**. You also receive a 10 percent discount at a nearby restaurant. $–$$

The Seawall Campground. 600 Seawall Road #1, South West Harbor; (207) 244–3600. Open from late May to late September. This is a first come, first served campground where reservations cannot be made. The campground is very busy during late July and August. If you don't get there early, you may end up waiting in line. $

The Wonder View Inn. 50 Eden Street; (207) 288–3358 or (888) 439–8439; www.wonderviewinn.com. This seventy-nine-unit motel on fourteen acres overlooking Frenchman Bay has extensive and nicely landscaped grounds for strolls, plus a swimming pool and dining facilities. Pets and children are welcome. $–$$

For More Information

Bar Harbor Chamber of Commerce. (800) 345–4619; www.barharborinfo.com.

Southwest Harbor/Tremont Chamber of Commerce. (800) 423–9264; www.acadiachamber.com.

Games People Play

Tennis players can use the courts at **Atlantic Oakes by the Sea** (207–288–5801). Golfers have the **Kebo Valley Golf Club** (207–288–3000; www.kebovalleyclub.com). Located on Eagle Lake Road, this eighteen-hole course has been seeing divots for more than one hundred years. Another option is the **Bar Harbor Golf Course** (207–667–7505) in Trenton. Younger golfers will enjoy **Pirate's Cove Adventure Golf** (207–288–2133; www.piratescove.net), a three-acre miniature golf extravaganza. Picnic tables and a snack bar help make an afternoon or evening here pleasurable.

Amazing
Maine Facts

Maine is about 320 miles long and 210 miles wide, with a total area of 33,215 square miles, which is as big as the other five New England states combined.

Acadia

The acreage now known as Acadia National Park came under the protection of a public land trust formed in 1901 through the efforts of the island's wealthiest summer residents, among them Charles W. Eliot, then president of Harvard University. This group of citizens was greatly assisted by its director, George Door, who spent his fortune and energy taking control of some 11,000 acres for the park. By designating the area as protected space, portable sawmills were kept off the property and overdevelopment was controlled. By 1916 Door had convinced the federal government to give the trust national monument status and later, in 1919, to establish it officially as a national park, the first such park east of the Mississippi. Acadia National Park currently accounts for about one-half of the entire island, covering some 40,000 acres. About five million people visit the park each year. Most of them never see the finer points that you and your family can enjoy in relative peace and seclusion.

Other towns you might want to visit before leaving the island include Southwest Harbor and Bass Harbor. Mount Desert Oceanarium, in Southwest Harbor, and Ship Harbor on Route 102A near Bass Harbor offer great opportunities for strolling. Bass Harbor Head Light is a picture-perfect lighthouse. You can also take ferries out of Bass Harbor to visit Swans Island or Long Island.

Once you leave Acadia National Park and the Bar Harbor area, there are no more big-name tourist places Down East. This is not to say that there are no attractions and activities—it's just that they are scattered and are not as well known. The downside of moving

FYI: **Pedaling Maine**

Acadia is a popular place to bike, but there are many scenic routes throughout the state. Tour de Web to find forty of the most picturesque, least traveled routes in Maine. At www.pedaling.com you'll find self-guided bicycle routes for both the novice and the experienced rider. Choose rides by region, terrain, mileage, and difficulty.

Amazing
Maine Facts

Cadillac Mountain, located in Acadia National Park, rises 1,530 feet. It is the highest spot on the Atlantic coast

out of a well-known tourist area is that you have to drive a bit more to reach special places and attractions. On the plus side, you will find fewer crowds and see more of what Maine life is really like. How far you go and how frequently you meander down country roads is up to you. There are, however, plenty of other attractions in Down East Maine.

Acadia National Park (all ages)

The visitors center at the Hulls Cove entrance on Park Loop Road is open from May through October (207–288–5262; www.nps.gov/acad/). Main headquarters is at Eagle Lake on Route 233 (207–288–3338). For information, write to Superintendent, P.O. Box 177, Bar Harbor, ME 04609; www.acadia.net/anp. A seven-day pass for autos using the Park Loop Road costs $10.00. Hikers and bikers are charged $5.00. $$

Hiking is a favorite activity within the park, as is rock climbing. You can take an easy, 3½-mile walk around Jordan Pond Loop Trail, or you can opt for a more vigorous climb along the Precipice Trail. Although it is less than 2 miles in length, this trail is very steep and in some places has iron rung ladders. Strenuous even for experienced hikers, this trail is not recommended for young children. Consult a ranger. The park has many other hikes appropriate for families.

The park has magnificent views, clean air, and excellent trails. Industrialist and philanthropist John D. Rockefeller Jr. donated more than 50 miles of single-lane, gravel carriage roads that provide cyclists, equestrians, joggers, and hikers access to some of the park's prettiest acreage. Cross-country skiing is popular on the carriage roads in winter. Seventeen stone bridges connect the roadways. These trails put you in touch with remote areas without interference from motorized traffic.

The 27-mile Park Loop Road is also a prime tourist trail, but it is open to automobiles.

Park Land

Maine's natural assets include 542,629 acres of state and national parks, including Acadia National Park, the second most visited national park in the United States.

Take a **Dip**

Summer is rarely brutal in Maine, but it can get hot. Ocean water in this area can be as cool as 50 degrees Fahrenheit, which is pretty cold by most standards. If you want to swim, consider the lakes and ponds, which will be much warmer. Sand Beach, about 4 miles south of Bar Harbor, offers supervised swimming. Echo Lake, 11 miles west of Bar Harbor, is also a supervised swimming area. Seal Harbor, on Route 3, provides a town beach with parking and good swimming. Lake Wood is one of the warmer swimming holes. It's perfect for children, but there are no lifeguards on duty. To get to the lake, turn off Route 3 at the Cove Motel and take the second left, which is a dirt road. A small sign points the way to the lake. There is good parking and a short walk to the water.

Southwest Harbor

The Wendell Gilley Museum of Bird Carving (all ages)

A short walk from Great Harbor Marina in Southwest Harbor; (207) 244–7555; www.acadia. net/gilley/. Open June to October Tuesday through Sunday 10:00 A.M. to 4:00 P.M., May, November, and December Friday through Sunday 10:00 A.M. to 4:00 P.M. Closed January to April except to museum members or by group appointment. $

The work of Wendell Gilley, a Southwest Harbor native and world renowned bird carver, is showcased in this museum. Just one look and you'll understand why he is considered a pioneer of this American art form. Even better than looking at the finished product is watching a carver at work. Demonstrations are given almost daily.

If the exhibits really inspire you, workshops are available. Workshops range from one day to ten weeks in length. What could be a better souvenir to take home from your vacation than a bird carving you did yourself?

Mount Desert Oceanarium
(all ages)

Clark Point Road; (207) 244–7330; www.theoceanarium.com. Open 9:00 A.M. to 5:00 P.M., except Sundays, mid-May to late October. Admission is free for children 3 and under. $$

The "living room," where you can see many exhibits and displays of sea life, holds more than twenty tanks filled with

Tee **Time**

The Causeway Golf Club (207–244–3780) in Southwest Harbor is a nine-hole course with pull carts and a pro shop.

marine creatures from the coast of Maine. The touch tank allows kids to pick up crabs, snails, and other interesting species. The audiovisual room lets them experience the sights and sounds of the sea, and the whale exhibit gives them a chance to listen to the "songs" of whales. Before you leave, check out the gift shop, which offers dozens of trinkets from and about the sea. Visit this oceanarium and the one in Bar Harbor and save 25 percent on a combo ticket.

For More Information

Mount Desert Chamber of Commerce. (207) 276–5040.

Mount Desert Island Information Center. (207) 288–3411.

Acadia Information Center. (800) 358–8550; www.acadiainfo.com.

Southwest Harbor/Tremont Chamber of Commerce. (800) 423–9264; www.acadia chamber.com.

Lamoine Beach

At Lamoine Beach, located at the end of Route 184 in Frenchman Bay, you'll find more area residents than tourists. It's a very good saltwater swimming beach, with more than 2,700 yards of beach frontage.

When you've explored Lamoine, you might want to sidetrack to towns like Winter Harbor, Milbridge, and Jonesport, which are all worth a look. Most of what they offer are scenery and relaxation, but sometimes that is all it takes to have a good time.

Lamoine Beach State Park (all ages)

Near the end of Route 184 at Frenchman Bay, 23 State Park Road; (207) 667–4778 (off-season) or (207) 941–4014 (in season); www.state.me.us/doc/prkslnds/lamoine.htm. Open April 15 through October 15. Admission is free for children 4 and under. $

This state park is not your typical tourist trap. In fact, it's one of the better-kept secrets of the region. The fifty-five-acre park is often ignored, but it shouldn't be. Picnicking is always in season here, and the pebble beach is fun to walk on and safe for swimming. Kids can always enjoy skipping a few flat rocks on the water. There are more than fifty campsites available, many with water views.

While here, enjoy spectacular views of Cadillac Mountain. There is a boat launch and a dock on which to sit and watch the sun set. You can also fish and hike here. The park is only about 11 miles from Acadia's Hulls Cove Visitor's Center, so it's not far from other scenic sites. The only disadvantage is that the park has no hot showers.

Visiting during the colder months? The park is open after October 15 for cross-country skiers.

For More Information

Mount Desert Island Information Center. (207) 288–3411.

Amazing
Maine Facts

Famous for its shellfish, Maine averages an annual harvest of nearly 40 million pounds of lobster. The combined total of all shellfish and finfish harvested annually is more than 200 million pounds.

Steuben

Steuben is a little town on Route 1 that offers some superb hiking opportunities. Petit Manan National Wildlife Refuge is 6 miles off Route 1 on Pigeon Hill Road. A 5-mile trail here will take you around woods and coastline. Pine trees, cedar bogs, marshes, and blueberry fields provide habitat for many species of birds. Get out your binoculars and cameras for this walk.

Milbridge

Milbridge is another Route 1 town along the coast. McClellan Park is here, overlooking Narraguagus Bay. Picnic tables, fireplaces, campsites, and rest rooms make this a great place for families.

If you're happy just meandering, stop in Milbridge. Staying on Route 1 will take you to Cherryfield, which is somewhat inland. Driving up Route 1A will keep you along the water and guide you to Harrington. Once you pass through Harrington and Columbia Falls, head east on Route 187 and you will arrive in Jonesport.

Winter **Wonderland**

There's no such thing as winter blues here. You can glide through tranquil forests or across snow-covered fields on cross-country skis. The **Maine Nordic Ski Council** (800–754–9263; www.mnsc.com) has more information. Hop a snowmobile and crisscross miles of well-groomed trails. The **Maine Snowmobile Association** (800–880–7669 or 207–622–6983; www.mesnow. com) will hook you up. Schuss downhill, day or night, on expert or beginner slopes. **Ski Maine** (207–773–SNOW; www.skimaine. com) can tell you all you need to know.

Where to Eat

The Red Barn. Main Street; (207) 546–7721. A good place to take the kids. Pasta, steak, chicken, and seafood are some of what you can choose here. There's a children's menu. Open from 7:00 A.M. to 9:00 P.M. $–$$

Jonesport

A detour from Route 1 onto Route 187 will take you into Jonesport and to the bridge to nearby Beals Island. Both of these are lobstering villages with a flair unique to Maine. Great Wass Island is also accessible by bridge from Jonesport. Jonesport is deceiving. The village may seem small at first, but further investigation will reveal antiques shops, restaurants, a picture-perfect marina, and many more shops and lodging facilities. Lobsters are big business in Jonesport, but don't overlook the crabmeat—it's delicious.

Norton's Tours (all ages)

8 Sea Street; (207) 497–5933 or (888) 889–3222; www.machiassealisland.com. Cruises run from Memorial Day to the end of August, departing at 7:00 A.M. and returning at 1:00 P.M. $$$$

Captain Barna Norton has been offering bird-watching cruises to Machias Seal Island since the 1940s. He and his son run a good ship, and the island is a preferred nesting spot for puffins in June and July. These colorful birds pose perfectly for shutterbugs. Razor-billed auks and arctic terns take over the island in August and September.

Where to Eat

Tall Barney's Restaurant. Main Street; (207) 497–2403. Open from 7:00 A.M. to 7:00 P.M. for breakfast, lunch, and early dinner. You're likely to see many Mainers as you enjoy your meal at this local gathering place. Lobstermen favor the restaurant, as do tourists, and prices here will not burst your budget. $–$$

Where to Stay

Jonesport "By The Sea." 1 Main Street; (207) 497–2590. A good choice, with five guest rooms available. $–$$

For More Information

Downeast Coastal Chamber of Commerce. (800) 377–9748; www.downeast coastalchamber.org.

Other Things to **See** and **Do**

History buffs will enjoy a look at the **Sawyer Memorial Congregational Church.** Built in 1887, it is adorned with some of the finest stained-glass windows in the country. Model train enthusiasts will get a thrill from the 750 square feet of working track at the **Sandy River Model Railroad.** If you're visiting Jonesport on the Fourth of July, be sure to watch the **World's Fastest Lobster Boat Race.**

Beals and Great Wass Islands

If you venture across the bridges to the islands, check out the Downeast Institute (207–497–5769; www.hollyeats.com/bealshatchery.htm). Open from May through November from 9:00 A.M. to 4:00 P.M., this is a good place for your children to get a lesson in marine management and sea life.

After you've explored Beals Island, head over the Green Bridge to Great Wass Island. Walking trails are Great Wass Island's claim to fame. More than 1,500 acres are combined to create this piece of land. Many parents choose a short, 2-mile trail along the shore to Little Cape Point to hike and picnic. Kids love to scamper over the smooth rocks and look for hidden treasures. There are coastal peat lands to see, as well as Maine's largest jack pine stands. Camping is not encouraged on the island.

For More Information

Sunrise County Economic Council. (207) 255–0983; www.sunrisecounty.org.

Jonesboro

Head back over to the mainland on Route 187 to Jonesboro, the last major town before Machias. Situated along the Chandler River and Chandler Bay, the town offers scenery that is hard to beat.

Roque Bluffs State Park is about 6 miles outside Jonesboro on Roque Bluffs Road. As you near the park (keep an eye out for the small and obscure signs) take a right turn on Evergreen Point Road to the swimming area. Once in the park, you can choose between a saltwater pebble beach and a sand beach on fresh water. The sand beach is easier to walk on, and the water here is always warmer than the ocean. Hard sea breezes can be cold even in late summer on the pebble beach. Kids love the playground in the park, and parents like to relax at the many tables provided in the area. You will find diaper-changing facilities, grills, and rustic toilets to meet your needs.

FYI: **State Bird?**

Maine mosquitoes are big. In fact, they are jokingly called the "state bird." But they don't have to ruin your fun. If you're planning to be outside, especially at night, be sure to wear bug repellent. (The *official* state bird is the chickadee.)

Where to Eat

Whitehouse Restaurant. Route 1; (207) 434–2792. Right next door to the Blueberry Patch Inn (see Where to Stay), this restaurant opens before most people's eyes do (at 5:00 A.M.) and closes at 8:00 P.M. You can sit in a booth or opt for counter service. The staff is as friendly as can be, and the prices aren't bad. $–$$

Where to Stay

The Blueberry Patch Motel. Route 1; (207) 434–5411. Each unit has a refrigerator, TV, air-conditioning, and phone, and a pool is on the premises. $

Machias

The Machias River runs through Machias, offering good salmon fishing from mid-May through early June. The town is also the site of the first naval battle in the American Revolution.

Machias was once second only to Bangor as a lumber port. Today, it is famous for the Maine Wild Blueberry Company, which processes about 250,000 pounds of blueberries a day.

The Burnham Tavern (all ages)
Main Street; (207) 255–4432. Open 9:00 A.M. to 5:00 P.M. Monday through Friday from June through September. $

This 1770s tavern, filled with period furnishings, tells the story of how locals captured the British man-of-war Margaretta on June 12, 1775. When the local townspeople went out in *Unity*, a small sloop, to capture *Margaretta*, they triggered the first naval battle of the American Revolution.

Machias Wild Blueberry Festival (all ages)
Centre Street Congregational Church, Centre Street; (207) 255–6665; www.machiasblue berry.com. Held the third week of August each year. Admission is free.

Taste and see for yourself what makes Washington County blueberries different from those grown elsewhere. A firmer skin allows the berries to keep their shape—even during cooking—and helps hold in natural juices, creating a distinctive, mouthwatering flavor. At this festival you can sample blueberry muffins, pies, and pancakes, as well as other blueberry desserts.

Between blueberry treats enjoy the book sale, children's parade, and craft show. Run a race or enter a pie-eating contest. Whatever you do, don't miss the locally written, acted, and directed musical *Gold 'n' Blue Downeast*.

Where to Eat

Bluebird Ranch Family Restaurant. 3 East Main Street; (207) 255–3351. Open year-round from 6:00 A.M. to 8:30 P.M. It's a laid-back place until dinner, when the ambience and service become a bit more formal. $

Helen's Restaurant. 28E Main Street; (207) 255–8423. This place caters to big groups, but this is not to say that you and your family are not welcome. By all means, stop in. Sandwiches, seafood, various meats, and salads are all on the menu. Pies and other desserts are raved about here. Open 6:00 A.M. to 9:00 P.M. in season, 6:00 to 8:00 P.M. off-season. $

For More Information

Machias Bay Area Chamber of Commerce. (207) 255–4402 or (800) 377–9748; www.machiaschamber.org.

Machiasport

Not far from Machias on Route 92 is Machiasport. Fort O'Brien is also here. Used as an ammunition dump during the American Revolution and the War of 1812, today it is just a mound of earth. A more entertaining place in Machiasport is Jasper Beach. This pebble beach is rich in colored stones. If you continue down Machias Road through Machiasport, you will run out of land at Starboard, a beach with incredible views. This route features water views and down-home Maine living.

Lubec

When you leave East Machias on Route 1, take a right turn on Route 189 in Whiting. This road will take you to Lubec, on the border with Canada, and to the bridge from Lubec to Campobello Island in Canada. Once a center of the sardine industry, with twenty canning plants, Lubec still houses two active plants.

The West Quoddy Light State Park (all ages)
South Lubec Road, Box 1490, Lubec 04652; (207) 733–0911 in season, (207) 941–4014 off-season; www.westquoddy.com. Open from mid-May through October from sunrise to sunset. Free.

Because this is the easternmost tip of the United States, it is the place to be if you want to be the first in the country to see a sunrise. A lighthouse decked out with red and white stripes is on the property. It dates back to 1858 and is still operating. There are beaches here, but the water is cold. A 2-mile trail leads you along the cliffs to Carrying Place Cove, but due to dangerous heights, this is not a good hike for young kids. Certainly, this is a pleasant place to take a break from driving.

Where to Eat

Atlantic House Coffee & Deli Shop. 52 Water Street; (207) 733–8907; www.atlantic house.net. Open seven days a week. Dine on the upper or lower deck and you might spy seals in the harbor. Enjoy a sandwich or pizza. But save room for a homemade pastry or some ice cream—choose from twenty-six flavors. $–$$

Where to Stay

The Home Port Inn. 45 Main Street; (207) 733–2077 or (800) 457–2077; www.home portinn.com. Offers seven guest rooms. $

The Peacock House. 27 Summer Street; (207) 733–2403 or (888) 305–0036; www. peacockhouse.com. This 1880s house has five guest rooms, one of which is wheelchair accessible. $

For More Information

Lubec Chamber of Commerce. (207) 733–4522; www.downeastregion.com.

Other Things to **See** and **Do**

Another possibility for fun in Lubec is the Sunrise Air-Lubec (207–733–2124) adventures. You can go up for scenic views, fish watching, and aerial photography. Another spot for a photo is the Roosevelt Campobello International Park (just over the bridge from Lubec), Franklin D. Roosevelt's summer home.

Northern Maine

The crown of Maine is vast and beautiful. Rolling fields and scenic vistas seem endless. Up north, native pride runs deep and country roads run long. This tranquil haven is the perfect place to get away from it all and get back to nature.

Most of the land is wild and undeveloped, so you won't find many amusement parks in the north woods. What you and your children will find, however, is great outdoor adventure and plenty of wholesome family fun. Enticing wide-open spaces reward you with both freedom and privacy. A chain of brooks, streams, and lakes forms a massive waterway rich in wildlife and solitude. Don't worry; you don't need to be an expert in wilderness survival to get the most out of the area.

In any season, dramatic territory, from Maine's largest lake to its loftiest mountain, will tempt the outdoor lover in you. When snow blankets the land, opportunities for skiing, snowmobiling, and ice fishing will spur you to brave the winter chill in search of winter thrills. In summer and fall, a river that drops more than 70 feet per mile, through a granite canyon, guarantees you some of the best white-water rafting in the East.

Camping is an economical way to see the north country, but rental cabins, cottages, and motel rooms are plentiful around key towns. You don't need four-wheel drive to reach most of the remote areas, as the roads provided for logging trucks are quite passable by car.

Bangor

Bangor is a pretty large town, by Maine standards—in fact, it's Maine's second largest city and the gateway to the north woods. Easily reached from I–95, this old logging town has become a business and shopping center. Bangor International Airport (207–947–0384; www.flybangor.com) is served by major airlines.

If you're heading north, Bangor is a great place to shop for necessities and little extras. Besides Bangor Mall, which has eighty stores, you might want to try **West Market Square**.

NORTHERN MAINE

Stores at the square such as The Briar Patch, featuring children's books and toys, and The Grasshopper Shop, which also carries toys, are good places to purchase something to keep the children occupied while you travel.

If you'd like something to read while you relax at northern camps or cabins, check out Bett's Bookstore on Main Street, Mr. Paperback at Main Square, BookMarc's on Harlow Street, or The Booksource at Crossroads Plaza.

In addition to shopping, there are museums to visit, places to fish, courses to golf, and live performances to enjoy.

Cole Land Transportation Museum (all ages)

405 Perry Road; (207) 990–3600; www.colemuseum.com. Open daily May 1 to November 11 from 9:00 A.M. to 5:00 P.M. $$. Free for children under 19.

Aficionados of vehicles of all kinds will enjoy a stop at this museum, which displays old-time wagons, snowplows, trucks, sleds, and rail equipment. This collection exhibits some interesting models and provides a good history lesson.

Bonnie's
Top Ten Picks for Northern Maine

1. Watching a performance by the Penobscot Theatre Company, Bangor; (207) 947–6618.
2. Racing a go-kart at Blackbeard's USA, Bangor; (207) 945–0233.
3. Seeing stars at Maynard F. Jordan Planetarium, Orono; (207) 581–1341.
4. Exploring the Hudson Museum, Orono; (207) 581–1901.
5. Experiencing living history days at Leonard's Mill at the Maine Forest and Logging Museum, Bradley; (207) 866–0811.
6. Playing at Lily Bay State Park, Beaver Cove; (207) 695–2700.
7. Cruising Moosehead Lake aboard the SS *Katahdin*, Greenville; (207) 695–2716.
8. Enjoying a family adventure with Unicorn Expeditions, Jackman; (207) 668–7629.
9. Hiking in Baxter State Park, Millinocket; (207) 723–5140.
10. Discovering the wildlife exhibits at Nylander Museum, Caribou; (207) 493–4209.

Photo Op: **Tall Paul**

Few characters from American folklore have the stature of Paul Bunyan. His enormous size and great strength became symbolic of America. He and Babe, his giant blue ox, are credited with forming many geographic features throughout the United States and Canada. His work can be seen from the Great Lakes all the way to the Pacific Ocean. But a 31-foot statue of the famous folk hero can only be seen on Main Street in Bangor.

Penobscot Theatre Company (ages 5 and up)
131 Main Street; (207) 947–6618 (admission office) or (207) 942–3333 (box office); ptc.maineguide.com. $$–$$$

Housed in a beautifully renovated historic building dating from 1888, the Penobscot Theatre Company has been entertaining audiences for more than twenty-five years. Originally founded in 1973 as a summer theater, the company now offers performances throughout the year.

The company's Maine Shakespeare Festival has brought life to Bangor's downtown waterfront. Preshow entertainment features fire-torch jugglers, Renaissance singers and dancers, and animated swordplay. You can purchase food from on-site vendors, then, under starlit skies, enjoy productions such as *Cymbeline* and *Henry IV, Part One*.

There is a special children's theater series offered in the spring and fall. Youngsters will marvel at live productions such as *The Secret Garden*. Creative arts workshops, offered during the summer, put kids in the spotlight as they learn everything from acting to staging.

Blackbeard's USA (all ages)
339 Odlin Road; (207) 945–0233; www.blackbeardsusa.com. Open Monday through Saturday 10:00 A.M. to 10:00 P.M., Sunday 10:00 A.M. to 8:00 P.M. $$

This is the closest you'll get to an amusement park in northern Maine. You can sail a remote-controlled pirate ship, play putt-putt on Treasure Island, practice for the majors in a batting cage, or cruise in an Indy-style go-kart. After all the fun, get a bite to eat at the Ship's Galley, or feed rainbow trout in a half-acre trout pond.

Check out the Web site for a coupon good for discounts on either adventure golf or a go-kart ride.

Myths and Legends:
The Things We Do for Love

The cliffs along Kendukeag Stream in Bangor are dubbed "Lover's Leap" because lovers reputedly jumped to their deaths from one of the granite ledges.

Maine Discovery Museum (all ages)
74 Main Street; (207) 262–7200; www.mainediscoverymuseum.org. Open Tuesday through Saturday 9:30 A.M. to 5:00 P.M., Friday evenings until 8:00, Sunday 11:00 A.M. to 5:00 P.M. Closed Monday except for school vacations; extended summer hours. $$

This museum, which opened in February 2001, is a playground for your mind. In the historic Freese's building in downtown Bangor, you and your kids will discover three floors of stimulating interactive exhibits. There are seven major exhibit areas, each offering something fun and educational.

Send a boat down a 20-foot waterway and learn about Maine's ecosystem at the *Nature Trails* exhibit. Visit Australia, Peru, and Ghana in *Passport to the World*. Enter the pages of Maine children's literary classics in *Booktown*. Snap a picture of the kids with Wilbur from *Charlotte's Web* while you're there. Conduct an orchestra in *Sounds Abound* or create an original masterpiece in *Artscape*. Try your hand at robotics at the *Mission Discovery* exhibit or find out how your body works in *Body Journey*. You may never look at yourself the same after you travel through a giant intestine.

If all this wasn't enough, you can listen to a story in the *Head Down Baseball Diamond,* or uncover trinkets and toys and bundles of books at the museum's gift shop, Treasure Island Too.

Having fun here is easy and so is parking. Slip into a spot in the Pickering Square parking garage for two free hours of parking.

Amazing
Maine Facts

Maine boasts 6,000 lakes and ponds, 32,000 miles of rivers and streams (including the 92-mile Allagash Wilderness Waterway), and seventeen million acres of forest.

Bangor State Fair (all ages)

100 Dutton Street, Bass Park; (207) 947–5555; www.bangorstatefair.com. Held the last week of July and first week of August. $$

The fair recently celebrated its 150th year. There are performances by country stars, kid shows like Magic & Mayhem, and agricultural exhibitions featuring livestock and Maine-made products. You'll also find carnival rides, a midway full of games, a petting zoo, and all the food you can eat.

Where to Eat

Governor's Take Out and Eat In. 643 Broadway; (207) 947–3113. Open from 6:00 A.M. to midnight. Hamburgers and steaks are on the menu, along with German potato soup and fresh strawberry pie and ice cream. $

Miller's Restaurant. 427 Main Street; (207) 942–6361. Miller's offers a great buffet with many choices, including make-your-own sundaes. Prices are family friendly. Open seven days a week. $–$$

Nicky's Cruisin' Diner. 957 Union Street; (207) 942–3430. For nearly thirty-five years Nicky's has served up homestyle meals at down-home prices. The menu offers everything from seafood to lasagna. On Friday nights you'll enjoy live music, and every other Wednesday (May through September) is "cruise night." $

Thistle's Restaurant. 175 Exchange Street; (207) 945–5480. This four-star restaurant offers appetizers such as lobster brioche—a fresh pastry filled with lobster in a creamy brandied sauce. Dinner entrees include Aberdeen chicken—a boneless chicken breast sautéed with smoked trout and fresh lime juice. Sandwiches, light fare, pasta, and steak are also available. $$

Where to Stay

Bangor Motor Inn. 701 Hogan Road; (207) 947–0355 or (888) 244–0355; www.bangor motorinn.com. Features two-room suites, free shuttle service to the airport, free deluxe continental breakfast, and a daily paper. $

Four Points Hotel. 308 Godfrey Boulevard; (207) 947–6721; www.bangorsheraton.com. If you're flying into Bangor, this is a great choice because when you land your accommodations are waiting for you. Four Points, a full-service hotel, is connected to the Bangor International Airport via an enclosed skywalk. Once there enjoy the outdoor pool, fitness, or game room, or grab a bite to eat at the Wright Brothers American Grille & Lounge. $$–$$$

Holiday Inn. 404 Odlin Road; (207) 947–0101 or (800) 914–0101. The largest hotel property in Bangor offers an indoor heated pool with Jacuzzi, an outdoor pool with courtyard dining, and a fully equipped Gold's Gym on-site. Eat at Pete & Larry's Grill and enjoy entertainment nightly. $$

Paul Bunyan Campground. 1862 Union Street; (207) 941–1177. Open April to November. There are fifty-two sites with picnic tables and fire rings. A heated pool, a play area, a rec hall, hayrides, paddleboat rentals, and planned activities on weekends throughout the summer make this a great place for families. $

For More Information

Bangor Convention and Visitors Bureau. (207) 947–5205 or (800) 91–MOOSE; www.bangorcvb.org.

Bangor Region Chamber of Commerce. (207) 947–0307; www.bangorregion.com.

Orono

Home to the University of Maine, Orono is a typical college town—bustling with activity and lots of things to do.

Hudson Museum (ages 6 and up)

University of Maine, 5746 Maine Center for the Arts; (207) 581–1901; www.umaine.edu/hudsonmuseum. Open Tuesday through Friday from 9:00 A.M. to 4:00 P.M., and Saturday from 11:00 A.M. to 4:00 P.M. Closed Sunday, Monday, and holidays. Admission is **free.**

Anthropological exhibits and programs explore traditional cultures. Special programs for children include the Just for Kids series on Saturdays and during school vacations, Museum Mornings in the summer, and Games Day during February school break. Activities include making a colorful beadwork patch, wall painting with Indian rice paste, and going on an art collector's hunt for symmetry.

Maynard F. Jordan Planetarium and Observatory (ages 4 and up)

5781 Wingate Hall, University of Maine; (207) 581–1341; www.ume.maine.edu. $. Planetarium presentations are given on Friday at 7:00 P.M. and Sunday at 2:00 P.M. There are also special daytime showings during school vacations. There is an admission charge for the planetarium. The observatory is open on clear Friday and Saturday evenings from 8:00 to 10:00. Public viewing in the observatory is **free.**

View the universe from Maine's first planetarium. You'll see stars, planets, and the Milky Way. Travel to the center of the earth or the edge of the universe. Journey back to the

birth of the solar system or the beginning of time itself. Special presentations just for young sky watchers provide a fun and educational experience. Chat with Father Sun and each of the planets in *Our Sky Family*, or catch *Follow the Drinking Gourd* and learn how Southern slaves used the sky to escape to the North. Special events like Astrofest offer a full day of astronomy activities for the whole family.

Maine Forest and Logging Museum (all ages)

Leonard's Mills, 403 Main Street, Bradley, P.O. Box 456, Orono 04473; (207) 866–0811 or (207) 581–2871; www.leonardsmills.com. Open daily year-round for exploration and self-guided tours, as well as cross-country skiing and snowshoeing in season. Living history days are held on designated weekends in the summer and fall. $$

The centerpiece of this museum is Leonard's Mill, which is located on 265 acres in Bradley, Maine. The site of a pioneer settlement, visitors are free to walk the self-guided nature trails and enjoy the pond. Living history days bring the village to life as volunteers, in period dress, perform tasks common to a logging and milling community of the 1790s.

October brings special activities like dipping candles, pressing apples for cider, and making cedar shakes—all activities in which children can participate. In winter take a horse-drawn sleigh ride through the woods. Special events throughout the year such as Children's Day, Woodsmen's Day, and the Blacksmith Roundup give visitors a real feel for life in the eighteenth century.

Where to Eat

Bear Brew Pub. 36 Main Street; (207) 866–2739. A family-friendly restaurant offering indoor or outdoor dining, live entertainment, and a varied menu. $–$$

Margarita's Mexican Restaurant. 15 Mill Street; (207) 866–4863. In the mood for Mexican? Then this is the place for you. The children get their own menu too. $–$$

Where to Stay

Best Western Black Bear Inn & Conference Center. 4 Godfrey Drive; (207) 866–7120 or (800) 528–1234; www.black bearinnorono.com. This full-service hotel offers spacious rooms and suites, an exercise room and sauna, a **free** continental breakfast, and in-room coffeemakers. $–$$

University Motor Inn. 5 College Avenue; (207) 866–4921 or (800) 321–4921; www.universitymotorinn.com. This forty-eight-room motor inn is not luxurious but it is economical. Clean rooms, an outdoor pool, and a continental breakfast are all part of the package. Pets are welcome. $

For More Information

Bangor Region Chamber of Commerce. (207) 947–0307; www.bangorregion.com.

Greenville

When you arrive in Greenville, you will find a town with plenty of modern conveniences, but you won't find any elevators or skyscrapers. You're on your way to Maine's wilderness.

Greenville borders Moosehead Lake. Running about 40 miles long and up to 10 miles wide, with a shoreline that covers about 420 miles, it is Maine's largest lake. Boats are available on a rental basis, but this is not a lake to explore on your own. Hire a licensed guide if you want to enjoy the water. Unexpected waves can swamp a 16-foot boat in a blink of an eye.

Penny **Pinching**

Besides renting mountain bikes, Northwoods Outfitters (207–695–3288 or 866–223–1380; www.maineoutfitter.com) also offer guided moose safaris. You'll have to maneuver a canoe or kayak, but this is the only company that guarantees a moose sighting. If you don't spot a moose, you get another trip free.

Besides boats, colorful floatplanes dot Moosehead Lake. These planes are used to deliver mail, people, and supplies. You can hire a flying service to give you and your family an aerial tour. If you're up north in the winter, snowmobiling and ice fishing on the lake are very popular.

The Greenville area provides opportunities for golfing, fishing, hiking, moose watching, swimming, and horseback riding. You can even rent mountain bikes, from Northwoods Outfitters (207–695–3288) on Main Street. Fine food and good lodging are also available in and around town.

Moose Safaris and Scenic Cruises (all ages)

Route 15; (207) 695–3241 or (888) 624–3993; www.mainelodge.com/cruise.html. Daily tours mid-May through mid-October. Cruises depart at 5:00 P.M. through August 1 and at 4:00 P.M. after August 1. $$$$

There are a couple of reasons this tour is worth mentioning. If you stay at one of their lodges, you get a free safari. Also, the 30-foot pontoon *Discovery* offers foul-weather curtains to protect you from Mother Nature; this can be important for the little ones. Complimentary beverages are served during the cruise, and there are rest room facilities onboard.

June and July are the best months for sightings of moose, but you'll also enjoy the beauty of Mount Kineo and its 700-foot cliffs. Don't forget to bring the camera or to make reservations—they're required.

FYI: **Boating Moosehead**

The Wilderness Boat (207–534–7305) offers Moosehead lake excursions. Call for rates and schedules. If you'd rather create your own boat excursion, talk to the people at Cozy Moose Lakeside Cabins & Recreation (207–695–0242; www.mooseheadcabins.com), where you can rent a motor boat, canoe, or kayak. Beaver Cove Marina (207–695–3526; beavercovemarina.com) is another place to rent boats for those with an independent, adventurous spirit.

Amazing
Maine Facts

Moosehead Lake was made famous in the writings of Henry David Thoreau.

Lily Bay State Park (all ages)

Beaver Cove; (207) 695–2700 in season, (207) 941–4014 off-season. Open May 1 through October 15. $. **Free** for children 4 and under.

A small beach on Moosehead Lake is part of this 942-acre recreational area. You'll find a playground, rest rooms, and plenty of picnic spots. Canoe rentals are available, and there is a ramp to launch your own boat. Swimming is good, but the water can be pretty cold. There are campsites and trails in the area.

SS *Katahdin*/Moosehead Marine Museum (all ages)

P.O. Box 1151, Greenville 04441; (207) 695–2716; www.katahdincruises.com. Cruises Memorial Day through October. Three-hour, five-hour, and eight-hour cruises are available. $$$ Children under 6 ride **free.**

One way for you and your family to tour Moosehead Lake is on a cruise aboard the SS *Katahdin*. Kate, as she is called locally, is a 1914 steam vessel that once hauled pulpwood. A standard cruise around the southern tip of Moosehead takes about an hour. Once a month, from June to September, you can arrange for the 80-mile Head of the Lake cruise. Another variation is the Mount Kineo cruise, which goes out to Mount Kineo Island.

Founded in 1976, the Moosehead Marine Museum houses an extensive collection of photographs and displays depicting Moosehead Lake's steamboat history. The museum's star exhibit, however, is the SS *Katahdin* itself.

Where to Eat

Auntie Em's. Main Street; (207) 695–2238. Offers pizza and other home-cooked specialties. $

Bair Hill Inn. 351 Lily Bay Road; (207) 695–0224; www.bearhill.com/dining.html. Ranked as one of the top ten romantic restaurants in Maine by *Down East* magazine, Bair Hill is open to the public Thursday, Friday, and Saturday evenings from 6:00 P.M. to 8:00 P.M. Choose from a five-course menu and drink in the beautiful view which extends as far as Mount Washington and Quebec. Best for families with older children. $$$–$$$$

Flatlander's. Pritham Avenue; (207) 695–3373. Features steak, ribs, and burgers. $$

The Greenville Inn. Norris Street; (207) 695–2206 or (888) 695–6000; www.green villeinn.com. Open May through October, the inn offers an upscale menu to guests as well as other diners. Children's specials are available. $$$$

Kelly's Landing. Route 15, Greenville Junction; (207) 695–4438; www.kellysatmoose head.com. Home cooking is their specialty. $$

Where to Stay

Chalet Moosehead Motel. Birch Street, Greenville Junction; (207) 695–2950 or (800) 290–3645; www.mooseheadlodging.com. Moosehead's only lakefront motel, the Chalet offers motel rooms, two-room efficiencies, and a lakeside cabin. Guests have use of docks, gas grills, picnic tables, canoes, and paddleboats. $$

The Greenville Inn. Norris Street; (888) 695–6000 or (207) 695–2206; www.green villeinn.com. Open from April through November, this impressive inn sits atop a hill with a commanding view of Moosehead Lake. The building's paneled interior walls of cherry, mahogany, and oak richly set off the fireplaces and a leaded-glass window, capturing a rustic yet elegant mood. Breakfast is included in the rate, and the dining room offers some of the best food in northwestern Maine. $$–$$$$

The Greenwood Motel. 314 Rockwood Road, Greenville Junction; (800) 477–4386. Good service, fair price. Pets are allowed, and rooms are air-conditioned. Actually, you can win this motel, not just stay in it. They are raffling off the motel for $200 a ticket. $

Kelly's Landing. Route 15, Greenville Junction; (207) 695–4438 or (800) 498–9800; www.kellysatmoosehead.com. Rental suites with air-conditioning, a private beach, and free docking. $–$$$

The Lodge at Moosehead. Upper Lily Bay Road, P.O. Box 1167, Greenville 04441; (207) 695–4400; www.lodgeatmooseheadlake. com. Built in 1916 as a hunting lodge; four of the five guest rooms have lake views. Each room features a distinct decorating theme, for instance, the "trout room" and the "loon room." All have cable television, a gas fireplace, a private bath, and a whirlpool tub. Rates are a bit steep, but they include breakfast. $$$$

For More Information

Moosehead Lake Region Greenville Chamber of Commerce. (207) 695–2702 or (888) 876–2776; www.mooseheadlake.org.

Other Things to **See** and **Do**

Take an aerial tour of Moosehead with Folsom's Air Service (207–695–2821; www.folsomsairservice.com), the oldest and best-known service on the lake. Currier's Flying Service (207–695–2778; www.curriersflyingservice.com) and Jack's Flying Service (207–695–3020) also offer flying excursions.

During the winter, downhill skiing at the Squaw Mountain Resort (207–695–1000) is popular. If you have the courage, take a chairlift ride here in the summertime for an outstanding view of Moosehead Lake. Cross-country skiing is also available throughout the region.

Rockwood

There's plenty of beautiful scenery to be taken in as you enter the westerly wilderness of Rockwood. When you arrive, you will be greeted by the sight of Mount Kineo, which stands some 700 feet above Moosehead Lake. The entire mountain is made of green flint. Abenaki Indians used this flint to make arrowheads and tools.

Unless you think fishing, hiking, cruising, camping, and other outdoor fun is not good for children, you'll find plenty to keep you busy in Rockwood. You might even want to stay a few days.

Where to Stay

The Birches Resort/Wilderness Expeditions. Birches Road, P.O. Box 41, Rockwood 04478; (207) 534–7305 or (800) 825–9453; www.birches.com. Open year-round, the resort includes a large lodge with guest rooms, plus fifteen log cabins along the lake, some of which have floating docks. The cabins have one to three bedrooms and either Franklin stoves or fireplaces; a few are equipped with kitchens. An outdoor hot tub and sauna are available, along with sailboats, kayaks, canoes, fishing boats, and mountain bikes. Cross-country skiing is offered in winter. Pets are not allowed. $–$$

Maynards in Maine. Route 6/15 on the Moose River; (207) 534–7703 or (888) 518–2055; www.maynardsinmaine.com. This lodge was founded in 1919. About a dozen cabins are scattered around the grounds, all with indoor plumbing. Rates are around $48 a day, including three meals a day, two served in the dining room and one packed for the trail. The decor in the dining room is worth a look, even if you don't spend the night. $

For More Information

Moosehead Lake Vacation Association. (207) 534–7300; www.rockwoodonmoosehead.org.

Jackman

Close to the Canadian border, this area is known as the Switzerland of Maine. Jackman itself is a frontier town. To this day, you may spot a moose walking down Main Street. If the town feels to you like a jumping-off point to the wilderness, it is. Jackman is the last developed township before crossing the mountains into Canada. Bring some angling gear with you; the area boasts some of the best freshwater fishing in all of Maine. A famed canoe expedition known as the Moose River Bow Trip covers 46 miles of nearby waterways. Because it is long and somewhat arduous, this trip is not recommended for young children, but it can be quite an adventure for older children and teens. Contact any local outfitter for more information.

Other Things to **See** and **Do**

Take a break from all the rafting, hunting, and fishing and stroll through the **Jackman Moose River Historical Museum** (207–668–4171; www.jackmanmaine. org/museum.html). Admission is **free.** Need a little competition? Try your swing at **Moose River Golf Course** (207–668–4841; www.jackmanmaine. org/golf.html), a small nine-hole course with the historic Captain Samuel Holden House (1829) built right in. If you hit one out of bounds between the third and fifth greens, you'll also discover an 1829 cemetery. The course is open May through October.

Unicorn Expeditions (ages 8 and up) ⚠ 🍴 ⚠

Lake Parlin Resort, HC 64, Box 564, Jackman 04945; (207) 668–7629 or (800) UNICORN; www.unicornraft.com. Open year-round. Rafting trips along the Dead, Kennebec, and Penobscot Rivers offered April through October. One-, two-, and four-day packages are available. Prices vary by length of trip, time of year, and river. $$$$

One of the best outfitters for families, Unicorn has been offering outdoor adventure trips for more than twenty years. Today you can participate in year-round activities, including rafting, canoeing, hiking, mountain biking, snowmobiling, and hunting.

Rafting trips for families include a one-day "no experience necessary" trip along the Dead River, with intermediate rapids like Elephant Rock and Poplar Falls. A four-day family package includes rafting, lodging in a lakefront cabin, and use of resort facilities.

The best part is the Unicorn guarantee: If you're not satisfied with your rafting, canoeing, or biking adventure, your trip is free.

For More Information

Jackman–Moose River Region Chamber of Commerce. (207) 668–4171; www. jackmanmaine.org.

The Forks

When you enter the Forks, you enter white-water country. The Forks is where the Dead River and the Kennebec River join forces. Many rafting and canoe companies ply their trade in this area as well as in Millinocket, where they raft the Penobscot River. If you're into rafting, you will usually find that May and June provide the highest water, July and August the warmest temperatures, and September and October smaller crowds and Maine's famous foliage.

Penny **Pinching**

White-water rafting is a popular weekend sport. However, if you raft during the week with Northern Outdoors, children 8 to 15 are half price with a paying adult (one child per adult).

While you're visiting The Forks, consider taking a short, easy hike up to Moxie Falls. This 90-foot waterfall is the tallest in New England. The waterfall is on the south side of the bridge crossing the Kennebec River. You can park off the road at the trailhead sign.

Northern Outdoors, Inc. (ages 8 and up)

Route 201, P.O. Box 100, The Forks 04985; (207) 663–4466 or (800) 765–RAFT (7238); www.northernoutdoors.com. Daily rafting trips on the Kennebec and Penobscot Rivers, with selected trips on the Dead River, are offered April through October. $$$$

This is the first and largest rafting outfitter on the Kennebec River. In conjunction with rafting, this company offers many other services. Its resort center at The Forks provides good food and entertainment. You can swim in a pool, soak in a hot tub, and go fishing or mountain biking. Accommodations range from campsites for tenters to private cabins and condos. Rafting is the most popular activity here in warmer weather, with skiing and snowmobiling in the winter.

Magic Falls Rafting (ages 10 and up)

P.O. Box 9, Route 201, West Forks 04985; (800) 207–7238; www.magicfalls.com. Rafting trips on the Kennebec, Dead, and Penobscot Rivers are offered May through mid-October. $$$$

Here rafting is more than just a business. It is a time "to shed worries and stress and get a natural high." A one-day family rafting trip is along the Kennebec River Gorge. You'll enjoy the beauty of steep rock walls banking the river and the thrill of waves swelling 4 to 6 feet high. You'll paddle through rapids with names like Big Mama and Magic Falls. After you pass the rapids, you can jump in and float with the current. Your trip ends with a delicious homemade meal and a video show of your trip. Family overnight trips are also available, with almost everything you need provided. Alcohol is not permitted on these expeditions.

Moxie Outdoor Adventures (ages 5 and up)

HC 63, P.O. Box 60, The Forks 04985; (800) 866–6943; www.moxierafting.com. Daily rafting trips on the Kennebec, Penobscot, and Dead Rivers are offered May through October. The Family River Trip is $110 for a family of four and a great deal. $$$$

This outfitter offers family specials through the week that include inflatable kayaking, white-water rafting, canoeing on Lake Moxie, and lodging. All trips begin with a full orientation to river techniques and are led by experienced licensed guides.

FYI: **Four-Season Outfitters**

Many of the outfitters that operate in The Forks also have bases in Millinocket. Most are open year-round, offering hunting, fishing, snowmobiling, and skiing. For more information, contact Raft Maine at (800) 723–8633, or check out the Web site at www.raft maine.com.

For More Information

Kennebec Valley Tourism Council. (800) 393–8629; www.kennebecvalley.org.

Upper Kennebec Valley Chamber of Commerce. (207) 672–4100; www.kennebec valley.com.

Kokadjo

If you're heading from Moosehead Lake to Baxter State Park, odds are you'll travel through this town. Just a few years ago, Kokadjo boasted a population of three. There were more moose than people. The settlement has grown a little, and the new population report indicates the number of town residents as "not many."

Where to Eat

Kokadjo does have some modern dining facilities as well as a general store.

Kokadjo Snack Bar. Kokadjo Trading Post, HC 76, Box 590, Kokadjo 04441; (207) 695–3993. One of two eating options that offer good food at family prices. Open from 7:00 A.M. until "when everybody leaves." $$

Northern Pride Lodge. HC 76, Box 588, Kokadjo 04441; (207) 695–2890; www. northernpridelodge.com. In sight of the Trading Post, it is open only for dinner; reservations are required. $$–$$$

Where to Stay

Kokadjo Camps. Located next to the Trading Post, Kokadjo; (207) 695–3993; www. campstorent.com/kokadjo/kokadjo9.html. Featuring rustic accommodations along the Roach River. You can't beat the fishing, but it's fly-fishing only. Pets are allowed, but there is no electricity. $

Millinocket

Millinocket is possibly Maine wilderness at its best. As you reach the outskirts of town, turn right on Golden Road. A small vehicle fee is charged for this high-quality dirt road, which takes you on an unbelievable tour of the North Woods and accesses many recreational areas such as Baxter State Park. Controlled by paper companies, the Golden Road is often busy with lumber trucks, which have the right-of-way.

Golden Road parallels the western branch of the Penobscot River, providing some spectacular views. A favorite is the Ripogenus Dam. Locals call it Rip Dam. The view over the gorge and along the river is outstanding. Be careful with young children in this area. The rocks can be slippery, and a fall into the river could be disastrous. Excellent fishing and white-water rafting are some of the recreational options along this river.

During your drive you will discover numerous places perfect for picnics and scenic photographs. You'll also find gas and country-store supplies along Golden Road, as well as many sporting camps that offer places to stay for the night. Most of these camps are rustic, and many don't have electricity unless it is generated on-site. Basic amenities usually include beds, linens, and gas lamps.

Photo Op: **Mainely Moose**

If you'd like to get up-close and personal with these large creatures, Mainely Photos (207–723–5465; www.mainelyphotos.com) offers moose photo tours through Baxter State Park. Averaging a 100 percent sighting rate for the last two years, you're virtually guaranteed to get the shot you want. Family rates are $25 per person, and tours are offered May through September. As many as thirty-six moose have been sighted in one tour, but the average is between six and twenty.

Baxter State Park (all ages)

64 Balsam Drive; (207) 723–5140. Summer camping from May 15 through October 15. Winter camping from December 1 through April 1. No vehicular traffic during the winter. Camping reservations are accepted after January 1. A flat fee vehicle day pass is available. Fees vary for overnight stays. $$

This 204,737-acre park is the wonderfully wild centerpiece of Millinocket. It boasts Mount Katahdin, which towers majestically over the area, and the northern terminus of the 2,050-mile-long Appalachian Trail.

There are forty-six mountain peaks and ridges in the park, eighteen of which are more than 3,000 feet tall. The thrilling Knife Edge is one of many rigorous and scenic hiking trails spanning these mountains. The park has a total of 175 miles of hiking trails. Some are diffi-

FYI: **Bug Warning**

If you visit Baxter State Park during the summer months, you'll run into dense bug populations. Always bring insect repellent. It's also a good idea to keep your windows rolled up when you leave your car during bug season—otherwise, tons of unwanted guests will be waiting for you when you get back.

cult, but many are easy enough for young children, especially the Daicey Pond Nature Trail. A free pamphlet on the trail is available from the ranger's station at Daicey Pond Campground. All hikers and climbers should check in at park gatehouses or campgrounds and pick up detailed maps of the area. If you would rather tour the park by car, allocate at least two hours for the trip.

Good swimming and canoeing can be enjoyed at South Branch Pond, where rental canoes are available. Abol Pond is another good swimming hole. If you and your family enjoy bird-watching, you will have an opportunity to see about 170 species in the park. Moose and deer can often be seen along the roads and ponds. Bears inhabit the area, but they rarely are a problem. Take precautions nonetheless; this park is pure wilderness. There is no running water for domestic use, no electricity, and no food or supplies.

The park offers so many recreational activities that you should spend a few days and enjoy them. Camping is available, but reservations are essential. This park attracts a lot of visitors, so make camping plans early. There are ten campgrounds with varying facilities, including cabins, bunkhouses, lean-tos, tenting sites, fireplaces, and picnic tables. However, narrow roads prohibit large trailers.

New England Outdoor Center (ages 10 and up)

Old Medway Road, Rice Farm, P.O. Box 669, Millinocket 04462; (800) 766–7238; www.neoc.com. Daily rafting trips on the Penobscot and Kennebec Rivers, with selected trips on the Dead River, offered April through October. Lodging/rafting packages are available. $$$$

Once you check in at Rice Farm, a bus ride along the scenic Golden Road will take you to the starting point for a run of the lower, calmer part of the Penobscot River. After a hearty riverside lunch, you'll travel to Ripogenus Gorge. This upper section of the Penobscot offers some of the most challenging class-5 white water in the East. You have to be 15 or older to run the entire river. Families with younger children can return to base camp after lunch. There are showers, changing facilities, a hot tub, and a restaurant at Rice Farm—enough to keep you busy until it's time for a slide and video show of your day's adventure.

If you want to stay over, you have your choice of accommodations. Cabin tents are available at Rice Farm, and sporting camp cabins at Twin Pine Camps, just 14 miles away. This outfitter also operates the Sterling Inn in Caratunk, near The Forks. Now a bed-and-breakfast, the inn was once a nineteenth-century stagecoach stop.

North Country Rivers (ages 10 and up)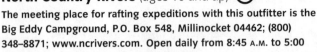
The meeting place for rafting expeditions with this outfitter is the Big Eddy Campground, P.O. Box 548, Millinocket 04462; (800) 348–8871; www.ncrivers.com. Open daily from 8:45 A.M. to 5:00 P.M. from late April to early October. $$$$

Families with children 10 and older can enjoy a ride down the lower section of the Penobscot River. Passengers must be at least 16 years of age to raft the Upper Gorge. The company rents wet suits for spring and fall trips. Check out the Web site for details on winning a **free** rafting trip.

Amazing
Maine Facts

Baxter State Park was a gift to the state of Maine from former Maine Governor Percival P. Baxter. The summit of Mount Katahdin (Maine's highest peak at 5,267 feet) is called Baxter Peak in his honor.

Where to Stay

Big Moose Campground. P.O. Box 98, Millinocket 04462; (207) 723–8391; www.big moosecabins.com. Whether you're looking to stay in a quaint inn, a cozy lakeside cabin, or camp beneath the stars, Big Moose can make all your wishes come true. A store on the premises provides you easy access to necessities. On those nights when you want to eat well and leave the dishes for someone else, enjoy homemade meals and Maine hospitality at the Big Moose Restaurant. $–$$$

Hidden Springs Campground. 224 Central Street; (207) 723–6337 or (888) 685–4488; www.hiddenspring.com. Free hot showers, bike trails, and a swimming pool make this a pleasant place to camp. Pull your RV right in or pop up a tent; either way it's a good spot for exploring Baxter State Park or the Allagash Waterway. $

For More Information

Katahdin Area Chamber of Commerce. (207) 723–4443; www.katahdinmaine.com.

FYI: **Rating the Rapids**

White-water rapids are rated on a scale of 1 to 6, with 6 being the most difficult. The rapids on the Penobscot River range from 3 to 5, with 5 being the Upper Gorge. For a complete listing of licensed outfitters, contact the Maine Department of Inland Fisheries and Wildlife (207–287–8000).

Medway

Medway is a great place to start your family adventure in the Maine woods. If you like to fish, you can find excellent waters for smallmouth bass. Kids can swim and play along the sandy shore of the Penobscot River. Floatplanes will take you for aerial tours, and campgrounds are close by.

A nice public access just up Route 157 leads to a small playground, a boat ramp, and a sandy beach on the eastern branch of the Penobscot River. The water is shallow at shore and grows deeper gradually. River currents are not a problem, even for young children who stay close to the beach. This is a great place to take a break. There's even a country store at the intersection of Routes 157 and 11, just before you get to the parking area for the river access.

Where to Stay

Katahdin Shadows Campgrounds. P.O. Box 606, Medway 04460; (800) 794–5267; www.katahdinshadows.com. Open year-round, this facility caters to campers. Cabins with lofts are also available. Kids will love the arcade, outdoor pool, and playground. The owner can help you make arrangements for trips by plane, canoe, or raft. $

Pine Grove Campground and Cottages. HCR 86, Box 107K, Route 11, Medway 04460; (207) 746–5172; www.mainerec.com/pine grove.html. Open from May 20 to September 30. Fees are inexpensive, and the campground has sites for tenting, RVs, and cabin dwellers. A small store is on the premises. Pets are allowed, and so is swimming in the calm river waters near the campground. This facility is suitable for children, but it's a little rough around the edges (older furnishings and rustic cabins). $

Patten

The Lumbermen's Museum (all ages)

Shin Pond Road, P.O. Box 300, Patten 04765; (207) 528–2650; www.lumbermensmuseum. org. Open Memorial Day to September, Tuesday through Saturday from 9:00 A.M. to 4:00 P.M., Sunday from 11:00 A.M. to 4:00 P.M. The museum stays open through October on weekends only. Admission is free for children 5 and under. $

A working model of a sawmill is part of this museum. Other attractions include a blacksmith shop, old tractors, and artifacts from the logging industry.

Presque Isle

Presque Isle is considered by many to be the heart of Aroostook County. Known to locals as "The County," Aroostook is bigger than Connecticut and Rhode Island combined. Presque Isle is the shopping and entertainment hub for people in this area. Caribou, a city about 11 miles northwest, provides the only other option within miles for what most people consider creature comforts.

The County is not known for its lavish lifestyle. Residents in what is often called potatoland are wholesome, hardworking, down-to-earth people. If you are inclined to visit the working farmlands of the north, Presque Isle is one of your best choices as a home base.

Recreational themes in the Presque Isle region include swimming, playing tennis, skiing, golfing, snowmobiling, hunting, fishing, and camping. Presque Isle doesn't offer numerous attractions for children, at least not in terms of amusement parks, beaches, or zoos. But what you will find in this rural town is a natural environment with modern conveniences.

Aroostook State Park (all ages)

87 State Park Road; (207) 768–8341 or (207) 768–7751. For camping reservations, call (207) 287–3824. Open May 15 through October 15, sunrise to sunset. Free for children 4 and under. $

The park is the main attraction in the Presque Isle area. Hikers will find comfortable trails here. The North Peak Trail covers 1¼ miles, starting at the day-use parking area. Magnificent views abound among the hardwoods and conifers. The North-South Peak Ridge Trail meanders along a ridge between two peaks for a distance of about 1 mile. South Peak Trail is short, less than 1 mile, but it is a rugged walk. The trail is steep and rocky. During winter, enjoy miles of cross-country ski trails.

A lakeside picnic area offers tables, charcoal grills, a swimming area, and a place to change into bathing suits. You can launch your own boat or canoe, or you can rent a canoe, along with needed accessories, to explore the pristine waters within the park.

If you and your family enjoy camping, you will find thirty wooded sites with tables and fireplaces available for tents and camping trailers. Whether you have a day or a week to spend, Aroostook State Park is an excellent choice for families.

Presque Isle Historical Society (ages 6 and up)

16 Third Street; (207) 762–1151; www.katahdin.mfx.net/~pihs. The Estey House Museum is open April through August on Tuesday from 10:00 A.M. to 2:00 P.M. Free admission.

This is a nice place to visit if you're interested in the history of Presque Isle. The society was founded in 1963 to collect items of interest that illustrate life in the Presque Isle region.

Where to Eat

Finding food in Presque Isle is not a problem. If you're in the mood for fast food, you can find everything from tacos to roast beef along the main drag through town. Most major food franchises are represented along this route. Sit-down restaurants are also plentiful.

Mai Tai. 449 Main Street; (207) 764–4426. Offers Polynesian, Chinese, and American cuisine. $

Riverside Inn. 399 Main Street; (207) 764–1447; www.mainerec.com/riversde.shtml. You can get breakfast here all day long. There are seafood specials daily, and other specials like meat loaf on Tuesday, beef stew on Wednesday, and liver 'n' onions on Sunday. $–$$

Winnie's Restaurant and Dairy Bar. 79 Parsons Street; (207) 769–4971. Home of the famous "Winnie's Burger." $$

Where to Stay

Arndt's Aroostook River Lodge and Campground. 95 Parkhurst Siding Road; (207) 764–8677; www.arndtscamp.com. You and your family could have a complete vacation here. You will enjoy swimming, biking, fishing, canoeing, and golfing on an adjacent golf course. There are tent sites and pull-throughs for big rigs. Views from most sites are spectacular. $

The Budget Traveler Motor Lodge. 71 Main Street; (207) 769–0111. Offers sixty-two modern rooms, with laundry facilities and kitchen units. $

Northeastland Hotel. 436 Main Street; (207) 768–5321. Has fifty-one rooms, a restaurant, and a lounge. $

Northern Lights Motel. 72 Houlton Road; (207) 764–4441. Located near the park. $

Presque Isle Inn's Conference Center. 116 Main Street; (207) 764–3321 or (800) 533–3971; www.presqueisleinn.com. Offers 151 rooms, a restaurant, lounge, and indoor pool. Pets are welcome. $

For More Information

Aroostook County Tourism. (888) 216–2463; www.visitaroostook.com.

Presque Isle Chamber of Commerce. (800) 764–7420; www.pichamber.com.

Caribou

Caribou doesn't offer any glitz or glamour, but it does provide a variety of activities for families. The town is a favorite jumping-off point for those interested in visiting Canada or seeing a different part of Maine. In contrast to the Maine coast, Caribou boasts of woods and fields. The economy here centers on agriculture, especially potato farming. You are likely to see more farm tractors than sports cars on the roads.

Outdoor activities, such as fishing, canoeing, and hiking, are popular in this little-known haven in northern Maine.

Check It Out: Winter Fun

If snow is on the ground, consider renting snowmobiles. Gliding across miles of groomed trails is an experience you and your older children will not forget. **Earl's Snowsled Sales and Service,** 595 New Sweden Road (800–451–5281), will set you and your family up with top-quality snowmobiles. A deposit is required, and during peak season reservations are recommended.

Crystal Snowmobile Tours (ages 8 and up)

Fort Fairfield Road, P.O. Box 1448, Caribou 04736; (207) 498–3220; www.mainerec.com/ crystal.shtml. Rates vary according to customized package.

Aroostook County offers more than 1,600 miles of prime trails for your riding pleasure. Distances range from as little as 8 to more than 170 miles.

This company offers tours on more than 1,200 miles of groomed trails. Tour packages include lodging, meals, snowmobiles, and guides.

Caribou Country Club (ages 8 and up)

New Sweden Road, Route 161; (207) 493–3933. $$

This nine-hole, par-72 course offers beautiful scenery and challenging greens. You'll want to avoid the woods and water hazards but not the restaurant and pro shop. Treat yourself to a nice lunch or a new club if you play well. If not, the driving range is open for practice.

Nylander Museum (all ages)

393 Main Street; (207) 493–4209; www.nylandermuseum.org. Open June through September, Tuesday through Sunday, 12:30 to 4:00 P.M. Admission is free.

Highlights of the museum include a mounted moose head, artifacts of early mankind, geological exhibits, butterfly and moth collections, and a section on marine life. An herb garden at the rear of the facility includes herbs once used by Native Americans and those introduced by early colonists. More than eighty herbs are represented.

The Nylander Museum also has one of the finest collections of fossils in the eastern United States.

FYI: **Pet** Motel

If you've brought the family pet along and need a place to leave it while you explore wild, wonderful Caribou, you can board it at Home Farm Kennels on Old Washburn Road (207–498–8803) for $9.50 per day.

Other Things to **See** and **Do**

If you're looking for something fast and fun, spend a Saturday night at the Caribou Motor Speedway (207–498–3309). Watch bombers, late models, and minis race around the ⅕-mile asphalt track. Something more classic and cultural your style? Spend an evening at the Caribou Performing Arts Center (207–493–4278). While the center is part of the local high school, it holds an audience of 800 and hosts nationally acclaimed performers as well as local talent.

Where to Eat

Frederick's Southside Restaurant. 507 Main Street; (207) 498–3464. Another good choice. $

Jade Palace Restaurant. Skyway Plaza; (207) 498–3648. Craving an egg roll? This restaurant can satisfy you. $

Reno's Family Restaurant. 117 Sweden Street; (207) 496–5331. Enjoy breakfast, lunch, or dinner at affordable family rates. When pizza strikes your fancy, it's hard to beat Reno's. $–$$

Where to Stay

Caribou Inn and Convention Center. 19 Main Street; (207) 498–3733 or (800) 235–0466; www.caribouinn.com. A good choice if you want something a bit elegant. There are seventy-three rooms, a restaurant, a lounge, a laundry, an indoor pool, and kitchen units. $–$$

Crown Park Inn. P.O. Box 662, Caribou 04736; (207) 493–3311 or (888) 493–3311; www.mainerec.com/parkinn.shtml. This inn offers sixty-one rooms, free continental breakfast, a weight room, and access to a snowmobile trail. $–$$$

For More Information

Aroostook County Tourism. (888) 216–2463; www.visitarroostook.com.

Caribou Chamber of Commerce. (207) 498–6156 or (800) 722–7648; www.cariboumaine.net.

Central Maine

C entral Maine offers plenty of fun despite the fact it's not known for amusement parks, salt beaches, or mountains. Take your time and enjoy the trip. Augusta, the capital, offers a great museum for you to learn about the state and the ways of life that have made Maine what it is today.

The Maine Wildlife Park in Gray is a wonderful place to conclude your trek to Central Maine. You and your family can enjoy a picnic lunch while seeing wildlife that is indigenous to the state.

Augusta

Augusta, the state capital, is often called the heart of Maine. Its pulse is strong and steady, the tempo unhurried. Situated on the banks of the Kennebec River, Augusta has been a site of commerce since the 1600s, when a Pilgrim trading post was established here. Centuries of growth have transformed the city, making it a center of business with a quality of life that is hard to beat.

Augusta gained status as the capital city in 1827, seven years after the state of Maine was admitted to the Union. Located about 60 miles north of Portland and about 72 miles south of Bangor, Augusta's location makes it the hub of the state. Due to its convenient location and airport, Augusta attracts the attention of businesses and residents in a way that few Maine cities enjoy. There are plenty of hotels and restaurants in the greater Augusta area, and all of them are easy to find. Plan to spend a day or two in Augusta, and enjoy yourself.

Smaller towns, such as Hallowell and Gardiner, lie just outside the city and provide a variety of shopping experiences and history lessons.

CENTRAL MAINE

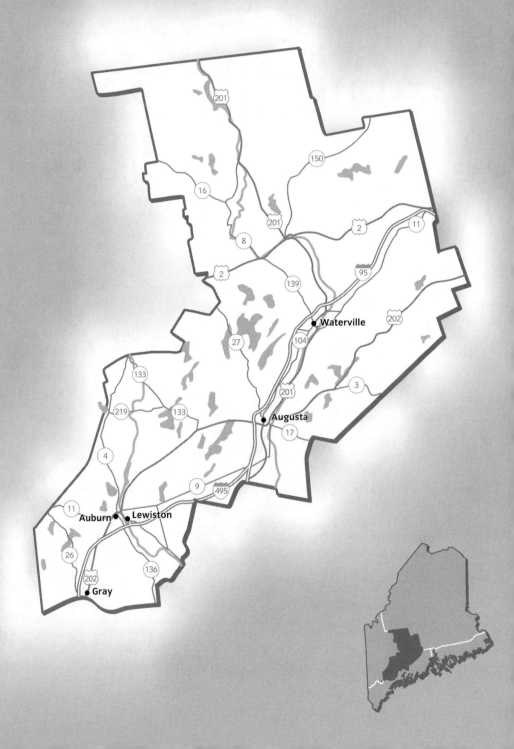

"Whatever" Family Festival (all ages) 🍴 🔒 🎵

Held throughout Augusta, culminating in Capital Park; (207) 623–4559; www.augusta maine.com. No admission fee.

This festival of fun is the equivalent of a whole town having a huge party that lasts for two weeks at the end of June and beginning of July. You've never brought in summer like this before.

There are so many things to do in so many places throughout town another book would be needed just to list them all. Your little ones might get the chance to shake hands or get a hug from Oakie the Oakhurst Acorn, Jimmy Neutron, Sleepy Bear, or "Slugger" the Sea Dog. They could get their faces painted, or you could have a caricature done. They can watch a puppet parade, breakdancing demo, or basketball shooting contest. How about riding in the Family Bike Rodeo, or taking a mini martial art lesson? Let them try tossing a bean bag, running an obstacle course, making bookmarks or tissue flowers, playing old-fashioned children's games, or riding a trolley.

Of course there's always live entertainment, delicious food, and colorful fireworks. You have to see this festival to believe it!

The Maine State Museum (all ages) 🖼️ 🔒

83 State House Station; (207) 287–2301; www.state.me.us/museum. The museum is open Tuesday through Friday from 9:00 A.M. to 5:00 P.M. and Saturday from 10:00 A.M. to 4:00 P.M. Admission is free for children 5 and under. $

Look for the big dome of the State House, and you will have no problem finding the facility. This is the largest museum of history in the state of Maine. Exhibits in the museum reach back 12,000 years into the past. The facility is handicapped accessible, and wheelchairs are available on the premises.

The museum is not extremely large, but it does offer a lot. A gem collection is intriguing. Old cars attract a lot of attention. The history of Maine's lumber industry is a major

Bonnie's
Top Picks for Central Maine

1. Going back in time at Old Fort Western, Augusta; (207) 626–2385.
2. Enjoying *This Land Called Maine* exhibit at the Maine State Museum, Augusta; (207) 287–2301.
3. Playing at the Children's Discovery Museum, Augusta; (207) 622–2209.
4. Seeing the hot-air balloons at the Balloon Festival, Great Falls Plaza, Auburn; (800) 639–6331.
5. Visiting animals at the Maine Wildlife Park, Gray; (207) 657–4977.

Power House: Come on In

Guided tours of the Maine State House are offered Tuesday through Friday from 9:00 A.M. to 1:00 P.M. Enjoy a forty-five-minute tour including the Old Museum, the Hall of Flags, and the House of Representatives and Senate chambers. Orientation lectures are presented in the chambers when the legislature is not in session

topic, as is the procedure used to take ice from Maine's lakes and rivers. Marine life and the fishing industry are represented in the museum. A favorite of children is the natural history section, where you will find life-size mounts of many of Maine's animals. Even the textile industry is shown in a real-world environment. You and your family can spend hours investigating all of the interesting exhibits and still have time to visit the Children's Discovery Museum.

Samantha Smith Memorial (all ages) 🏛
Maine State Capitol Complex, Augusta.

If you're visiting the Maine State Museum or the Maine State House, don't miss this memorial. In December 1982, ten-year-old Samantha Smith from Manchester, Maine, wrote Yuri Andropov a congratulatory letter regarding his appointment as Soviet premier. In the letter she confided her fears and concerns about nuclear war and strained relations between the United States and Russia. Andropov responded to the letter with an invitation to Samantha and her family to visit him and experience his culture firsthand. Samantha died in a 1985 plane crash, but her voice still rings strong, showing that one little girl can make a difference.

Amazing
Maine Facts

Maine's state motto is *Dirigo*, which means "I direct" or "I lead."

Amazing
Maine Facts

Maine was admitted to the Union on March 15, 1820, as part of the Missouri Compromise. Maine, a free state, being admitted along with Missouri, a slave state, kept the number of free and slave states equal.

The Children's Discovery Museum (ages 2 to 10)
265 Water Street; (207) 622–2209; www.ohwy.com/me/c/chidismu.htm. Open weekdays during the summer from 9:00 A.M. to 4:00 P.M., Saturday from 10:00 A.M. to 4:00 P.M., and Sunday from 1:00 to 4:00 P.M. Winter hours are Tuesday through Thursday 9:00 A.M. to 4:00 P.M., and Friday 9:00 A.M. to 8:00 P.M. In the fall, Friday from 6:30 to 8:00 P.M. is Family Festival with special activities. Free for children under 1. $

This museum emphasizes a hands-on approach to learning and having fun. Most of the exhibits are for younger children, up through fifth grade. Children can partake in real-life scenarios, such as a diner, a grocery store, and a post office. They can enjoy workshops, arts and crafts demonstrations, family festivals, and birthday parties.

Special programs such as science workshops, performing arts, and family events are scheduled on a regular basis.

Old Fort Western (all ages)
16 Cony Street; (207) 626–2385; www.oldfortwestern.org. Open May through October with special events every Sunday afternoon. Admission is free for children 5 and under. $$

Constructed in 1754, this National Historic Landmark is New England's oldest surviving wooden fort.

Kids will get a real sense of history from costumed interpreters demonstrating military, community, and family life in the 1700s. The blast of a musket fired during a military drill or war encampment might surprise them. Sweet smells from the kitchen will make them hungry, and they'll savor the taste of homemade bread toasted by the open fire and topped with freshly churned butter. They'll see the modest toys of the time and play games enjoyed by children long ago.

Check It Out: One of the Best

The Maine State Museum is one of the most visited museums in Maine, and for good reason. Its exhibits are award-winning, and it is rated as an "outstanding" attraction by AAA.

A Merrill Family Advenure:
Lessons Learned

As a parent, I have to admit I don't always give my kids enough credit, so the impression left on my oldest daughter after visiting Fort Western surprised me. During our trip back in time, we tried out a rope bed, helped "toast" bread over an open fire, and learned games children played in the 1700s. For weeks she talked of how grateful she was for all she has as a child of today. She even took better care of her toys—for a while, anyway.

I also learned a lesson. A 208-year-old clock, with no minute or second hand, showed me that in the 1700s knowing the exact time was not important—all that mattered was the hour. For weeks I tried to be less conscious of time, less ruled by the clock. I didn't even get upset when we were running a few minutes late—for a while, anyway.

The Blaine House (all ages)
192 State Street; (207) 287–2121 (general information) or (207) 287–2301 (tour reservation). Public tours are available Tuesday, Wednesday, and Thursday from 2:00 to 4:00 P.M. except during special events. Call to confirm tour dates. Free.

Built in 1833 as the family home of presidential candidate James G. Blaine, the Blaine House has been the official residence of Maine governors since 1919. A tour of this twenty-eight-room mansion will teach your children about architecture and show them a different type of Maine history.

The Civic Center (all ages)
76 Community Drive; (207) 626–2405; www.augustaciviccenter.org. $$–$$$$

In addition to the auditorium, which can hold 7,000 people, the facility can accommodate 500 diners in the Augusta Room. Events at the Civic Center range from musical concerts to conventions and exhibitions. Check the schedule of events.

Amazing
Maine Facts

Maine has sixteen counties, twenty-two cities, 435 towns, thirty-two plantations, 422 unorganized townships, and three Native American voting districts.

Amazing
Maine Facts

Maine's flag is the state's coat of arms on a blue field. It was adopted by the legislature in 1909.

Pine Tree State Arboretum (all ages)

Corner of Hospital Street and Piggery Road; (207) 621–0031. Guided tours available. $

This 200-acre arboretum is blooming with flora and fauna and fun. Enjoy hiking, biking, picnicking, or bird-watching among various trees, shrubs, and plants that make the air sweet and the landscape beautiful. Many of the seedlings were planted for educational and scientific purposes, but you'll also find sixty-eight white pine trees planted in honor of each of Maine's governors.

Where to Eat

Augusta offers a smorgasbord of eating establishments. All the major fast-food chains are represented, mostly along Western Avenue.

Augusta House of Pancakes. 100 Western Avenue; (207) 623–9775. Looking for a hearty breakfast? Look no further. $

The Ground Round. 110 Community Drive; (207) 623–0022. A fine family eatery. $–$$

Hattie's Chowder House. 103 Water Street, Hallowell; (207) 621–4114 or (877) 621–4114; www.hattieslobsterstew.com. Located in the next town over from Augusta, Hallowell, Hattie's is worth mentioning just for the lobster stew. If you're staying locally, they'll even deliver their stew to your door. Open seven days a week, serving lunch and dinner. $

Margaritas. 390 Western Avenue; (207) 622–7874. Outstanding Mexican dishes. Happy hour from 4:00 to 7:00 P.M. $$

Capital **Entertainment**

Nature lovers and history buffs will relish a stroll through the Cony Cemetery, where eighteenth century slate headstones bear interesting epitaphs. A walk through Monument Park, the mustering ground for the area's Civil War troops, will unearth war memorials from five different wars. Those looking for more up-to-date activities can skate around **Kennebec Ice Arena** (207–622–6354) or hit the alley at **Interstate Bowling Center** (207–623–6000).

Where to Stay

Comfort Inn. 281 Civic Center Drive; (800) 228–5150 or (207) 623–1000. Here you will enjoy comfortable accommodations, a restaurant, a lounge, a health club, and an indoor swimming pool. $–$$

Econolodge. 390 Western Avenue; (888) 63–MAINE or (207) 622–6371. Offers 128 rooms, an outdoor pool, and **free** continental breakfast. $

Holiday Inn. 110 Community Drive; (207) 622–4751. Offers a fitness center, a restaurant, and a lounge at rates that won't ruin your vacation. $–$$

Senator Inn's Spa. 284 Western Avenue; (207) 622–5804 or (877) 772–2224; www.senatorinn.com. A great place if you're looking for a bit of luxury. You can take advantage of elegant rooms and suites, award-winning dining, a fitness center, sauna, heated pool, hot tub, and nature trails for walking or jogging. Rates are a bit higher, but not as high as you might expect. Kids 18 and under stay for **free.** $–$$$

For More Information

Kennebec Valley Chamber of Commerce. (207) 623–4559; www.augustamaine.com.

Waterville

The thriving small Maine community of Waterville is located 20 miles northeast of Augusta. Museums, cruises, golf, and theater can be found within its borders. Another attraction in Waterville is Colby College, founded in 1813. The beautiful campus is worth a visit. Several lakes, snowmobiling trails, and more are within driving distance.

The Waterville Opera House (ages 7 and up) 🎵
93 Main Street; office (207) 873–5361, tickets (207) 873–7000; www.operahouse.com. Ticket prices vary by performance. $$–$$$

Built in 1902, and originally called the City Opera House, this theater has had its share of ups and downs. Strong in its early days, it suffered during the vaudeville days and even closed for a short time in the 1950s. Today, however, the opera house is alive and well. Come in, sit down, and enjoy local, national, and international performances.

Photo Op

Two-Cent Bridge in Waterville is the last known toll footbridge in the country. Bring the camera and some change.

Amazing
Maine Facts

Colby College was the first all-male college to offer admission to women. Mary Low enrolled at Colby in 1871. She graduated four years later, valedictorian of her class.

Colby College Museum of Art (ages 6 and up)
5600 Mayflower Hill Drive; (207) 872–3228; www.colby.edu/museum. Open Monday through Saturday 10:00 A.M. to 4:30 P.M., Sunday 2:00 to 4:30 P.M. Admission is free.

While you're strolling the beautiful campus, this museum is worth a peek. It houses a permanent collection of eighteenth-, nineteenth-, and twentieth-century American art. There are also many temporary exhibit programs, gallery talks, lectures, and receptions, which the general public is welcome to attend.

Where to Eat

Buen Apetito. 4 Chaplin Street; (207) 861–4649. A fiesta of authentic Mexican food. Fire it up a notch with their fresh salsa. Add a homemade desserts and you'll need a siesta after this fiesta. $–$$

Killarney's Restaurant. 375 Main Street; (207) 873–0111; www.holiday-inn.com. Located in the Waterville Holiday Inn, it's a great place to eat even if you're not staying. You can get something extravagant like beef tenderloin stuffed with lobster or something simple like a sandwich. $$–$$$

Where to Stay

Comfort Inn & Suites. 332 Main Street; (207) 873–2777; www.choicehotels.com. One- and two-bedroom suites include a complimentary hot breakfast, a fitness room, and an indoor heated pool. $–$$

Holiday Inn. 375 Main Street; (207) 873–0111; www.holiday-inn.com. A full service hotel in the heart of Maine. Enjoy in-house movies, coffeemaker, and Nintendo for the kids. Take advantage of the pool, hot tub, sauna, and fitness center. $$–$$$

For More Information

Mid-Maine Chamber of Commerce. (207) 873–3315; www.midmainechamber.com.

Par Tee:
Pick a Club

You have a couple choices if you want to practice your swing: Pine Ridge Municipal Golf (207–873–0474) or Waterville Country Club (207–465–9861).

Lewiston/Auburn

The city of Auburn lies along the banks of the Androscoggin River. A bridge connects Auburn with its sister city, Lewiston. The Lewiston-Auburn area is the second largest population center in the state. The L/A area, as it is called by local residents, is not rich in recreational activities within the city limits, but both cities are positioned to give travelers access to outlying areas. For example, there are five major ski areas within two hours. The Oxford Plains Speedway is less than an hour away. Augusta, the capital city, is only a short drive up the Maine Turnpike, and L. L. Bean in Freeport is about thirty minutes away.

Lewiston: **Rich and Recognized**

Lewiston is rich in French Canadian heritage and is one of "The 100 Best Small Arts Towns in America" (according to John Villani's book of the same name).

Lewiston's first official settlement was established in 1770. A single cabin was constructed by Paul Hidreth of Dracut, Massachusetts, on the east side of the Androscoggin River. By 1795 the town was officially incorporated. The population grew to more than 1,000 residents by the year 1810. In 1861 Lewiston was incorporated as a city, with a population in excess of 5,000.

The development of Auburn was not as simple as that of Lewiston. Auburn went through many name changes. The city began as Bakersville, changed to Poland, then to Minot. Finally, in 1869, the name Auburn was chosen. At the time of its incorporation, Auburn was made up of settlements covering more than 66 square miles. This made Auburn one of the largest cities in the United States.

The Great Falls waterfall, created by the Androscoggin River, drops 54 feet and can be seen from the bridge that connects the two cities. Lewiston was first to harness the power of Great Falls. A long canal created for Lewiston was instrumental in making the city an important center in the textile industry.

Auburn became known for a different industry. In 1836 it became home to the first organized shoe company in the state. The Minot Shoe Company was established in West Auburn and took advantage of the railroad system. In 1865 approximately 600,000 pairs of shoes were made. This number grew to more than six million by 1900.

Around 1905 a dam was built above the falls that provided Auburn with plenty of power. Within fifteen years, Auburn was the fifth largest shoe manufacturing center in the country. Growth was fast and good. However, during the depression of the 1930s, the sister cities suffered terribly and never fully recovered. Today, the region is adapting to the new rigors of economic success.

If you and your family enjoy lakeside picnics or dynamite bass fishing, check out Lake Auburn. This large, deep lake is located about 2 miles outside Auburn, on Route 4. Bass and salmon are the two major attractions for anglers. Recreational boating is another attraction, as is the public swimming at the outlet of the lake. Taylor Pond, near Young's Corner, is another spot where public swimming is allowed.

FYI: **Housing Pets**

If you need a place to board your pet while you're in the L/A area, call Central Maine Veterinary Hospital, R.R. 3, Box 630, Auburn (207–225–2726). The center comprises a boarding kennel and veterinary hospital.

There is a variety of outdoor activities in the area. Rates in Lewiston-Auburn are affordable, and accommodations are comfortable and plentiful. The twin cities are well worth a look when you're touring the state of Maine.

Lost Valley Ski Area (ages 6 and up)
Lost Valley Road, P.O. Box 260, Auburn 04210; (207) 784–1561; www.lostvalleyski.com. Rates vary depending on sport. Children 5 and under ski free with paying adult.

Within about 2 miles of the L/A area, you will find good slopes and one of the largest and best learn-to-ski schools in the state. You can ski day or night and take advantage of fifteen trails that range from beginner to expert. Everything you need to hit the slopes can be rented on-site. You'll find a cafeteria, a restaurant, and a lounge. Cross-country skiing is also available.

Lost Valley also offers paintball (the only one in Lewiston/Auburn) and mountain biking. A day of paintball consists of a variety of games, each lasting twenty-five to forty-five minutes. You'll play single- and double-objective games as well as speedball. There's also recreational paintball in the woods. Equipment can be rented on the premises, and kids must be 10 to play.

Come for mountain biking in early May through November. Ride from dawn to dusk. You'll need a trail access ticket that costs $3.00, but it's an all-day pass.

Auburn Municipal Beach (all ages)
Lake Auburn Outlet, Route 4, Auburn; (207) 784–0191. Open to the general public seven days a week 10:00 A.M. to 7:00 P.M. mid-June to mid-August. Call for entrance fee information. Free parking.

Secluded by a wall of evergreens, this beach is the only place where swimming is permitted in Lake Auburn. The beach is staffed by a certified lifeguard for your safety and features a water slide and diving board for your fun. The park has a playground, a basketball court, a horseshoe pit, volleyball courts, and an open field for soccer and Frisbee.

Barbecue grills enable you to easily prepare your own fare, or grab a bite at the new concession stand. Rest room facilities are also on the premises for your comfort and convenience.

FYI: **Tiger to Be**

If golf is your game, there are plenty of great courses to choose from throughout Maine. The Golf Maine Association (207–883–9160; www.golfme.com) can list them all for you. Play them all and you just might give Tiger a little competition.

College Street Driving Range and Mini Golf (ages 2 and up)

601 College Street, Lewiston; (207) 786–7818. Open 10:00 A.M. to dark from April 1 through the end of May, 9:00 A.M. to 9:00 P.M. through late October. $–$$

Test your golfing skills on twenty-five artificial grass tees and twenty-five grass tees. There are three target greens, a video training facility, a practice sand bunker, and golf supplies and repairs. There are even lights for golfing after the sun goes down.

Ingersoll Arena/Pettengill Park (all ages)

48 Pettengill Road, Auburn; (207) 795–6375 (arena) or (207) 784–0191 (park). Arena open October through mid-March. Park open dawn to dusk year-round. $$

Ingersoll Arena, located within Pettengill Park, offers public ice-skating, and local hockey games. The park itself is forty acres right in the middle of town. Here you'll find a number of fields ranging from baseball to soccer, tennis courts, jogging trails, and three different playgrounds. There are also horseshoe pits, a pond, and a concession stand. Can't find anything to do outside? The Hasty Community Center is also located within the park.

Spare-Time Recreation (ages 4 and up)

729 Main Street, Lewiston; (207) 786–2695. Open 9:00 A.M. to 11:00 P.M. most days during the summer. $

This bowling alley offers thirty-four lanes of tenpin, auto scoring, and bumpers for the little ones—a nice way to spend an evening with the family. Also home to Porter's Family Restaurant in case bowling all those strikes works up an appetite.

Taber's Driving Range and Miniature Golf (ages 4 and up)

473 Lake Shore Drive, Auburn; (207) 784–2521. Open 10:00 A.M. to 9:00 P.M. mid-April through mid-September. $

After you play one round of minigolf, to play again only costs a buck. Another option for golf fans. In addition to a driving range, this facility offers miniature golf—a good alternative for young pros.

Twin Cities Air Services, Inc. (all ages)

Auburn-Lewiston Airport, 81 Airport Drive, Auburn; (207) 782–3882 or (800) 564–3882; www.flymaine.com. $$$$

If you're adventuresome, you can soar high above the twin cities. But more than just getting a scenic fight from this air service, you'll actually get to fly the plane! Several packages are offered ranging from $40 to $60—very reasonable for a half hour of flight time and the chance to fly an airplane. The super deluxe package also gets you an aviation T-shirt and ball cap, a log book recording your first flight, a photo of you and the plane, and a certificate.

Thorncrag Bird Sanctuary (all ages)

Highland Spring Road and Montello Street, Lewiston; (207) 782–5238; www.avcnet.org/ stanton/thorncrg.htm.

For a more down-to-earth adventure, you and your children can explore the 230 acres of one of the largest bird sanctuaries in New England.

Great Falls Annual Balloon Festival (all ages)

Great Falls Plaza, Auburn; general information (800) 639–6331, balloon ride hot line (207) 782–2637; www.greatfallsballoonfestival.org. The third weekend of August. Free parking at the Auburn Mall and Auburn Plaza with trolley rides into Great Falls Plaza and various festival events. Champagne balloon rides are $150 per person.

Carnival rides open on Thursday night, but the festival really kicks off with a 6:00 A.M. balloon launch on Friday (weather permitting). Balloon launches are typically at 6:00 A.M. and 5:30 P.M. Even if a romantic champagne balloon ride is out of the question, you'll thrill to the spectacle of dozens of colorful balloons soaring overhead. Don't miss Moon Glows on Friday and Saturday evenings: Tethered hot air balloons lit up with propane are on display.

Although hot air balloons are the highlight of the festival, there are plenty of things to keep you and the kids entertained on the ground. If you're hungry, make your way to a pancake breakfast; at supper enjoy the lobster/clambake. Watch a parade, stock car racing, or live entertainment. Test your skill at the climbing wall, your courage on the carnival rides, or your luck at bingo. There are also walking tours and various children's activities. It's great fun for the whole family.

Check It Out

Bates College, founded in 1855, was the first coeducational college in the East. Today it is ranked among the country's top twenty liberal arts colleges. Take a campus tour and visit the Carnegie Science Hall, the Ladd Library, and the college chapel (modeled after King's College Chapel, Cambridge University). You'll also enjoy the Olin Arts Center, which houses an art museum and a concert hall offering popular Tuesday noon concerts. Check out the Web site at www.bates.edu, or call (207) 786–6255 for more information.

Where to Eat

Eli's Restaurant. Turner Highlands Country Club, P.O. Box 28, Green 04236; (207) 224–7090. If you're in the mood for a more adult setting, visit Eli's, situated on a nine-hole golf course that is open to the public. Remember to pack your clubs along with your appetite. The menu features char-roasted rack of lamb, grilled bacon-wrapped filet mignon, and sea scallop sauté. $–$$

Georgio's Pizza & Donut Shop. 740 Minot Avenue; (207) 783–2981. Pizza and doughnuts may seem like a strange combination, but don't knock it until you've tried it. Doughnuts are on the menu, but pizza is the specialty. $

The Ground Round. 180 Center Street; (207) 784–1200. Features steak, barbecued ribs, chicken, salads, and fresh seafood. Children pay by the pound on Tuesday and Thursday. And, oh, don't overlook the free popcorn; your children will love it. $

The Heartland Restaurant. 20 East Avenue, Lewiston; (207) 784–3688. Chicken, steak, seafood, salads, and eighty-one dessert choices are just part of the menu. Kids' meals are available and served cheerfully. This is a true family-style restaurant. $

Lisbon Street Dairy Joy. 133 Lisbon Street, Lewiston; (207) 784–3245. An excellent place for frozen yogurt and hand-dipped ice cream. Cakes and pies also available. $

Luiggi's Pizzeria. 63 Sabattus Street, Lewiston; (207) 782–0701. Great pizza. Open seven days a week, until midnight from Sunday through Thursday, 1:00 A.M. on Friday and Saturday. $

Mac's Grill. 1052 Minot Avenue; (207) 783–6885; www.macsgrill.com. Steak and seafood at budget prices. $

Margaritas. 838 Lisbon Street, Lewiston; (207) 782–6036. Features steak and Mexican dishes. $$

Where to Stay

Regardless of what side of the river you decide is best for your home base, you can find comfortable lodging.

Other Things to **See** and **Do**

Municipal facilities for recreation are numerous. Try local YMCAs and YWCAs. The Lewiston Multi-Purpose Center is another recreational option. There are about thirty public tennis courts, twenty baseball fields, five outdoor hockey rinks, five outdoor swimming pools, and several soccer fields.

For another kind of outdoor fun, take a walking tour of Lewiston. There are one hundred stops highlighting the town's history. Great Falls, on the Androscoggin River, is one of them. In Auburn take a hike to Mount Apatite. During the summer enjoy two great festivals: the Bates Dance Festival (207–786–6381) and the Festival de Joie (207–782–6231; www.festivaldejoie.org).

Fireside Inn's Suites. 1777 Washington Street; (207) 777–1777. Features recently renovated rooms (both smoking and non-smoking), outdoor pool, full-service restaurant, and lounge. Children 12 and under stay **free.** $

Ramada Conference Center. 490 Pleasant Street, Lewiston; (207) 784–2331. A sauna, whirlpool tub, heated pool, large suites, king-size beds, cable TV, and in-room movies are just some of the features. There is on-site entertainment every night of the week, and the rates will not break your budget. Rates include a deluxe continental breakfast. $$

Super 8 Motel. 1440 Lisbon Street, Lewiston; (800) 843–1991 or (207) 784–8882. Offers nonsmoking rooms with cable TV, **free** local calls, king-size beds, and recliners at affordable rates. $

Travel Inn. 1968 Lisbon Road, Lewiston; (207) 784–5476. Offers an outdoor pool, cable TV, air-conditioning, and a laundry room. $

For More Information

Androscoggin County Chamber of Commerce. (207) 783–2249; www.androscoggincounty.com.

Gray

Just a short drive south of Auburn is Gray, an out-of-the-way town that anyone with kids who love animals should take the time to visit. Since this area is off the beaten path, not many tourists come through here. They don't know what they're missing.

Maine Wildlife Park (all ages)

Route 26; (207) 657–4977. Open 9:30 A.M. to 4:30 P.M. daily from mid-April through Veterans Day. Guided tours on Saturday from 11:00 A.M. to 1:00 P.M. and wildlife programs on Sunday from 1:00 until 3:00 P.M. Admission is **free** for children 4 and under. Guided tours are an additional $1.00 per person. $

Although the park offers structured events that guarantee a good time, you and the kids are free to roam about the grounds any day during the operating season.

When you enter the game farm, you'll drive past picnic tables under a pine canopy. Chain-link fence enclosures on both sides of the road behind the picnic areas reveal the protected inhabitants: coyotes, foxes, skunks, pheasant, and vultures, to name a few.

You'll also find white-tailed deer, black bear, and moose compounds (you can feed the deer).

After chasing the kids back up the hill, stop at the bird pens to see turkeys, pheasant, and peacocks. Then head down to the fish hatchery. No fishing gear is allowed, but food is available for feeding the trout.

Amazing
Maine Facts

Gray is the site of America's first woolen mill.

The paved paths are stroller-friendly, but some of the hills are a little steep. Access is good for the most part. The animals here are essentially wards of the state, waiting to be reintroduced to the wild or living out their lives here in relative comfort.

For More Information

Gray Business Association. (207) 657–7000; www.gbamaine.org.

Western Maine

addle a canoe on a glassy lake, or hike to a mountain summit yielding spectacular views. Drive down country lanes, shaded by trees painted with autumn colors, or stroll through historic museums. Snowboard awesome verticals by day, or thrill to a downhill run at night. In any season, western Maine has a lot to offer both nature lovers and adventure seekers. Yet it is often overlooked by travelers.

You don't want to ignore the state's western lakes and mountains. Although not as vast as the north country, western Maine offers plenty of outdoor activities amid the beauty of unspoiled wilderness. Fun for the kids abounds here as well. There are towns to visit, like South Paris, Norway, and Naples, and much to be seen from Bethel to Rangeley.

Sebago Lake Region

The Sebago Lake Region encompasses the towns of **Casco**, **Raymond**, **North Windham**, and **Naples**, as well as **Sebago Lake**, **Sebago**, and **North** and **East Sebago**. Sebago Lake is the hub of the area and at 46 square miles is Maine's second largest lake. The lake is a source of pleasure for both boaters and anglers. It was here that a lucky angler reeled in the state's record catch for landlocked salmon (20–plus pounds).

Photo Op: Burning Bridges

There are nine covered bridges in Maine. Babb's Bridge, spanning the Presumpscot River in Windham, is the oldest. A National Historic Site, the bridge was built in 1856 by seven men who were paid less than $78 apiece. Destroyed by arsonists in 1973, the bridge has since been rebuilt.

WESTERN MAINE

Carrabassett Valley

Rangeley
Rangeley Lake

Mooselook-meguntic Lake

Phillips

Byron ● ● Weld

White Mountain National Forest

Bethel

West Paris ●

South Paris
Norway

Harrison
Bridgton

Fryeburg

Naples

Sebago Lake

Windham

While in the area, you can view glass and ceramics from around the world at a local museum. Enjoy a day at the state park, and climb to the top of Douglas Mountain for picture-perfect views of the lake. If you like snapping pictures, Babb's Bridge in Windham is a good subject.

Sebago Lake State Park (all ages)

Located just off Route 302 between Casco and Naples; (207) 693–6613 June 20 through Labor Day, (207) 693–6231 after Labor Day through June 19. Open May 1 through October 15. $

Basically a day-use area, Sebago Lake State Park offers beaches (with lifeguards), bathhouses, tables, grills, and, of course, the lake. A separate campground has its own beach. There are guided tours along nature trails and presentations in an amphitheater. Camping is available.

Seacoast Fun/Snow Park (all ages)

932 Roosevelt Trail, Windham; (207) 892–5952. Snow Park admission varies. Fun Park admission offers options such as the Multi-Pass or the Max-Pass. You can also purchase individual tickets for certain attractions. $$–$$$

Nestled in the Sebago Lakes region, this recreation park offers everything from miniature golf and bumper boats to a slingshot trampoline and Skymax, 100 feet of free-fall fun. During winter months there's snow tubing and snowboarding.

Bonnie's
Top Ten Picks for Western Maine

1. Relaxing at Sebago Lake State Park, Sebago Lake; (207) 693–6613.
2. Cruising on the *Songo River Queen II,* Naples; (207) 693–6861.
3. Enjoying the Fryeburg Fair, Fryeburg; (207) 935–3268.
4. Catching a concert at Deertrees Theatre, Harrison; (207) 583–6747.
5. Mining gems in Perham's quarries, West Paris; (207) 674–2341.
6. Trekking with llamas at Telemark Inn and Llama Farm, Bethel; (207) 836–2703.
7. Panning for gold along the Swift River, Byron; (800) 685–2537.
8. Picnicking in Rangeley Lake State Park, Rangeley; (207) 864–3858.
9. Playing at the Big Adventure Center, Bethel; (207) 824–0929.
10. Turbo tubing at Sugarloaf/USA, Kingfield; (800) 843–5623.

A Merrill Family Adventure: **Stunned**

The first time I swam in a lake we were spending the day at Sebago Lake celebrating my husband's grandparents' fiftieth anniversary. After we hiked, fished, and ate, family members started jumping, one by one, from some nearby rocks into the lake. It looked like fun, so I jumped in too, forgetting my southern blood (I'm originally from Virginia). I was so stunned by the cold water that I nearly drowned. My husband literally had to jump in and save me.

Douglas Hill Orchard (all ages)

Orchard Road, Route 107, Sebago; (207) 787–2745. Open sunrise to sundown through October.

A great place to stop if you're visiting the area in late summer or early fall. Pick delicious apples at the orchard, located in the foothills of the White Mountains. Enjoy weekend hayrides. If you come in October, pick pumpkins instead of apples. Apple cider is available all season.

After experiencing the great outdoors and munching some healthy fruit, you might want to take a little hike. The Douglas Hill trails, located nearby, will accommodate you.

Chunky's Cinema (all ages)

765 Roosevelt Trail, Windham; (207) 892–6677, movie hotline (207) 892–4777; www.chunkysmaine.com. $$

Feel like dinner and a movie? Chunky's will save you time and money. You'll get more than popcorn with your flick, and ordering can be fun. How about Wizard of Ozzarella Sticks for starters? Then try the Kevin Bacon Burger, the Charlton Heston Chicken, or the Dom DeLuise Delight. End the show with an Any Given Sundae Brownie, or Strawberry Fields Forever Shortcake.

A **Peak** Experience

When the weather is good and the sky is clear, a stroll to the top of Sebago's Douglas Mountain is a good idea. The hiking trail is child-friendly and should take less than thirty minutes. Once you reach the 1,415-foot peak, you'll discover a stone tower offering views that stretch from the Atlantic to New Hampshire's White Mountains.

Where to Stay

Aimhi Lodge. 14 Aimhi Woods Road, North Windham; (207) 892–6538; www.aimhilodge.com. Since 1919 this family lodge has been beckoning guests to come in and stay awhile. Here you'll find twenty-three cozy cottages along the shore of Little Sebago Lake, complete with screened porches, fireplaces, and docks. Enjoy water sports, backyard sports, and three home-cooked meals each day. Two high points are the Friday Night Lobster Bake and the supervised children's activities. A great place for families. Accommodations are by the week. $$$$

Point Sebago Resort. 261 Point Sebago Road, Casco; (207) 655–3821 or (800) 530–1555; www.pointsebago.com. This 775-acre resort is located on the shores of Sebago Lake. Enjoy all kinds of water sports. Play on one of ten tennis courts or the eighteen-hole championship golf course. There are supervised children's programs and nightly entertainment. Families can even join in for songs around the campfire. Rates vary, but Family Fun Value Weeks help families save. $–$$$$

For More Information

Greater Windham Chamber of Commerce. (207) 892–8265; www.windhamchamber.sebagolake.org.

Naples

Naples is a boaters' paradise. The Songo Locks, which date back to 1830, are a series of twenty-seven hand-operated locks that once connected Portland and Harrison. Although the lock system is no longer used for transportation, it does provide 50 miles of waterway for recreational boating. Golfing (both regular and miniature), tennis, windsurfing, parasailing, and antiquing are some of the activities in the Naples area.

Songo River Queen II (all ages)
Route 302, on the Causeway, P.O. Box 1226, Naples 04055; (207) 693–6861 (summer) or (207) 929–4705 (winter). Operates daily from July through Labor Day. Call for schedule in June and September. Ticket prices vary depending on length and time of cruise. $$

This 90-foot stern-wheeler riverboat is one of the biggest attractions in the Naples area. You and your family can enjoy a one- or two-and-a-half-hour ride. Your destination is Brady Pond, which you reach through the only surviving lock from the 1830 Songo Locks.

Steamboat Landing Miniature Golf (ages 4 and up)
Route 114, Naples; (207) 693–6782; www.steamboatlandingminigolf.com. Open daily 10:00 A.M. to 10:00 P.M. May through Labor Day, weekends only September and October. Children under 5 play free with paying adult. $–$$

Play putt-putt on an eighteen-hole course surrounded by gardens and shaded by oaks and pines. Going through this course is like taking a trip through the Pine Tree State and its history. You'll see a lighthouse, Old Fort Western, and a covered bridge.

Cruisin' Songo Lake

Mailboat rides on Songo Lake (207–693–6861 summer, 207–929–4705 winter) are available Monday through Saturday. The trips run from the last Saturday of June through the Saturday before Labor Day. This pontoon-style boat does not have toilet facilities, and rides last between one and two-and-a-half hours, so it may not be a good idea to take this trip with young children.

Grab a bite at the snack bar after your game is done, or cool down with some Gifford's ice cream at the new ice parlor. Don't worry if bad weather stops you from finishing your game. Steamboat offers rain checks for just such occasions.

Where to Eat

Flight Deck Restaurant. On the Causeway, Naples; (207) 693–3508. A Naples tradition for many years. You can enjoy your meal on the lakeside deck while watching all the activity on Long Lake. On hot days you might choose to dine indoors. The varied menu promises something for everyone, and the kids get a menu of their own. $

Where to Stay

The Augustus Bove House. Located at the corner of Routes 302 and 114, R.R. 1 Box 501, Naples 04055; (207) 693–6365 or (888) 806–6249; www.naplesmaine.com. Here you will enjoy a hearty breakfast and lake-view rooms. $–$$$

The Bay of Naples Campground. Route 114/11, Box 240N, Naples 04055; (800) 348–9750 or (207) 693–6429; www.bayof naples.com. Geared to families, this camp-ground offers 150 shady campsites, trailer hookups, a sandy beach, hot showers, laundry facilities, and a wide array of recreational activities. Two playgrounds, table tennis, pool

Other Things to See and Do

Golf enthusiasts should check out the Naples Country Club on Route 114 (207–693–6424). Tennis fanatics can turn to Brady Pond Camps on old Route 114 (207–693–3129). Horseback riding can be arranged at Secret Acres Stables at 670 Lambs Mill Road (207–693–3441).

tables, volleyball courts, horseshoe pits, badminton, and an adjoining public golf course are all available here. Swimming, fishing, hayrides, waterskiing, and boat and canoe rentals also available. $

Inn at Long Lake. P.O. Box 806, Lake House Road, Naples 04055; (207) 693–6226 or (800) 437–0328; www.innatlonglake.com. Built in 1906, the Inn at Long Lake has sixteen guest rooms decorated in early-twentieth-century elegance. A buffet continental breakfast is included. Ask about special murder-mystery weekend packages. $–$$$$

For More Information

Naples Business Association. (207) 693–3285; www.napleschamber.com.

Bridgton

Bridgton offers several good places to take a dip and cool off during the hot weeks of Maine's summer. Sound refreshing? Check out the beach on Long Lake. You'll find it just off Main Street. Two other freshwater beaches in the area are Woods Lake on Route 117 and Highland Lake right on the edge of town. All are **free**, fun, and easy to find.

The area offers other activities for children, but most of what you will find is aimed at older children and adults.

The Cool Moose (all ages)

63 Main Street; (207) 647–3957; www.thecoolmoose.com.

The Cool Moose is a cool place. Christened Maine's original moose store, the clothing, belts, leather goods, toys, and crafts you will find here all celebrate our state's unofficial mascot. Muddy Duddy and Maynard Moose, Sebago the Loon, and Harry Bear are soft, cuddly creatures that will attract the kids. Magnets, stickers, T-shirts, and sweatshirts are fun gifts to get for yourself.

The Bridgton Historical Society Museum and Narramissic
(ages 8 and up) 🧩

Gibbs Avenue; (207) 647–3699; www.megalink.net/~bhs. The museum is open Monday through Saturday 1:00 to 3:00 P.M. in July and August. Narramissic is open Wednesday through Sunday from 1:00 to 4:30 P.M. in July and August. Admission is free, but donations are accepted.

Founded in 1953, the Bridgton Historical Society operates a museum and research center in downtown Bridgton, as well as Narramissic, the nineteenth-century restored Peabody-Fitch House, which includes a working blacksmith shop, in South Bridgton. The collection includes a 1911 Sears "horseless carriage" and slides of the old narrow-gauge railroad that used to run in these parts. The museum is located in the former fire station.

Bridgton Highlands Country Club (ages 5 and up)

Highland Ridge Road, R.R. 3 Box 1065, Bridgton 04009; (207) 647–3491; www.bridgton highlands.com. Open from sunrise to sunset April to November. $$$–$$$$

Shoppers Corner:
Maine Goods from A to T

"A" is for the antiques you'll find at Favorite Past-Time Antiques (207–647–4486; www.maine-antiques.com). "T" is for the original Maine T-shirts at Sportshaus, 61 Main Street (207–647–5100). It's open from 9:00 A.M. to 5:00 P.M. Friday and Saturday only.

An eighteen-hole golf course and four tennis courts are open to the public. A junior golf program for children 5 to 16 is held on Wednesday throughout July and August.

Shawnee Peak Ski Area (all ages)
Mountain Road, R.R. 1 Box 734, Bridgton 04009; (207) 647–8444; www.shawneepeak.com. Open from December through March. Lift ticket prices vary, depending on day and time. There is a free beginner lift ticket for children under 6 when accompanied by a paying adult. A Family Deal is available—four family members ski all day for $125. $$–$$$$

Maine's oldest downhill ski area, Shawnee Peak offers a vertical drop of 1,300 feet. There are more than thirty trails, and night skiing is available. The facility offers child care, equipment rentals, and lessons.

Special programs designed for young skiers include Skiwee for kids 4 to 6, Junior Mountaineers for ages 7 to 12, and a Youth Racing Program for kids 5 to 18. These successful programs are offered in full- and half-day segments and include lift ticket, instruction, skiing or snowboarding time, constant supervision, and inside play, as necessary.

Sneak **Peak**

Skiing is always great at Shawnee Peak, but on select days throughout the season the good times are even better. Family Fun Day adds a magic show and noontime barbecue to your peak experience. The Spring Fling Beach Party brings with it pond skimming, reggae music, and more. Let the good times roll.

Where to Eat

The Black Horse Tavern. 8 Portland Street; (207) 647–5300. Enjoy casual dining in a comfortable equestrian atmosphere. Menu items such as steak, ribs, chicken, fresh seafood, and pasta are served with hospitality. A full children's menu is available. $–$$

Where to Stay

Grady's West Shore Motel. RR 3, Box 39, Bridgton 04009; (207) 647–2284; www.mega link.net/~gradywst/. Grady's is located on Highland Lake, and you can stay in an efficiency unit or in a lakeside cottage. Relax on the sandy beach, take a canoe, rowboat, or pedal-boat out on the lake, spend time fishing. During the colder months you can night slide on a lighted hill, ski, or go snowmobiling. $–$$

For More Information

Bridgton Lakes Region Chamber of Commerce. (207) 647–3472; www. mainelakeschamber.com.

Fryeburg

Nestled in the foothills of the White Mountains, Fryeburg is a picturesque village known for its fertile farmlands. Visit in the fall, and you're in for a treat; the foliage is breathtaking. Fall is also the time for the Fryeburg Fair, Maine's largest agricultural fair. Held for a full week in October, it goes out with a bang on Columbus Day weekend.

    If you arrive in the summer, you should investigate the water fun on the Saco River. The sandy shores offer ideal picnic spots, and the river is perfect for canoeing.

Fryeburg Fair (all ages)

P.O. Box 78, Fryeburg 04037; (207) 935–3268; www.fryeburgfair.com. Held the first week of October at the Route 5 fairgrounds. Children under 12 get in free. $2.00 parking fee. $

What has become Maine's largest agricultural fair began on a blustery day in March 1851, when local farmers and merchants got together to show their wares to the community. Today the weeklong celebration guarantees good times for all. Each day is filled with a variety of programs, from the society pig scramble to a parent/child cookie contest. Each night brings a free concert under the stars featuring top performers.

Amazing Maine Facts

Maine has more moose per square mile than any state in the United States, including Alaska. The word *moose* is derived from the Algonquin *mong-soa*, which means "twig eater." A full-grown moose can consume in one day about sixty pounds of plants and herbs.

Family-Friendly **Canoeing**

The calm waters of the Saco River offer easy and safe canoeing for the entire family. There are several local outfitters ready to provide you with everything you'll need for your adventure. Saco River Canoe and Kayak (207–935–2369 or 888–772–6573) provides canoe rentals and shuttle service, when needed. If you have your own canoe, there are many places where you can put it into the river on your own. Call (207) 935–3639 for information.

There is literally something for everyone. Animal shows, harness racing, tractor pulls, and parades are just some of the activities to be enjoyed—not to mention the great food. Children will especially appreciate McDonald's Farm Park, where they'll be entertained by puppeteers, storytellers, magicians, and clowns. Catch the hurdy-gurdy man with his monkey and miniature antique auto as he roams the fair throughout the week. And don't miss the grand finale, as fireworks light up the crisp autumn sky.

Where to Stay

The Admiral Peary House. 9 Elm Street; (207) 935–3365; www.admiralpeary house.com. This stately house was once home to Maine's famed Arctic explorer Robert Edwin Peary. Now five large guest rooms with private baths and air-conditioning await your arrival. A clay tennis court, a billiards room, and an outdoor spa are among the amenities here. Bicycles are also available. $–$$

Photo Op: **Covered Bridge**

Hemlock Bridge, located off Route 302, spans an old channel of the Saco River. It was built in 1857 of Paddleford truss construction with supporting wooden arches.

Harrison

Harrison is a small town situated on the shores of Long Lake and Crystal Lake.

Deertrees Theatre (ages 6 and up)
Deertrees Road, P.O. Box 577, Harrison 04040; (207) 583–6747; www.deertreestheatre.org. The season starts the last week of June and runs until Labor Day. All shows begin at 8:00 P.M. $$

A State and National Historic Landmark, Deertrees Theatre has been offering live shows since 1936. Its stage has been graced with such celebrities as Ethel Barrymore, Vivian Vance, Rudy Vallee, Fabian, and Shirley Knight.

Named "Maine's most enchanting playhouse," Deertrees Theatre was born from the vision of opera coach and singer Enrica Clay Dillion. She wanted to build a world-class opera hall within an idyllic forest setting. Today, although opera performances are still held here, you can also enjoy dance performances, plays, and a variety of concerts from classical music to rock.

Where to Eat

Caswell House Restaurant. 22 Main Street; (207) 583–6550. Good food, reasonable prices, and Maine hospitality are what you'll find here. Built in the 1850s, Caswell House has a classic but casual New England atmosphere. Enjoy the house specialty, "Puffa Steak" (named for the way it puffs up when cooked), or savor the lobster roll, a house favorite. Open for lunch and dinner, with extended hours on weekends and daily specials. Children are always welcomed; their portions are half priced. $–$$

Where to Stay

Greenwood Manor Inn. Tolman Road, Route 117; (207) 583–4445; www.green woodmanorinn.com. Open year-round, the inn offers nine guest rooms with private baths. Set on one hundred acres of sloping hills, this facility includes a social room in the old icehouse, a dining area, and a lounge that overlooks spectacular gardens. Children under 2 stay for **free,** but you will need your own portable crib. Rent bicycles or a canoe to see the sights after enjoying a complimentary breakfast. $$

Snowbird Lodge. Route 2, 83 Templehill Road; (207) 583–2544. This lodge is set on fifty acres lush with birch and pine trees. Amenities include a private pond, complete with beach, and a recreation room with a large stone fireplace, a piano, TV, VCR, and games. $

Norway/South Paris

Northeast of Harrison are the towns of Norway and South Paris. If you want to check out some of the out-of-the-way areas of Maine, there's a little picnic area and boat ramp right outside Norway. This is not a trendy place, so it shouldn't be too crowded if you decide to pull in here for a break or for a picnic lunch.

FYI: **The Best Pine**

In the history of shipbuilding, Norway pines were considered the finest for the masts of ships. However, these magnificent white pines do not get their name from the country, but rather from the town of Norway, Maine, where they grew in abundance.

The Celebration Barn Theater (ages 6 and up)

190 Stock Farm Road, South Paris; (207) 743–8452; www.celebrationbarn.com. Live performances every Friday and Saturday evening in summer. Call for schedule. $$

This barn theater is located on ten acres in the foothills of western Maine. Summer workshops are held in mime, voice, and various performing arts. There are classes for professionals and those with aspirations for the stage and screen. Students and staff come from all over the world. The facility encompasses two rehearsal studios, the 125-seat theater, and housing for eighteen students.

Even if you don't take a workshop, you'll enjoy the performances held each weekend throughout the summer, many of which host world-class artists.

CAN-AM Wheelers (ages 10 and up)

140 Emerson Road, Norway; (207) 743–9018; www.canamwheelers.com. Call for tour schedule and pricing. $$$$

Offering one- and two-week biking tours throughout Maine and Canada, CAN-AM is the place for those of you in good shape. Age is no barrier, but lack of training is. CAN-AM provides support vehicles, baggage transport, maps and a marked route, campsites with hot showers, and more. You provide the muscle, knowledge, and equipment to keep your bike wheels turning.

The MOOSA (Maine's Original Outstanding Super Adventure) and Lighthouse are both weeklong camping tours. MOOSA begins in Rangeley, Maine, and takes you to Quebec and back. Notre Dame des Bois, Levi, and the waterfall at St. Anne de Beaupre (higher than Niagra Falls) are some of the sites you'll enjoy. Lighthouse begins in Portland, where you board the *Scotia Prince* for an overnight cruise to Nova Scotia. Once in Canada you'll ride along St. Mary's Bay, through Kejimkujik National Park, Liverpool, and Shelburne (where *The Scarlet Letter* was filmed). This tour ends with a relaxing day cruise back to Maine.

The McLaughlin Foundation (all ages)

101 Main Street, South Paris; (207) 743–8820; www.mclaughlingarden.org. The garden is open and free to the public from May through October. The gift shop is open year-round from 10:00 A.M. to 3:00 P.M. Friday through Tuesday. The Tea Room is open Wednesday through Saturday 11:00 A.M. to 4:00 P.M. from June through August.

A wonderfully beautiful place to take a quiet stroll, the three-and-a-half acre perennial garden was started by Bernard McLaughlin in 1936. While working in a local grocery store, he worked the garden in his spare time. After retiring in 1967, McLaughlin poured all his energy into the garden. He wanted it to be something he and his wife, Rena, could enjoy in their old age.

It has become much more than that. Voted the Best Public Garden in Maine in a *Maine Times* readers poll, it's hard to imagine that when the McLaughlins first acquired the land, the house and barn were surrounded by hay fields. Now everyone can enjoy Bernard's garden. After a walk around, you can also enjoy a light snack or sandwich in the Tea Room.

Amazing
Maine Facts

Abraham Lincoln's first vice president, Hannibal Hamlin, came from South Paris, Maine.

Where to Eat

Country Way Restaurant. 187 Main Street, South Paris; (207) 743–9783. Good food and reasonable prices. $

Shaner's Family Restaurant. 193 Main Street, South Paris; (207) 743–6367. Open year-round for breakfast, lunch, and dinner. Their specialty is homemade ice cream. A children's menu is available. $

West Paris

West Paris may not have a lot of flashy stuff to pull in tourists, but it does have some hidden nuggets of sorts. This part of Maine is known for its natural gem deposits, and you can mine the quarries yourself. The treasures you find are yours to keep.

Perham's Store (all ages)
194 Bethel Road; (800) 371–GEMS or (207) 674–2341. Open daily from 9:00 A.M. to 5:00 P.M. May through December, and Tuesday through Sunday 9:00 A.M. to 5:00 P.M. January through April.

The place to be for rock hounds, this gem, mineral, and rock shop was founded in 1919 by Stanley Perham. On the premises is a small museum, where admission is **free.** Your children will get a first-class introduction to gems and minerals here. The impressive stone displays include some specimens of tourmaline, quartz, gold, and others in their rough, natural setting, some in finished form as jewelry, and even some that glow in the dark.

This is a store that welcomes the novice and satisfies the seasoned collector. You can buy rock hammers, gold pans, chisels, lapidary equipment, and metal detectors. Rentals are available on some items, such as the metal detectors. Even if you have never had an

Check It Out: Sparkling Rocks and Water

While you're at Perham's ask them to show you how to get to Snow Falls Gorge. It's right off Route 26, but it's unmarked. You'll find a waterfall that cascades into a gorge. Walk out on the bridge and enjoy the view. There are also hiking trails.

interest in rocks, you will fall in love with this store. The polished stones and intricate carvings fascinate children and adults alike.

Perham's also controls several quarries in the area. You can ask at the store for directions and search these areas without charge. What you find is yours to keep. Access is easy, and the rock piles are generally safe for even young children to poke around in. The only problem with Perham's is that there is so much neat stuff to buy that you will certainly leave wishing that you could have spent more money. Don't leave without purchasing at least one dish for gold panning. You'll be needing one when you arrive at the profitable banks of the Swift River (see page 178).

Bethel

Along the way to Bethel you will pass through the picturesque town of Bryant Pond. The small town of Locke Mills will also be a landmark for you. Once you reach Bethel, you are in for some four-season fun. The warmer seasons bring hikers and antiques buyers to the area, and winter, of course, draws skiers. Bethel is known for great skiing, both downhill and cross-country. Convenient to the popular tourist spot of North Conway, New Hampshire, Bethel's proximity to the White Mountain National Forest literally guarantees some of the best ski conditions in the East.

Popular in hiking season as well as in the ski season, Bethel is a quiet, down-home town that serves as a year-round stopover for travelers going in many directions. Whether you are just traveling through or staying for a while, you will enjoy the outstanding scenery. White birch trees line the roads out of town, and the Androscoggin River meanders through meadows, calling to anglers.

Once known as a farming and trading community, Bethel is still very much a working town. Lumber mills produce pine clapboards, furniture parts, and a great number of broom handles. Yes—broom handles. In addition, three local dairy farms ship some 7,000 gallons of milk a week out of this mountainous region.

FYI: **Ear Protectors**

In 1873 a 15-year-old boy named Chester Greenwood invented earmuffs, or as he called them "Greenwood's Champion Ear Protectors." Born and raised in western Maine, Greenwood's first invention was born from necessity—he suffered from cold ears while ice skating on a local pond. As an inventor, Greenwood went on to obtain more than one hundred patents from the U.S. Patent Office. He was also selected by the Smithsonian Institution as one of fifteen outstanding American inventors.

Before you leave Bethel, you might enjoy browsing through some shops and stores. A favorite is **Groan and McGurn's Tourist Trap and Craft Outlet** on Route 2 (207–836–3645), which has all the stuff you need and a lot of goodies you don't. **Mountainside Country Crafts** on Sunday River Road (207–824–2518) lives up to its name, offering crafts galore. **Bonnema Potters** at 146 Main Street (207–824–2821) is known for its fabulous stoneware.

If you enjoyed Perham's Store in West Paris, you will probably like **Mt. Mann Jewelers** on Main Street (207–824–3030). This gem and rock shop is not as extensive as Perham's, but it is well worth your time. You can gather a wealth of information here and buy some fine jewelry at the same time. Many other stores are worth a look. They aren't hard to find, so take your time and explore this mountain town.

Check It Out: Take a Hike

Other hiking areas near Bethel include Grafton Notch State Park on Route 26 between Newry and Upton and Screw Auger Falls, about 1 mile past Grafton Notch. Step Falls, Mother Walker Falls, and Moose Cave are also in the region.

The Bethel Inn and Country Club (ages 8 and up)
1 Broad Street; (207) 824–2175 or (800) 654–0125; www.bethelinn.com. The inn is open year-round, but the dining room is closed in April, November (but open for Thanksgiving), and the first two weeks of December. The golf course operates from May through October. $$$$

This country club pulls in golfers from far and wide. The eighteen-hole, championship-length course is challenging. The club's driving range allows you to tune up your short game and your driver. Clubs and golf carts are available for rent.

The golf course is open to cross-country skiers in the winter.

White Mountain National Forest (ages 6 and up)
Call (207) 824–2134 for maps and other information. $–$$$

If you like to hike mountain trails, Bethel is one of the best places to do it. Although the 42,000-acre White Mountain National Forest is mostly in New Hampshire, enough of it stretches into Maine to provide ample entertainment for outdoor types. The local ranger can provide trail maps.

A good way to enter the park is off Route 113 near Gilead (a short distance from Bethel). It will bring you to the national forest at the point where the Wild River and the Androscoggin River meet. Stop at one of the many pull-offs along Route 113 to fish, picnic, or wade in the shallows of the river. This really is a great place for kids to get a little break from riding. Wilderness campsites are farther down Route 113. For information, call (877) 444–6777.

Telemark Inn and Llama Farm (ages 6 and up)

Located 10 miles outside Bethel at 591 Kings Highway; RFD 2, Box 800, Bethel 04217; (207) 836–2703; www.telemarkinn.com. Tours offered from July through August. Tour price includes a fully catered trailside buffet lunch. One-, three-, four-, and six-day treks are available. $$$$

If you would like some help along the trail, you should call Telemark. This farm features llamas trained as pack animals that will accompany you and your family into the woods on guided tours. The folks at Telemark will arrange day trips or overnight camping trips of up to six days. The llamas carry the gear. An overnight package includes meals, camping, or lodging at the inn. Reservations are required. Also open in the winter for private ski tours.

Sunday River Inn & X-Country Ski Center (ages 8 and up)

23 Skiway Access Road, R.R. 3 Box 1688, Newry; (207) 824–2410; www.sundayriverinn.com. Trails are open from December through March. $$$$

These well-maintained trails hold snow when other trails don't. The center offers Friday guided night skiing, equipment rentals, lessons, and snacks.

Carter's X-Country Ski Center II (ages 6 and up)

786 Intervale Road; (207) 539–4848; www.cartersxcski.com. Skiing is free for children under 6. $$

The center has about 1,000 acres of cross-country trails open in season; some of these run along the Androscoggin River. Cabins are available too.

Sunday River Ski Area (all ages)

Sunday River Road, P.O. Box 450, Bethel 04217; (207) 824–3000 or (800) 543–2754; www.sundayriver.com. Open year-round. A day lift ticket is free for children 5 and under. $$$$

Strong snowmaking ability, good grooming, eight interconnected mountains, and 126 trails allow for skiing well into the spring. There is even a train that runs from Portland to Sunday River on the historic Grand Trunk Railroad route. Skiwee classes are available for children 4 to 6.

During the warmer months, enjoy the Sunday River Mountain Bike Park and the Adventure Center, featuring a skate park, a BMX track, a climbing wall, a water slide, and more. Packages are available.

Mount Abram (all ages)

Howe Hill Road, Route 26, Greenwood; (207) 875–5002; www.skimtabram.com. A day lift ticket is free for children 5 and under. $$$$

Although not technically in Bethel, it's close by, in Greenwood. The site has thirty-five trails and slopes, as well as sixty condominiums. There is also a nursery for young children and a ski shop. Rental equipment is available. Because Locke Mills is such a short drive from Bethel, you might find it fun to ski in both places.

Big Adventure Center (ages 4 and up)

12 North Road; (207) 824–0929; www.bigadventure.com. Summer hours 11:00 A.M. to 11:00 P.M. daily. Hours vary for school vacations, and from April to June. The water park is open June to Labor Day and usually closes at 5:00 P.M. You can play individual games or buy a day pass for $29.00. $–$$$$

Play laser tag in a huge three-level arena, featuring ramps, bridges, mazes, and even a forest. Find the four hidden GEMs (Game Enhancement Modules) and get "special powers." This dark world is full of fog and fun.

Hold on, more fun and games await you. Take a swing at a round of mini golf on a course complete with a river, covered bridge, waterfall, and old-fashioned gristmill with working waterwheel. Beware of water hazards.

Speaking of water, grab a partner and slide Double Down, 40 feet high and snaking 360 feet to the pool. On Blue Heat you'll experience a swirling 360-degree loop at the end of the slide. Parents, comfortably watch your kids from the heated spa at the landing pool.

But that's not all. Try your hand at mini-bowling, a scale of candlepin. Seem a little tame? Attempt bowling when the black lights are switched on. You might just need a time-out. Full of the latest video games, the game room is a perfect place to chill. You can also enjoy a classic game of pool.

Those looking for a more strenuous challenge should look no further than the Rock Climbing Gym. There are twenty-six rope courses in this vertical canyon, extending to heights of 24 feet.

Where to Eat

Bethel Inn and Country Club. Town Common, Bethel; (207) 824–2175; www.bethel inn.com. A good choice if you're looking for a more formal setting. $$$

Crossroads Diner & Deli. 24 Mayville Road; (207) 824–3673. Open seven days a week for breakfast and lunch. Friday and Saturday you can get dinner as well. Good food at a fair price. Check out the daily specials when you visit. $

Legends at the Summit. Sunday River Road; (207) 824–3500. A great place for creative Maine cuisine. Breakfast, lunch, and dinner. $$

Mother's. 43 Main Street; (207) 824–2589. Open for lunch and dinner, this establishment has unique decor and kid-friendly food. Prices are very reasonable. $

Winter Sports

If you prefer skating over skiing, you can head to the Bethel Common. It is flooded in winter to provide safe outdoor skating. People who don't own skates can rent them from the Bethel Inn. There are snowmobiling trails in the Evans Notch/Gilead area, and sleigh rides are offered at Sunday River Ski Resort, the Bethel Inn, and the Telemark Inn and Llama Farm.

Rebel Family Restaurant. 157 Barker Road, Bethel; (207) 836–3663. A great place to enjoy a pizza. Subs and hot sandwiches are also on the menu. Daily specials and family dinners are available. $–$$

Sudbury Inn. Main Street, P.O. Box 369, Bethel 04217; (207) 824–2174; www.the sudburyinn.com. Enjoy fireside dining in this warm country inn. Entrees include rack of lamb, grilled duck, and lobster Sudbury. Closed in May. $$$

Where to Stay

Bethel Inn and Country Club. Town Common, P.O. Box 49, Bethel 04217; (207) 824–2175; (800) 654–0125; www.bethelinn.com. Enjoy candlelight dining with piano music, relax in the fireside lounge, warm up in the saunas, or take a dip in the pool. Overnight packages include dinner, breakfast, cross-country skiing, ice-skating, and free downhill skiing at Mount Abram for kids 15 and under. $$–$$$$.

The Bethel Spa Motel. 88 Main Street; (800) 882–0293 or (207) 824–3341. Offers ten upstairs units over shops. These rooms aren't fancy, but they're clean and comfortable. $

The River View Resort. 357 Mayville Road; (207) 824–2808 or (888) 224–8413. An attractive building that offers 32 two-bedroom suites. Each suite has its own kitchen, living room, dining area, and large modern bathroom. One queen-size bed and two twin beds are in each unit. Air-conditioning, telephone, maid service, and TV are included in the modest room charges. You can enjoy nature walks along the river, as well as a playground, whirlpool, sauna, tennis court, and game room. $–$$

Sunday River Ski Area. Sunday River Road; (800) 543–2754. Offers a variety of lodging packages. Call for information. $$–$$$$

For More Information

Bethel Area Chamber of Commerce. (800) 442–5826; www.bethelmaine.com.

Rangeley Lake Area

Rangeley is a sportsman's town with a reputation. Fish and animals far outnumber the human residents, and no amusement parks or ocean beaches will attract you here. If you want to escape the pressures of urban living, however, Rangeley is a wonderful place to go. Good, wholesome fun can be had by nature lovers, young or old. This is a place where you can ski, fish, hike, hunt, or simply relax in nice accommodations.

One of Maine's favorite wilderness areas, Rangeley is wild, but not as wild as the North Woods. Mainers have a saying: "You can't get theah from heah." This might seem to ring true as you make your way to Rangeley. You can make the journey more enjoyable by stopping at interesting places, like the Swift River, along the way. You'll also discover numerous mountains along the way offering trails to hike. South Rangeley near Rangeley Lake State Park, Rangeley Lake, Mooselookmeguntic Lake, and Cupsuptic Lake, are wonderful places for the family to stop and enjoy freshwater activities.

Photo Op: **Snap a Moose**

Moose watching is a very popular activity in Rangeley for both adults and children. You can simply ride around in your car and see a number of the large brown animals, or you can take a different approach. **Rich Gacki** (207–864–5136) is a registered Maine guide who will be happy to show you moose from a canoe. His trips normally leave from the Rangeley Inn at 51 Main Street at around 5:00 A.M. Trips last about three hours and are followed by breakfast. The tour, including breakfast, is $40 for adults, with a sliding scale for children. Reservation are required the day before your excursion.

Fish in Rangeley don't just jump into your boat, but they are abundant. Brook trout are the most common catch in the streams, while landlocked salmon are king of the lakes. Numerous camps and lodges in the area offer fishing packages that include lodging, food, and boats. For information call the Rangeley Lakes Chamber of Commerce at (800) MT–LAKES. The **Rangeley Region Sport Shop** on Main Street (207–864–5615) is a good place to load up on tackle, get some free advice, and inspect a list of registered guides who will show you where the fish are.

Hiking in this part of Maine can be rugged. There are many good trails for adults and children in good physical condition, but some trails are too challenging for children under 6. A 1-mile hike up **Bald Mountain** might be of interest to you if your kids are young. Bald Mountain lies between South Rangeley and Oquossoc on Route 17. Many portions of longer trails can be traversed by young children. It's a good idea to purchase a trail guide or talk to a ranger about trail conditions and the advisability of hiking with youngsters on specific trails.

Travel by **Canoe**

Canoeing is always exciting in the Rangeley area. If you want some serious canoe travel, you can take an 8-mile trip from Rangeley to Oquossoc. Or you can opt for a longer trip on Lake Mooselook-meguntic, where a water trail takes you up to 20 miles around the lake. Canoe rentals are available in the area.

Swift River (all ages)
Route 17, Byron.

The Swift River is known for its trout and its gold. Yes, I said gold! Real gold that you and your kids can pan for. The gold found along this river is placer gold, usually in flake form, but some gold nuggets have also been discovered here. Some of the larger ones are displayed in the Maine State Museum in Augusta. Rumor has it that one old man lived along the river and supported himself entirely with the gold he panned.

Since you will be driving right through gold country on your way to Rangeley, it makes sense to stop and try your luck. The friendly people at Perham's Store in West Paris may have sold you some gold-panning supplies and books and given you some good free advice. Here's where you're going to use them. Can you really find gold in these parts? I suppose it depends a little on luck and a little on skill, but gold is found regularly in the areas near the towns of Byron and Roxbury.

Whether you're angling for trout, panning for gold, or just cooling your heels in the pleasant waters of the Swift River, this area offers a nice diversion from driving. Camping facilities and canoe trips can also be found near Byron. The canoeing can be fast and furious, however, so it may not be wise to arrange a trip with young children. Much of the river is shallow with lots of rocks and ripples. Children enjoy poking around the edges and wading in the shallow water. Good photo opportunities abound here.

Other Things to See and Do

Tennis lovers flock to the public courts in downtown Rangeley's Lakeside Park and just outside Rangeley, in the village of Oquossoc. Golfers head to Mingo Springs Golf Course on Proctor Road (207–864–5021), an eighteen-hole course with club and cart rentals.

Rangeley Lake State Park (all ages)
(207) 864–3858, off-season (207) 624–6080. Open May 15 through September. A day-use fee is charged. $

The park covers nearly 700 acres and more than a mile of shoreline along Rangeley Lake. Picnic areas are abundant, and swimming is available. Your kids will enjoy the play area, and there is a boat launch for those who own their own watercraft. Showers and toilets, along with a dumping station for RVs, are also located in the park. Snowmobiling is a favorite winter activity here.

Saddleback Ski Area (ages 6 and up)
Dallas Hill Road, P.O. Box 490, Rangeley 04970; (207) 864–5671; www.saddleback skiarea.com. $$$$

If it's snow season when you roll into Rangeley, consider going skiing. This ski facility can accommodate alpine skiers of all levels of expertise. The Nordic Touring Center at Saddleback provides plenty of cross-country skiing opportunities as well.

Where to Eat

Country Club Inn. Country Club Drive, P.O. Box 680, Rangeley 04970; (207) 864–3831. The prices are moderate, and the views of the lake are spectacular. $$

The Four Seasons Cafe. Cary Road, Oquossoc; (207) 864–2020. Choose from a full range of dinner specials for two. $$

Gingerbread House. Route 4, P.O. Box 273, Oquossoc 04964; (207) 864–3602. This kid-friendly restaurant with a marble soda fountain is sure to attract attention. $–$$

Our Place Cafe. Main Street and Richardson Avenue, Rangeley; (207) 864–5844. A good place for breakfast or lunch. Order anything from pancakes to seafood. All the locals come here, so it must be good. $

The Rangeley Inn. 51 Main Street, Rangeley; (800) MOMENTS or (207) 864–3341; www.rangeleyinn.com. Located in downtown Rangeley, serves fine food at moderate prices. $$

Red Onion. 77 Main Street, Rangeley; (207) 864–5022. Pizza lovers will want to stop here. $–$$

Where to Stay

Accommodations are plentiful in Rangeley, but they fill up fast, so call ahead for reservations.

Bald Mountain Camps. P.O. Box 332, Oquossoc 04964; (207) 864–3671 or (888) 392–0072; www.baldmountaincamps.com. Open from Memorial Day to Labor Day. Founded in the late 1800s, this camp has fifteen cabins with fireplaces. The sandy beach is perfect for children, and tennis courts and lawn games are available. The cabins are nestled on Mooselookmeguntic Lake. All meals are included. Prices are lower in May and June. $$$$

Country Club Inn. Country Club Drive, Route 16, Rangeley 04970; (207) 864–3831; www.countryclubinn.com. This charming inn overlooks mountain and lakes. During your stay enjoy activities such as golf, swimming, cross-country skiing, and snowmobiling. $$

Cupsuptic Campground. P.O. Box 326, Route 16, West Oquossoc 04964; (207) 864–5249; www.cupsupticcampground.com. Black Brook Cove offers fifty-five sites, tenting, electricity and water, a dump station, store, laundry, recreational hall, swimming, boating, fishing, and more. $

Grant's Kennebago Camps. Kennebago Lake Road West, P.O. Box 786, Rangeley 04970; (800) 633–4815; www.grantscamps.com. Open from ice-out (usually in May) to late September. Cabins are rustic; woodstoves provide heat. Keep the danger of a hot stove in mind with young children. Every cabin has its own dock and boat for your enjoyment. The charge includes three meals, which are hearty. If you can stay for a full week or more, the weekly rate is lower than daily rates. $$$$

North Country Inn B&B. 429 Main Street, Rangeley; (207) 864–2440 or (800) 295–4968; www.northcountrybb.com. This 1912 house offers four guest rooms. $–$$

Rangeley Inn and Motor Lodge. 51 Main Street, P.O. Box 160, Rangeley 04970; (800) 666–3687 or (207) 864–3341; www.rangeleyinn.com. Choose between a century-old inn furnished with antiques or a modern motel. Some of the motel rooms have kitchens, fireplace/stoves, and private two-person whirlpool baths. $–$$

Check It Out: Weekly Cabins

Several cottages in the area are available on a weekly basis. Rates run from $265 to $750, with $500 about average. Most cottages have lake or river access. For more information, contact Sundown Lodge and Cottages (207–864–3650), Hunter Cove (207–864–3383), Rangeley Lake Rentals (877–409–3300), Sunset Point Cottages (207–864–3712), Mountain View Cottages (207–864–3416), North Camps (207–864–2247), and Clearwater Sporting Camps (207–864–5424).

Rangeley Lake State Park. Located between Routes 4 and 17; (207) 864–3858. This is one campground that is both easy to reach and geared for children. Nonresidents of Maine pay $20 a night for a site. In addition to one of the fifty or so campsites in the park, this fee gives you access to a swimming beach on the lake, a boat ramp, picnic sites, and a play area. $

For More Information

Rangeley Lakes Chamber of Commerce. (800) MT–LAKES; www.rangeley maine.com.

Phillips

Using Rangeley as a base camp, you can find some interesting activities in the surrounding countryside. The town of Phillips, east of Rangeley on Route 4, offers a train ride.

Sandy River–Rangeley Lakes Railroad (all ages)

Route 4, P.O. Box B, Phillips 04966; (207) 779–1901; www.srrl-rr.org. Open May through October. Trains run at 11:00 A.M., noon, 1:00, 2:00, and 3:00 P.M. weekends only. Free for children under 6. $

Rail fans will be thrilled with this narrow-gauge railroad. It was built in 1873 and had an original length of 115 miles. Now you can ride for 1 mile to get a feel for what it was like in the good old days. The train depot contains an assortment of railroad memorabilia.

Weld

The township of Weld on Route 142 south of Phillips has a few goodies for the kids. In fact, you may want to spend several days in the Weld area.

Mount Blue State Park (all ages)
299 Center Hill Road; (207) 585–2347 or (207) 585–2261 off-season. Open year-round. $

This park is best known for its extensive cross-country skiing trails and 140 miles of snowmobile trails, but its lakeside setting is also perfect for swimming, fishing, hiking, camping, and other summer fun. Campsites, bathhouses, picnic tables, fireplaces, dump stations, boat ramps, and even boat rentals make the park ideal for day or overnight trips.

Webb Lake, which borders the state park, is also a fun place to spend the day.

Where to Stay

Lake Webb House. Route 142, Main Street; (207) 585–2479. Nice place, and the rates are quite reasonable. $

For More Information

Greater Farmington Chamber of Commerce. (207) 778–4215; www.farmington chamber.org.

Carrabassett Valley

Another area in western Maine worth mentioning is the Carrabassett Valley, where Sugarloaf Mountain is located. If you approach this region from Rangeley, you go through the town of **Stratton**. If you have wandered down to Phillips from Rangeley, you will encounter the towns of **Salem** and **Kingfield** on your way to the valley.

When you arrive in Carrabassett Valley, **Sugarloaf Mountain** will be the center of attention. Sugarloaf has a 2,820-foot vertical drop, making it the biggest ski and snowboard mountain in the East. Cross-country skiing is also big business in the valley during the snow season. If skiing doesn't interest you, consider going on a dogsled ride.

To explore the area, rent mountain bikes at Sugarloaf Mountain Bike Shop. For fishing, try Thayer Pond at the Carrabassett Valley Recreation Center on Route 27. This catch-and-release pond is open to the public. You can take fly-fishing lessons and rent a boat for a nominal fee. This is a good place to introduce your young anglers to the sport of fishing.

Want to play an outstanding eighteen holes of golf? Try the **Sugarloaf Golf Club**. If golf is not your game, head out for some hiking or swimming. Hiking along Mount Abraham and Bigelow Mountain is popular for enthusiastic hikers, but the trails can be tough for younger children. Call the **Sugarloaf Area Chamber** (800–843–5623) for information. Swimming at **Cathedral Pines** on Route 27 in Stratton is fun for the whole family. This public beach is **free**. There's much more for you and your family to enjoy in this glorious section of western Maine.

Check It Out: X-C Skiing

Those who prefer the fields to the hills will find several places in the area to accommodate their cross-country needs. Sugarloaf Ski Touring and Outdoor Center (207–237–6830) has 52 miles of trails to explore. Titcomb Mountain Ski Touring Center (207–778–9031) in Farmington offers fewer trails but lower rates.

The Stanley Museum (all ages)

40 School Street, Kingfield; (207) 265–2729; www.stanleymuseum.org. Open June through October Tuesday through Sunday, and November through May Tuesday to Friday 1:00 to 4:00 P.M. $

The museum is housed in an old school, circa 1903, that was donated by the Stanley family. The Stanley twins invented the airbrush and found their fortune. The museum displays everything from violins to steam cars, which happens to be what the Stanleys are best known for—the Stanley Steamer.

Sugarloaf/USA (all ages)

Route 27, R.R. 1, Kingfield; (207) 237–2000 or (800) THE–LOAF; www.sugarloaf.com. Open year-round. A one-day lift ticket is **free** for children under 5. Call for rates on summer outdoor adventure camps.

In operation since 1955, this complex offers more than one hundred trails, with a vertical drop of 2,820 feet. There's an on-site nursery, as well as instructional programs for interested rookies 3 and older.

During the summer months kids can participate in outdoor adventure camps. Their days will be filled with fun activities such as swimming, biking, hiking, tennis, golf, and rock climbing.

Sugarloaf Sports and Fitness Center (ages 8 and up)

Sugarloaf Inn Resort, Main Street, Route 27, Carrabassett Valley; (207) 237–2000. $$–$$$

This operation in the Sugarloaf Inn Resort offers such amenities as a pool, racquetball courts, hot tubs, steam rooms, whirlpool tubs, saunas, and even a beauty salon to make you feel better about yourself. New racquetball and wallyball courts as well as an indoor climbing wall have been added.

Where to Eat

There are numerous restaurants in the Carrabassett Valley area. Here are just some of your options.

The Bag and Kettle. Sugarloaf Mountain; (207) 237–2451. Get burgers in a bag or pizza to go. If you prefer, you can eat in the restaurant. $

D'Ellies. Village West, Carrabassett; (207) 237–2490. Here you can make your own sandwiches. $

Hug Italian Cuisine. 3001 Townline Road; (207) 237–2392. This is a perfect spot for family eating. Both the food and the service are excellent. $–$$

Java Joe's. North Maine Street, Kingfield; (207) 265–2326; www.carrabassett coffee.com. A quick stop here enables you to take the chill off with a piping hot cup of joe. This roaster/retail shop has beans to go so you can brew some java for yourself at home. $

Maine Street Cafe. 250 Main Street, Kingfield; (207) 265–2323; www.mainestcafe. com. Small shop, big flavor. The place for espresso, cappuccino, and lattes. Get a continental breakfast or a hearty soup for lunch. $

The Seasons Restaurant. Sugarloaf Inn, Route 27, 5 miles south of the Sugarloaf access road; (207) 237–2701. Serving breakfast and dinner. $$–$$$

Tufulio's. Valley Crossing Building, Kingfield; (207) 235–2010. Open from 4:30 P.M. for good Italian food. $$

The White Wolf Inn. Main Street, Stratton; (207) 246–2922. You can get breakfast for a buck, and lunch for not much more. The dinner menu starts with a big burger for under $5.00. $–$$

Where to Stay

Grand Summit Resort Hotel. Slopeside at Sugarloaf/USA, Carrabassett Valley; (800) THE–LOAF; www.sugarloaf.com/staying/lodging/grand_summit.html. Grand is a fitting name for this hotel as it sits in the center of all the action, majestically representative of mountain hotels of long ago. The views are spectacular, and you have your choice of suites, studios, condos, and even penthouse accommodations. $$–$$$

The Herbert Inn. Main Street at the corner of Routes 16 and 27, Kingfield; (207) 265–2000 or (800) THE–HERB; www.maine mountaininn.com. If your parental body is feeling the aches and pains of too much childlike activity, you might need to visit a relaxing spa. The inn can fix you right up with a sauna and whirlpool tub, sure to do the trick on the old lumbar muscles. $$

Judson's Sugarloaf Motel. Route 27, Box 2150, Carrabassett Valley 04947; (207) 235–2641; www.sugarloafusa.com. You might want to snowmobile up to the front door instead of driving; Judson's is located along one of Maine's major snowmobile trails. Hang out in the game room and enjoy pool, air hockey, Foosball, or video games. Grab a bite at the restaurant, or lounge in your room and order in. $–$$

Sugarloaf Inn. Slopeside Sugarloaf/USA, Carrabassett; (800) THE–LOAF; www.sugar loaf.com/staying/lodging/sugarloaf_inn.html. The Sawduster chairlift is right outside the front door. Hop on for a shot at the Birches trail. This forty-two-room country inn houses the Seasons Restaurant and the Shipyard BrewHaus. $–$$$$

For More Information

Sugarloaf Area Chamber of Commerce. (207) 235–2100 or (800) THE–AREA; www. sugarloafareachamber.org.

General Index

A

A Small Wonder Gallery, 88
Abol Pond, 136
Acadia, 107
Acadia and Island Tours, 101
Acadia Bike and Canoe, 101
Acadia Information Center, 110
Acadia Mountain Guides, 102
Acadia National Park, 104, 107, 108
Acadia National Park Tours, 100
Acadia Outfitters, 101
Acadia Zoo, 97
Acadian, 102
Agamont Park, 102
Andre the Seal, 83
Androscoggin County Chamber of
    Commerce, 157
Androscoggin River, 152
Angler, 102
Aquaboggan Water Park, 31
Aroostook County Tourism, 139, 141
Aroostook State Park, 138
Artist's Gallery, 13
Arundel, 29
Atlantic Climbing, 102
Atlantic Exposure Cruise & Charter Ltd., 25
Atlantic Oakes by the Sea, 106
Atlantic Seal, 45
Auburn, 152
Auburn Municipal Beach, 153
Augusta, 143
Ayla's Sweet Shop, 13

B

Babb's Bridge, 159
Bailey Island, 57
Bald Mountain, 177
balloons, hot air, 46, 155
Balmy Days Cruises, 69
Bangor, 119
Bangor Convention and Visitors Bureau, 125
Bangor International Airport, 119
Bangor Mall, 119
Bangor Municipal Golf Course, 125
Bangor Region Chamber of Commerce, 125, 126
Bangor State Fair, 124
Bar Harbor, 99
Bar Harbor Bicycle Shop, 101
Bar Harbor Chamber of Commerce, 106
Bar Harbor Golf Course, 106
Bar Harbor Town Pier, 102
Bar Harbor Whale Watch Company, 102
Barrett's Cove, 84
Bass Harbor, 107
Bass Harbor Head Light, 107
Bates College, 155
Bath, 59
Bath-Brunswick Chamber of Commerce, 59,
    62, 64
Bath Heritage Days, 62
Bath Iron Works, 59
batting cages, 36
Baxter State Park, 134, 136
Bay Chamber Concerts, 85
Bay Ferries, Inc., 103
Bay View Cruises, 45
Bay View Gallery, 88
beaches, See Activities Index
Beals Island, 113
Beaver Cove Marina, 127
Belfast, 88
Belfast and Moosehead Lake R.R. Co., 89
Belfast Area Chamber of Commerce, 90
Belfast City Park, 89
Belfast Museum, The, 89
Ben and Jerry's, 50
Bethel, 172
Bethel Area Chamber of Commerce, 176
Bethel Common, 175
Bethel Inn and Country Club, 173
Betselma, 87
Bett's Bookstore, 121
Biddeford, 30
Biddeford/Saco Chamber of Commerce, 36
Biddeford–Saco Country Club, 31

Big Adventure Center, 175
Bigelow Mountain, 151
Blackbeard's USA, 122
Blackjack Sportfishing and Charters, 69
Blaine House, The, 148
Bonnema Potters, 173
BookMarc's, 121
Booksource, The, 121
Boon Island Light, 12
Boothbay Central, 68
Boothbay Chamber of Commerce, 71
Boothbay Harbor, 69
Boothbay Harbor Region Chamber of
    Commerce, 70, 71
Boothbay Railway Village, 68
Boothbay Region, 68
Boothbay Region Land Trust Preserves, 70
Boothbay Whale Watch, 69
Bowdoin College, 51
Bowdoin College Museum of Art, 53
bowling, 34, 57, 154
Brady Pond, 163
Brady Pond Camps, 164
Bray House, 5
Briar Patch, The, 121
Brick Store Exchange, 23
Brick Store Museum, The, 23
Bridgton, 165
Bridgton Highlands Country Club, 165–66
Bridgton Historical Society Museum and
    Narramissic, The, 165
Bridgton Lakes Region Chamber of
    Commerce, 167
Brunswick, 51
Brunswick Fishway, 55
Brunswick Navel Air Station, 51
Bryant Pond, 172
Bunny Clark, 14
Bunyan, Paul, 122
Bureau of Parks and Lands, viii
Burnham Tavern, The, 115
Byron, 178

C

Cadillac Mountain, 108
Camden, 82
Camden Civic Theatre, The, 85

Camden Hills State Park, 83
Camden–Rockport–Lincolnville Chamber of
    Commerce, 87
Camden Snow Bowl, 83
Camp Ellis Beach, 34
Campobello Island, 116
CAN-AM Wheelers, 170
Cape Arundel Golf Club, 29
Cape Neddick Lighthouse, 8
Cap'n Fish Boat Cruises, 69
Caribou, 139
Caribou Chamber of Commerce, 141
Caribou Country Club, 140
Caribou Motor Speedway, 141
Caribou Performing Arts Center, 141
Carousel Music Theatre, The, 68
Carrabassett Valley, 181
Carrabassett Valley Recreation Center, 181
Carrying Place Cove, 116
Carter's X-Country Ski Center II, 174
Cascade Golf Range, 31
Casco, 159
Casco Bay Islands, 44
Casco Bay Lines, 45
Castle Tucker, 65
Cathedral Pines, 181
Causeway Golf Club, 110
Celebration Barn Theater, The, 170
Central Maine Veterinary Hospital, 153
Chamber of Commerce of the Greater Portland
    Region, 46
Chandler Bay, 114
Chandler River, 114
Chapman-Hall House, 72
Cherryfield, 111
Children's Discovery Museum, The, 147
Children's Museum of Maine, 41
Chocolate Church Arts Center, 60
Chunky's Cinema, 162
Cinema Ten, 57
City Theatre, 35
Civic Center, The, 148
Civil War Monument, 12
Clearwater Sporting Camps, 180
Cliff Island, 45
Coastal Maine Botanical Gardens, 70
Coffin Pond, 55
Colby College, 151
Colby College Museum of Art, 151

Cole Land Transportation Museum, 121
College Street Driving Range and Mini Golf, 154
Colonial Pemaquid State Historic Site, 74
Colony Beach, 27
Columbia Air, 98
Columbia Falls, 111
Common Ground Country Fair, 89
Convention and Visitors Bureau of Greater
    Portland, 46
Cony Cemetery, 149
Cool Moose, The, 165
Country Shop, The, 13
Cove's End, 13
Cozy Moose Lakeside Cabins & Recreation, 127
Craig Brook National Fish Hatchery, 95
cribstone bridge, 58
cruises, *See Activities Index*
Crystal Snowmobile Tours, 140
Cundy's Harbor, 57
Cupsuptic Lake, 176
Currier's Flying Service, 129

D

Daicey Pond Campground, 135
Daicey Pond Nature Trail, 135
Damariscotta, 72
Damariscotta Lake State Park, 77
Damariscottta Region Chamber of
    Commerce, 73
Damariscotta Region Information
    Bureau, 73
Dead River, 131
Deertrees Theatre, 168
Department of Inland Fisheries and
    Wildlife, viii
Desert of Maine, 48
Devil's Oven, 74
Diver Ed Live Underwater Video Tours, 100
Dock Square, 27
Dolphin Mini Golf, 69
Douglas Hill Orchard, 162
Douglas Mountain, 162
Downeast Air, Inc. 81
Downeast Coastal Chamber of Commerce, 113
Downeast Institute, 113
Downeast Nature Tours, 100

Downeast Windjammer and Lighthouse
    Cruises, 103
Downs Club Restaurant, 40
Dyer Library, 34
Dutch Elm Golf Course, 29

E

Eagle Island State Historic Site, 45
Eagle Tours, Inc., 45
Earl's Snowsled Sales and Service, 140
East Point Sanctuary, 35
Echo Lake, 109
Edgecomb, 66
Edgecomb Potters, 67
Elizabeth Ann, 80
Ellsworth, 95
Ellsworth Area Chamber of Commerce, 98

F

Fall Foliage Festival, 71
Farnsworth Art Museum, Victorian Homestead,
    Library, and Wyeth Center, 78
Favorite Past-Time Antiques, 166
Ferry Beach State Park, 34
Festival de Joie, 156
Finestkind Scenic Cruises, 14
First Parish Church, 12
First/Second Chance, Inc., 25
Fishermen's Festival, 71
Fishermen's Museum, 75
Flagship Cinemas, 81
Folsom's Air Service, 129
Footbridge Beach, 15
Forks, The, 131
Fort Baldwin, 61
Fort Edgecomb, 67
Fort Knox State Historic Site, 92
Fort McClary State Historic Site, 5
Fort O'Brien, 116
Fort Point State Park, 92
Fort Popham, 61
Fort Pownal, 92
Fort William Henry, 74
Fort Williams State Park, 43

Fred's Bikes, 88
Freeport, 48
Freeport Merchants Association, 50
Frenchman Bay, 104
Frisbee's General Store, 4
Fryeburg, 167
Fryeburg Fair, 167
Funtown/Splashtown USA, 33

G

George B. Door Museum of Natural History, 99
George Tate House, 46
Georgetown, 63
Ghostly Tour, 3
Golden Sails, 13
Goldenrod, The, 10
golf, *See Activities Index*
Golf Maine Association, The, 154
Gooch's Beach, 23
Goose River Golf Club, 86
Goose Rocks Beach, 27
Grafton Notch State Park, 173
Grand Auditorium, The, 95
Grasshopper Shop, The, 121
Gray, 157
Gray Business Association, 158
Great Chebeague Island, 45
Great Diamond Island, 45
Great Falls Annual Balloon Festival, 155
Great Wass Island, 113
Greater Bookland & Cafe, 57
Greater Farmington Chamber of Commerce, 181
Greater Windham Chamber of Commerce, 163
Greater York Region Chamber of Commerce, 13
Greenville, 126
Groan and McGurn's Tourist Trap and Craft
    Outlet, 173

H

Harbor Square Gallery, 88
Hardy Boat Cruises, 74
Harraseeket River, 50
Harrington, 111
Harrison, 168

Harvestfest, 9
Hemlock Bridge, 168
Hendrick Head Light, 68
Herbert Inn, The, 183
Higgins Beach, 39
Hobb's Pond, 18
Hoyt's Brunswick Cinema, 57
Hudson Museum, 125
Hunter Cove, 180

I

Ingersoll Arena/Pettengill Park, 154
Interstate Bowling Center, 149
Isaac H. Evans, 80

J

Jackman, 130
Jackman–Moose River Region Chamber of
    Commerce, 131
Jack's Flying Service, 129
Jasper Beach, 116
Jefferds Tavern, 8
Jefferson, 77
John Hancock Warehouse, 8
Jones Memorial, John Paul, 7
Jonesboro, 114
Jonesport, 112
Jordan Pond Loop Trail, 108
Joshua L. Chamberlain Civil War Museum, 54

K

Katahdin Area Chamber of Commerce, 136
Kebo Valley Golf Club, 106
Kelmscott Rare Breeds Foudation, 84
Kennebec Valley Chamber of Commerce, 150
Kennebec Ice Arena, 149
Kennebec Valley Tourism Council, 133
Kennebunk, 22
Kennebunk Beach, 23
Kennebunk Free Library, 26
Kennebunk-Kennebunkport Chamber of
    Commerce, 26, 29

Kennebunk Plains, 24
Kennebunkport, 27
Kennebunkport Maritime Museum, 30
Kingfield, 181
Kittery, 1
Kittery–Eliot–South Berwick Chamber of
    Commerce, 7
Kittery Historical and Naval Museum, 4
Kittery Outlets, 5
Kittery Point, 1
Kittery Trading Post, 3
Kokadjo, 133
Kylies Chance, 25

L

L. L. Bean, 48, 49
Lady J. Sportsfishing Charters Inc., 26
Lady Pepperell House, 7
Lafayette Center, 23
Laite Memorial Park and Beach, 85
Lake Auburn, 152
Lake Mooselookmeguntic, 177
Lake Wood, 109
Lamoine Beach, 110
Lamoine Beach State Park, 110
Land's End, 58
Laudholm Farm, 3
Leavitt Fine Arts Theater, 17
Ledgewood Riding Stables, 66
Len Libby Candies, 39
Lewis R. Frech, 87
Lewiston, 152
Lewiston Multi-Purpose Center, 156
lighthouses, *See Activities Index*
Lily Bay State Park, 128
Lincoln County Museum and Jail, 65
Lincolnville, 82
Little Cape Point, 116
Lively Lady Too, 84, 87
Locke Mills, 172
Long Island, 107
Long Sands Beach, 11
Long Shot Golf Center, 57
Lost Valley Ski Area, 153
Louis T. Graves Memorial Library, 30
Lovers Leap, 123

Lowell Cove, 57
Lubec, 116
Lubec Chamber of Commerce, 117
Lulu Lobster Boat Ride, 104
Lumbermen's Museum, The, 137

M

Machias, 115
Machias Bay Area Chamber of Commerce, 115
Machias Seal Island, 112
Machias Wild Blueberry Festival, 115
Machiasport, 116
Mackerel Cove, 58
Mackerel Sky Studio, 70
Magic Falls Rafting, 132
Maiden's Cliff, 85
Maine Audubon Society, 35
Maine Coast Artists Gallery, 88
Maine Department of Inland Fisheries and
    Wildlife, 136
Maine Discovery Museum, 123
Maine Forest and Logging Museum, 126
Maine Island Kayak Co., 46
Maine Lobster Festival, 79
Maine Lobster Museum, 99
Maine Maritime Museum, 59
Maine Narrow-Gauge Railroad Co. and
    Museum, 42
Maine Nordic Ski Council, 112
Maine Office of Tourism, viii
Maine Shakespeare Festival, 222
Maine Snowmobile Association, 112
Maine State Museum, The, 147
Maine State Music Theatre, 51
Maine Tourism Association, viii
Maine Wild Blueberry Company, 115
Maine Wildlife Park, 157
Maine Windjammer Association, 80, 87
Mainely Photos, 134
Marginal Way, 3, 14
Marine Resources Aquarium, 68
Mast Landing Sanctuary, 49
Maynard F. Jordon Planetarium and
    Observatory, 125
McClellan Park, 111
McLaughlin Foundation, The, 170

Medway, 137
Megunticook Lake, 85
Mid-Maine Chamber of Commerce, 151
Milbridge, 111
Millinocket, 133
Mingo Springs Golf Course, 178
Monhegan Island, 75
Monhegan Boat Line, 80
Monument Park, 149
Moody Beach, 15
Moose Cave, 173
Moose Point State Park, 91
Moose River Bow Trip, 130
Moose Safaris and Scenic Cruises, 127
Moosehead Lake, 126
Moosehead Lake Region Greenville Chamber of
     Commerce, 129
Moosehead Lake Vacation Association, 130
Moosehead Marine Museum, 128
Mooselookmeguntic Lake, 176
Morning in Maine, 80
Morris Farm, 65
Morse-Libby House, 46
Morse Mountain Sanctuary, 62
Mosman Beach Park, 91
Mother Walker Falls, 173
Mount Abraham, 181
Mount Abram, 174
Mount Battie, 84
Mount Blue State Park, 181
Mount Desert Chamber of Commerce, 110
Mount Desert Island, 99
Mount Desert Island Information Center,
     110, 111
Mount Desert Oceanarium, 107, 110
Mount Katahdin, 136
Mount Kineo, 128
Mount Megunticook, 85
Mountain View Cottages, 180
Mountainside Country Crafts, 173
Moxie Falls, 132
Moxie Outdoor Adventures, 132
Mr. Paperback, 121
Mt. Mann Jewelers, 173
Museum at Historic First Meeting House, 19
Museum at Portland Head Light, 43
Musical Wonder House, The, 64
M/V Monhegan, 80

N

Naples, 163
Naples Business Association, 165
Naples Country Club, 164
Narramissic, 165
National Park Outdoor Recreation Center, 104
New England Outdoor Center, 135
New Harbor, 73
Newcastle, 72
Newfield, 30
Nickels-Sortwell House, 64
Nick's Chance, 25
Nordic Touring Center at Saddleback, 178
North Country Rivers, 136
North Windham, 159
Northern Outdoors, Inc., 132
Northwoods Outfitters, 127
Norton's Tours, 112
Norway, 169
Nott House, 30
Nylander Museum, 140

O

Ocean Winds Art Gallery, 13
Oceanarium Lobster Hatchery and Maine
     Lobster Museum, 99
Odyssey Park, 104
Ogunquit, 13
Ogunquit Beach, 14
Ogunquit Chamber of Commerce, 16
Ogunquit Museum of American Art, 17
Ogunquit Playhouse, 15
Olad, 87
Old Burying Ground, 7
Old Conway House Complex, The, 83
Old Fort Western, 147
Old Gaol, 8, 9
Old Orchard Beach, 36
Old Orchard Beach Chamber of
     Commerce, 38
Old Orchard Beach Country Club, 37
Old Schoolhouse, 8
Old York Historical Society Museum, 8
Oquossoc, 178
Orono, 125

Orrs Island, 57
Owls Head Light, 80
Owls Head Transportation Museum, 81

P

Palace Playland, 36
Parson's Beach, 23
Parson's Way, 30
Passagassawakeag River, 89
Patten, 137
Peaks Island, 44
Peaks Island Mercantile, 44
Peary-MacMillian Arctic Museum, 54
Pejepscot Museum, 54
Pemaquid Art Gallery, 75
Pemaquid Beach, 73, 74
Pemaquid Point, 73
Pemaquid Point Lighthouse, Art Gallery, and
    Museum, The, 75
Penobscot Bay, 90
Penobscot Marine Museum, The, 90
Penobscot River, 137
Penobscot Theatre Company, 122
Percy & Small Shipyard, 60
Percy's Store, 61
Perham's Store, 171
Perkins Cove, 13
Perry's Tropical Nut House, 88
Petit Manan National Wildlife Refuge, 111
Phillips, 180
Phippsburg, 59
Pine Point, 39
Pine Tree Shop, 88
Pine Tree State Arboretum, 149
Pineridge Municipal Golf, 151
Pirate's Cove Adventure Golf, 37, 106
Point Beach, 93
Point Sebago Resort, 163
Popham Beach, 60
Popham Beach State Park, 60
Portland, 40
Portland Head Light, 43
Portland Museum of Art, 42
Portland Performing Arts Center, 46
Portland Pirates, 43
Portland Sea Dogs, 43

Portsmouth Naval Shipyard, 7
Precipice Trail, 108
Presque Isle, 138
Presque Isle Chamber of Commerce, 139
Presque Isle Historical Society, 138
Prouts Neck, 39

R

Rachel Carson National Wildlife Refuge, 19
Rachel Carson Salt Pond Reserve, 74
Raft Maine, 133
rafting, white-water, 131, 132, 134–37
Rangeley, 176
Rangeley Lake, 176
Rangeley Lake State Park, 178
Rangeley Lakes Area, 176
Rangeley Lakes Chamber of Commerce, 180
Rangeley Region Sport Shop, 177
Reid State Park, 63
Ripogenus Dam, 134
Robert Abbe Museum, 100
rock climbing, 102
Rockland, 78
Rockland Breakwater Light, 79
Rockland–Thomaston Area Chamber of
    Commerce, 82
Rockport, 82
Rockport Marine Park, 83
Rockport Opera House, 85
Rockwood, 130
Roger Pond, 26
Roosevelt Campobello International Park, 117
Roque Bluffs State Park, 114
Round Pond, 74
Round Top Center for the Arts, 73
Round Top Ice Cream, 73

S

Saco, 30
Saco Drive-In, 33
Saco Heath, 31
Saco Museum, 34
Saco River, 168
Saco River Canoe and Kayak, 168

Saddleback Ski Area, 178
Salem, 181
Samantha Smith Memorial, 146
Samoset Golf Course, 86
Sand Beach, 109
Sandy Point Beach, 93
Sandy River Model Railroad, 113
Sandy River–Rangeley Lakes Railroad, 180
Sawyer Memorial Congregational Church, 113
Sayward-Wheeler House, 12
Scarborough, 39
Scarborough Beach, 39
Scarborough Downs, 40
Scarborough Marsh Nature Center, 39
School House, 30
Scotia Prince Cruises, 44
Screw Auger Falls, 173
Sea Gull Shop and Restaurant, 76
Seacoast Fun/Snow Park, 161
Seal Harbor, 109
Searsport, 90
Searsport Antiques Mall, 91
Searsport Economic Development
    Committee, 92, 93
Seashore Trolley Museum, 27
Sebago, 159
Sebago Lake Region, 159
Sebago Lake State Park, 161
Secret Acres Riding Academy, 164
Sequin Lighthouse, 63
Shantih II, 87
Shawnee Peak Ski Area, 166
Ship Harbor, 107
Shirttail Beach, 85
Shore Path, 102
Shore Village Museum, 79
Short Sands Beach, 11
Silkweeds, 91
Simplicity, 80
Ski Maine, 112
skiing, See Activities Index
Skolfield-Whittier House, 54
Smiling Hill Farm, 40
Snow Falls Gorge, 171
Songo Locks, 163
Songo River Queen II, 163
South Branch Pond, 135

South Paris, 169
South Rangeley, 176
Southwest Harbor, 109
Southwest Harbor/Tremont Chamber of
    Commerce, 106, 110
Spare-Time Recreation, 154
Sportshaus, 166
Spruce Bush Farm, 77
Squaw Mountain Resort, 129
SS Katahdin, 128
St. Anthony's Franciscan Monastery, 30
St. Patrick's Church, 72
Stanley Museum, The, 182
Starboard, 116
Steamboat Landing Miniature Golf, 163
Step Falls, 173
Sterling Inn, 135
Steuben, 111
Stockton Springs, 92
Stratton, 181
Strawberry Bazaar, 13
Sugarloaf Area Chamber of Commerce, 181, 183
Sugarloaf Golf Club, 181
Sugarloaf Mountain, 181
Sugarloaf Mountain Bike Shop, 181
Sugarloaf Ski Touring and Outdoor Center,
    181, 182
Sugarloaf Sports and Fitness Center, 182
Sugarloaf USA, 182
Sunday River Inn & X-Country Ski Center, 174
Sunday River Ski Area, 174
Sundown Lodge and Cottages, 180
Sunrise County Economic Council, 113
Surprise, 87
Swans Island, 107
Swift River, 178

T

Taber's Driving Range and Minature Golf, 154
Teddy Bear Factory, The, 47
Telemark Inn and Llama Farm, 174
tennis, 106, 178
Thayer Pond, 181
Thomas Point Beach, 55
Thompson Ice House, 73

Thorncrag Bird Sanctuary, 155
Timberwind, 80
Titcomb Mountain Ski Touring Center, 182
Tom's of Maine Inc., 24
train rides, *See Activities Index*
Twin Cities Air Services, Inc., 155
Two-Cent Bridge, 150

U

Ugly Anne, 14
Unicorn Expeditions, 131
Upper Kennebec Valley Chamber of
    Commerce, 133

V

Vacationland Bowling Center, 34
Vesper Hill Children's Chapel, 83
Victoria Mansion, 46
Victorian Homestead, 78
Victory Chimes, 80
Village Park Family Entertainment Center, 37

W

Wadsworth-Longfellow House, 46
Waldo County Craft Co-Op, 91
Waldo Theatre, 77
Waldoboro, 77
Waldoboro Town Office, 78
Walker's Point, 30
Waterville, 150
Waterville Country Club,151
Waterville Opera House, The, 150
Webb Lake, 181
Webhannet Golf Club, 29
Wedding Cake House, 24
Weld, 181
Wells, 17
Wells Auto Museum, 19
Wells Chamber of Commerce, 22
Wells Harbor, 18

Wells Historical Society, 20
Wells National Estuarine Research Preserve, 19
Wells Recreation Area, 17
Wendameen, 80
Wendell Gilley Museum of Bird Carving, 109
West Market Square, 119, 121
West Paris, 171
West Quoddy Light State Park, The, 116
Western Beach, 39
whale watching, *See Activities Index*
"Whatever" Family Festival, 145
White Mountain National Forest, 173
White's Beach, 55
Wiggly Bridge, 10
Wild Gardens of Acadia, 100
Wild River, 173
Wilderness Boat, The, 127
Willis Hodson Park, 85
Willowbrook at Newfield Restoration
    Village, 30
Windjammer Days, 71
Winslow Memorial Park, 49
Winter Harbor, 110
Wiscasset, 64
Wiscasset Raceway, 66
Wolfe's Neck Woods State Park, 49
Wonder Mountain, 17
Wood Island Light, 32
Woodlawn Museum—The Black House, 97
Wyeth Center, The, 78

Y

Yankee Lanes of Brunswick, 57
Yarmouth, 47
Yarmouth Chamber of Commerce, 47
Yarmouth Clam Festival, 47
YMCA, 88, 99
York, 7
York Days, 9
York Harbor Beach, 11
York Wild Kingdom Zoo and Amusement Park, 9
York's Annual Golf Tournament, 9
Yummies Candy & Nuts, 3

Activities Index

Amusement Parks

Aquaboggan Water Park, 31
Big Adventure Center, 175
Blackbeard's USA, 122
Funtown/Splashtown USA, 33
Odyssey Park, 104
Palace Playland, 36
Seacoast Fun/Snow Park, 161
Village Park Family Entertainment Center, 37
York Wild Kingdom Zoo and Amusement Park, 9

Beaches

Auburn Municipal Beach, 153
Barrett's Cove, 84
Camp Ellis Beach, 34
Coffin Pond, 55
Colony Beach, 27
Echo Lake, 109
Ferry Beach State Park, 34
Footbridge Beach, 15
Fort Popham, 61
Goose Rocks Beach, 27
Higgins Beach, 39
Jasper Beach, 116
Kennebunk Beach, 23
Laite Memorial Park and Beach, 87
Lake Wood, 109
Lamoine Beach, 110
Long Sands Beach, 11
Megunticook Lake, 85
Moody Beach, 15
Moosehead Lake, 126
Mosman Beach Park, 91
Ogunquit Beach, 14
Old Orchard Beach, 36, 37
Parson's Beach, 23
Pemaquid Beach, 73
Pine Point Beach, 39
Popham Beach State Park, 60
Rangeley Lake State Park, 178
Reid State Park, 63
Roque Bluffs State Park, 114
Sand Beach, 109
Sandy Point Beach, 93
Scarborough Beach, 39
Seal Harbor, 109
Sebago Lake State Park, 161
Shirttail Beach, 85
Short Sands Beach, 11
Starboard, 116
Thomas Point Beach, 55
Western Beach, 39
White's Beach, 55
Willis Hodson Park, 85
York Harbor Beach, 11

Boating/Cruises

Acadia Bike and Canoe, 101
Acadia Outfitters, 101, 105
Atlantic Exposure Cruise & Charter Ltd., 25
Atlantic Seal, 45
Bay Ferries, Inc., 103
Bay View Cruises, 45
Beaver Cove Marina, 127
Belfast and Moosehead Lake R.R. Co., 89
Betselma, 87
Blackjack Sportfishing and Charters, 69
Boothbay Whale Watch, 69
Bunny Clark, 14
Cap'n Fish Boat Cruises, 69
Casco Bay Lines, 45
Cozy Moose Lakeside Cabins & Recreation, 127
Diver Ed Live Underwater Video Tours, 100
Downeast Windjammer and Lighthouse
    Cruises, 103
Eagle Tours, Inc., 45
Elizabeth Ann, 80
Finestkind Scenic Cruises, 14
First/Second Chance Inc., 25
Hardy Boat Cruises, 74
Isaac H. Evans, 80
Kylie's Chance, 25
Lady J. Sportsfishing Charters Inc., 26
Lively Lady Too, 84, 87

Lulu Lobster Boat Ride, 104
M/V Monhegan, 80
Magic Falls Rafting, 132
Maine Island Kayak Co., 46
Maine Windjammer Association, 80, 87
Monhegan Boat Line, 80
Moose Safaris and Scenic Cruises, 127
Morning in Maine, 80
Mount Blue State Park, 181
Moxie Outdoor Adventures, 132
National Park Outdoor Recreation Center, 104
New England Outdoor Center, 135
Nick's Chance, 25
North Country Rivers, 136
Northern Outdoors, Inc., 132
Norton's Tours, 112
Olad, 87
Rangeley Lake State Park, 178
Saco River Canoe and Kayak, 168
Sandy Point Beach, 93
Scarborough Marsh Nature Center, 39
Scotia Prince Cruises, 44
Shantih II, 87
Simplicity, 80
Songo River Queen II, 163
SS *Katahdin,* 128
Surprise, 87
Timberwind, 80
Ugly Anne, 14
Unicorn Expeditions, 131
Victory Chimes, 80
Wendameen, 80
Wilderness Boat, The, 127

Fishing

Aroostook State Park, 138
Baxter State Park, 134, 136
Bunny Clark, 14
Northern Outdoors, Inc., 132
Swift River, 178
Ugly Anne, 14
Wells Harbor, 18
White Mountain National Forest, 173

Golfing

Bangor Municipal Golf Course, 125

Bar Harbor Golf Course, 106
Bethel Inn and Country Club, The, 173
Biddeford–Saco Country Club, 31
Blackbeard's USA, 122
Bridgton Highlands Country Club, 165
Cape Arundel Golf Club, 29
Caribou Country Club, 140
Cascade Golf Range, 31
Causeway Golf Club, 110
College Street Driving Range and Mini Golf, 154
Dolphin Mini Golf, 69
Dutch Elm Golf Course, 29
Goose River Golf Club, 86
Kebo Valley Golf Club, 106
Long Shot Golf Center, 57
Mingo Springs Golf Course, 178
Moose River Golf Course, 131
Naples Country Club, 164
Old Orchard Beach Country Club, 37
Pine Ridge Municipal Golf, 151
Pirate's Cove Adventure Golf, 37, 106
Samoset Golf Course, 86
Seacoast Fun/Snow Park, 161
Steamboat Landing Miniature Golf, 163
Sugarloaf Golf Club, 181
Taber's Driving Range, 154
Waterville Country Club, 151
Webhannet Golf Club, 29
Wonder Mountain, 17

Hiking/Walking Trails

Acadia National Park, 104, 107, 108
Aroostook State Park, 138
Bald Mountain, 177
Baxter State Park, 134, 136
Bigelow Mountain, 151
Boothbay Region Land Trust Preserves, 70
Brick Store Museum, The, 24
Camden Hills State Park, 83
Coastal Maine Botanical Gardens, 70
Daicey Pond Nature Trail, 135
Desert of Maine, 48
Douglas Mountain, 162
Downeast Nature Tours, 100
Eagle Island State Historic Site, 45
East Point Sanctuary, 35
Fort Baldwin, 61

Fort Point State Park, 92
Fort Popham, 61
Fort Pownal, 92
Ghostly Tour, 3
Grafton Notch State Park, 173
Great Wass Island, 113, 117
Jordan Pond Loop Trail, 108
Kelmscott Rare Breeds Foundation, 84
Kennebunk Plains, 24
Lamoine Beach State Park, 110
Lily Bay State Park, 128
Magic Falls Rafting, 132
Maine Forest and Logging Museum, 126
Maine Lobster Museum, 99
Maine Wildlife Park, 157
Marginal Way, 3, 14
Mast Landing Sanctuary, 49
McLaughlin Fountaion, The, 177
Mount Abraham, 181
Mount Blue State Park, 181
National Park Outdoor Recreation Center, 104
New England Outdoor Center, 135
Oceanarium Lobster Hatchery, 99
Petit Manan National Wildlife Refuge, 111
Popham Beach State Park, 60
Precipice Trail, 108
Rachel Carson National Wildlife Refuge, 19
Reid State Park, 63
Saco Heath, 31
Scarborough Marsh Nature Center, 39
Sebago Lake State Park, 161
Shore Path, 102
Sugarloaf/USA, 182
Sunday River Ski Area, 174
Telemark Inn and Llama Farm, 174
Thorncrag Bird Sanctuary, 155
Unicorn Expeditions, 131
Wells National Estuarine Research Preserve, 19
Wells Recreation Area, 17
White Mountain National Forest, 173
Wolfe's Neck Woods State Park, 49

Historic Sites

Babb's Bridge, 159
Blaine House, The, 148
Brick Store Museum, 24
Burnham Tavern, The, 115

Cape Neddick Lighthouse, 8
Castle Tucker, 65
Chapman-Hall House, 72
Chocolate Church Arts Center, 60
City Theater, 35
Colonial Pemaquid State Historic Site, 74
Craig Brook National Fish Hatchery, 95
Eagle Island State Historic Site, 45
Farnsworth Art Museum, Victorian Homestead,
    Library, 78
Fort Baldwin, 61
Fort Edgecomb, 67
Fort Foster, 5
Fort Knox, 92
Fort McClary State Historic Site, 5
Fort O'Brien, 116
Fort Point State Park, 92
Fort Popham, 61
Fort Pownal, 92
Fort William Henry, 74
Fort Williams State Park, 43
George Tate House, 46
Joshua L. Chamberlain Civil War Museum, 54
Lincoln County Museum and Jail, The, 65
Maine Forest and Logging Museum, 126
Morse-Libby House, 46
Museum at Historic First Meeting House, 19
Musical Wonder House, The, 64
Nickels-Sortwell House, 64
Old Fort Western, 147
Old York Historical Society Museum, 8
Owls Head Transportation Museum, 81
Pemaquid Point Lighthouse, The, 75
Portland Head Light, 43
Rockland Breakwater Light, 79
Sandy River–Rangeley Lakes Railroad, 180
Sawyer Memorial Congregational Church, 113
Seashore Trolley Museum, 27
Skolfield-Whittier House, 54
St. Patrick's Church, 72
Thompson Ice House, 73
Victoria Mansion, 46
Wadsworth-Longfellow House, 46
West Quoddy Light State Park, The, 116
Willowbrook at Newfield Restoration
    Village, 30
Woodlawn Museum—The Black House, 97
Wyeth Center, 78

Horseback Riding

Ledgewood Riding Stables, 66
Secret Acres Stables, 164

Lighthouses

Bass Harbor Head Light, 107
Boon Island Light, 12
Cape Neddick Lighthouse, 8
Hendrick Head Light, 68
Owls Head Light, 80
Pemaquid Point Lighthouse, 75
Portland Head Light, 43
Rockland Breakwater Light, 79
Sequin Head Light, 63
West Quoddy Light State Park, 116
Wood Island Light, 32

Museums

Belfast Museum, The, 89
Boothbay Railway Village, 68
Bowdoin College Museum of Art, 53
Brick Store Museum, The, 24
Bridgton Historical Society Museum and
    Narramissic, 165
Children's Discovery Museum, 147
Children's Museum of Maine, 41
Colby College Museum of Art, 151
Cole Land Transportation Museum, 121
Colonial Pemaquid State Historic Site, 74
Desert of Maine, 48
Farnsworth Art Museum, Victorian Homestead,
    Library, and Wyeth Center, 78
Fort Williams State Park, 43
George B. Door Museum of Natural History, 99
Hudson Museum, 125
Joshua L. Chamberlain Civil War Museum, 54
Kennebunkport Maritime Museum, 30
Kittery Historical and Naval Museum, 4
Lumbermen's Museum, The, 137
Maine Discovery Museum, 123
Maine Forest and Logging Museum, 126
Maine Lobster Museum, 99
Maine Maritime Museum, 59
Maine Narrow Gauge Railroad Co. and
    Museum, 42
Maine State Museum, 147

Maynard F. Jordan Planetarium and
    Observatory, 125
Moosehead Marine Museum, 128
Museum at Historic First Meeting House, 19
Museum at Portland Head Light, 43
Musical Wonder House, The, 64
Nylander Museum, 140
Oceanarium Lobster Hatchery, 99
Ogunquit Museum of American Art, 17
Old Conway House Complex, The, 83
Old Fort Western, 147
Old Gaol Museum, 8
Old York Historical Society Museum, 8
Owls Head Transportation Museum, 81
Peary-Macmillan Arctic Museum, The, 54
Pejepscot Museum, 54
Pemaquid Point Museum, The, 75
Penobscot Marine Museum, The, 90
Perham's Store, 171
Portland Museum of Art, 42
Presque Isle Historical Society, 138
Robert Abbe Museum, 100
Saco Museum, 34
Sandy River–Rangeley Lakes Railroad, 180
Seashore Trolley Museum, 27
Shore Village Museum, 79
Skolfield-Whittier House, 54
Stanley Museum, The, 182
Wells Auto Museum, 19
Wendell Gilley Museum of Bird Carving, 109
Willowbrook at Newfield Restoration Village, 30
Woodlawn Museum—The Black House, 97

Parks

Acadia National Park, 104, 107, 108
Agamont Park, 102
Aroostook State Park, 138
Baxter State Park, 134, 136
Belfast City Park, 89
Camden Hills State Park, 83
Damariscotta Lake State Park, 77
Eagle Island State Historic Site, 45
Fort Foster, 5
Fort McClary State Historic Site, 5
Fort Point State Park, 92
Grafton Notch State Park, 173
Ingersoll Arena/Pettengill Park, 154
Lamoine Beach State Park, 110

Lily Bay State Park, 128
McClellan Park, 111
Monument Park, 149
Moose Point State Park, 91
Mosman Beach Park, 91
Popham Beach State Park, 60
Rangeley Lake State Park, 178
Reid State Park, 63
Roosevelt Campobello International Park, 117
Roque Bluffs State Park, 114
Sebago Lake State Park, 161
West Quoddy Light State Park, The, 116
Willis Hodson Park, 85
Winslow Memorial Park, 49
Wolfe's Neck Woods State Park, 49

Performing Arts/Theaters

Bay Chamber Concerts, 85
Camden Civic Theatre, The, 85
Caribou Performing Arts Center, 141
Carousel Music Theatre, The, 68
Celebration Barn Theater, The, 170
Chocolate Church Arts Center, 60
City Theater, 35
Civic Center, The, 148
Deertrees Theatre, 168
Grand Auditorium, The, 97
Leavitt Fine Arts Theater, 17
Maine State Music Theatre, 51
Ogunquit Playhouse, 15
Penobscot Theatre Company, 122
Portland Performing Arts Center, 46
Round Top Center for the Arts, 73
Waldo Theatre, 77
Waterville Opera House, The, 150

Shopping

Artist's Gallery, 13
Ayla's Sweet Shop, 13
Bangor Mall, 119
Bett's Bookstore, 121
BookMarc's, 121
Booksource, The, 121
Briar Patch, The, 121
Cool Moose, The, 165
Country Shop, The, 13
Cove's End, 13
Edgecomb Potters, 67
Favorite Past-Time Antiques, 172
Glassworks, 166
Golden Sails, 13
Goldenrod, The, 10
Grasshopper Shop, The, 121
Greater Bookland & Cafe, 57
Groan and McGurn's Tourist Trap and Craft
    Outlet, 173
Kittery Outlets, 5
Kittery Trading Post, 3
L. L. Bean, 48, 49
Land's End, 58
Len Libby Candies, 39
Mackerel Sky Studio, 70
Mountainside Country Crafts, 173
Mr. Paperback, 121
Ocean Winds Art Gallery, 13
Perham's Store, 171
Perry's Tropical Nut House, 88
Searsport Antiques Mall, 91
Silkweeds, 91
Sportshaus, 166
Strawberry Bazaar, 13
Teddy Bear Factory, The, 47
Tom's of Maine, 24
Waldo County Craft Co-Op, 91
Yummies Candy & Nuts, 3

Skiing

Aroostook State Park, 138
Bethel Inn and Country Club, The, 173
Camden Snow Bowl, 83
Carter's X-Country Ski Center II, 174
Downeast Nature Tours, 100
Lost Valley Ski Area, 153
Maine Nordic Ski Council, 112
Mount Abram, 174
Mount Blue State Park, 181
New England Outdoor Center, 135
Rangeley Lake State Park, 178
Saddleback Ski Area, 178
Shawnee Peak Ski Area, 166
Ski Maine, 112
Squaw Mountain Resort, 129
Sugarloaf/USA, 182

Sunday River Inn & X-Country Ski
    Center, 174
Sunday River Ski Area, 174
Telemark Inn and Llama Farm, 174
Titcomb Mountain Ski Touring Center, 182

Sports

batting cages, 34
bowling, 34, 57, 154
CAN-AM Wheelers, 170
Caribou Motor Speedway, 141
Interstate Bowling Center, 149
Kennebec Ice Arena, 149
Portland Pirates, 43
Portland Sea Dogs, 43

tennis, 106, 178
Wiscasset Raceway, 66

Train Rides

Belfast and Moosehead Lake R.R. Co., 89
Boothbay Railway Village, 68
Maine Narrow Gauge Railroad Co. and
    Museum, 42
Sandy River–Rangeley Lakes Railroad, 180

Whale-Watching

Bar Harbor Whale Watch Company, 102
Boothbay Whale Watch, 69
First/Second Chance, Inc., 25

About the Author

Bonnie Merrill has lived in the Pine Tree State with her husband, Ken, a Maine native, for seven years. A freelance writer and second-grade teacher, she previously worked for the Maine Tourism Association as a publication assistant and writer. She has been published in *Maine Invites You* and *Exploring Maine*. Her girls, Kaitlyn, 12, and Jaclyn, 10, enjoy going on day trips and discovering all the beautiful state of Maine has to offer.